W9-DCC-429

Qualitative Methods in Sports Studies

Sport Commerce and Culture

Series ISSN: 1741-0916

Editor:
David L. Andrews, *University of Maryland*

The impact of sporting issues on culture and commerce both locally and globally is huge. However, the power and pervasiveness of this billion-dollar industry has yet to be deeply analyzed. Sports issues shape the economy, the media and even our lifestyle choices, ultimately playing an unquestionable role in our psychology. This series examines the sociological significance of the sports industry and the sporting world in contemporary cultures around the world.

Previously published books in the series:

Sport and Corporate Nationalisms, *edited by Michael L. Silk, David L. Andrews and C.L. Cole*
Global Sport Sponsorship, *edited by John Amis and T. Bettina Cornwell*

Qualitative Methods in Sports Studies

Edited by

David L. Andrews, Daniel S. Mason and Michael L. Silk

Oxford • New York

English edition
First published in 2005 by
Berg
Editorial offices:
First Floor, Angel Court, 81 St Clements Street, Oxford OX4 1AW, UK
175 Fifth Avenue, New York, NY 10010, USA

Berg is the imprint of Oxford International Publishers Ltd.

Library of Congress Cataloging-in-Publication Data
Qualitative methods in sports studies / edited by David L. Andrews, Daniel S. Mason
and Michael L. Silk.
p. cm. — (Sport, commerce and culture)
Includes bibliographical references and index.
ISBN 1-85973-784-6 (cloth) — ISBN 1-85973-789-7 (pbk.)
1. Sports—Study and teaching. I. Andrews, David L. II. Mason, Daniel S.
III. Silk, Michael L. IV. Series.

GV361.Q35 2005
796'.07'2—dc22

2005017084

British Library Cataloguing-in-Publication Data
A catalogue record for this book is available from the British Library.

ISBN-13 978 1 85973 784 2 (Cloth)
978 1 85973 789 7 (Paper)

ISBN-10 1 85973 784 6 (Cloth)
1 85973 789 7 (Paper)

Typeset by JS Typesetting Ltd, Porthcawl, Mid Glamorgan
Printed in the United Kingdom by Biddles Ltd, King's Lynn

www.bergpublishers.com

Contents

Notes on Contributors

John Amis is an Associate Professor at the University of Memphis, where he holds joint appointments in the Department of Health & Sport Sciences and the Department of Management. Amis's current research interests are predominantly centered on organizational change and the identification, utilization and management of intangible resources. His work has appeared in journals such as *Academy of Management Journal, Journal of Applied Behavioral Science, Journal of Sport Management, European Marketing Journal, European Sport Management Quarterly* and *Leisure Studies*. He has recently published a co-edited collection (with Bettina Cornwell), titled *Global Sport Sponsorship* (Oxford: Berg, 2005).

David L. Andrews is an Associate Professor in the Department of Kinesiology at the University of Maryland at College Park. He is assistant editor of the *Journal of Sport and Social Issues*, and an editorial board member of the *Sociology of Sport Journal*. He has published on a variety of topics related to the critical analysis of sport as an aspect of contemporary commercial culture.

Jennifer Chapman is an Assistant Professor in the Department of Theater at Albion College. Her research interests include issues of gender and sexuality in theater and drama education, especially in relation to high-school drama curricula.

Jim Denison is a lecturer in Coach Education and Sports Development at the University of Bath, UK. His first book, *Moving Writing: Crafting Movement in Sport Research* (Peter Lang), is a co-edited scholarly monograph outlining various ethnographic writing practices in sports studies. He has also published *Bannister and Beyond: The Mystique of the Four-Minute Mile* (Breakaway Books), a collection of in-depth interviews with a wide array of sub-four-minute milers; and *The Greatest* (Breakaway Books), the authorized biography of the Ethiopian long-distance running legend, Haile Gebrselassie. Denison is also the editor of *The Coach*, a bi-monthly magazine for track and field coaches. He is currently at work on a number of autoethnographic projects related to athletes' and coaches' experiences.

Samantha King is an Assistant Professor in the School of Physical and Health Education at Queen's University. Her research explores how individuals and populations are governed, within the realms of sport and health, through what are often described as "neoliberal" rationalities of thought and practice. As part of this work, she has recently completed a manuscript titled, "Pink Ribbons Inc: Breast Cancer Culture and the Politics of Philanthropy." A member of the editorial board for the *Journal of Sport and Social Issues*, her recent publications have appeared in *Social Text, the International Journal of Sport Marketing and Sponsorship* and the *Journal of Sport and Social Issues.*

Pirkko Markula is currently with the Department of Education at the University of Bath, UK. She is a co-editor with Jim Denison of *Moving Writing: Crafting Movement in Sport Research* (Peter Lang). She also edited *Feminist Sports Studies: Sharing Joy, Sharing Pain* (State University of New York Press). Her research interests include post-structuralist feminist analysis of dance, fitness and sport. In addition, she is interested in alternative ways of representing social science research, such as dance performance, performance ethnography and autoethnography.

Daniel Mason is an Associate Professor with the Faculty of Physical Education and Recreation and an adjunct professor with the School of Business at the University of Alberta, in Edmonton, Canada. His research takes an interdisciplinary approach and he has published in numerous journals, including *Economic Development Quarterly, European Journal of Marketing, European Sport Management Quarterly, Journal of Sport and Social Issues, Journal of Urban Affairs, Media History, Sport History Review, Sport in Society* and *Urban History Review.* In 2004, he was named a Research Fellow by the North American Society for Sport Management.

Darcy C. Plymire is an Assistant Professor in the Department of Kinesiology at Towson University. Her interest in sport and media reflects her life-long love for sporting spectacles. When she can tear herself away from the mediated sport, she coaches girls' field hockey and lacrosse at an independent school in the Baltimore, MD area.

Michael L. Silk is an Assistant Professor and a member of the Physical Cultural Studies Research Group located in the Department of Kinesiology at the University of Maryland. His work is committed to the critical, multidisciplinary and multi-method interrogation of sporting practices, experiences and structures. He has published a number of book chapters and journal articles in *Media, Culture, Society, the International Journal of Media & Cultural Politics*, the *Journal of Sport and Social Issues*, the *Sociology of Sport Journal*, the *International Review for the Sociology of Sport, Sport, Culture and Society*, the *Journal of Sport Management* and *Media Culture: A Review.*

Anne Swedberg is completing her dissertation with the assistance of an American Association of University Women fellowship. She is a PhD candidate at the University of Wisconsin-Madison and is writing about the politics of power and representation in community-based theater.

Heather Sykes is an Assistant Professor at the Ontario Institute for Studies in Education at the University of Toronto. She uses queer, psychoanalytic, feminist and postmodern theories to examine issues of gender/sexuality, embodiment and anti-homophobia pedagogy in physical education and sport. She has published articles in journals such as *Sociology of Sport Journal*, *International Journal of Qualitative Studies in Education* and *Journal of Curriculum Studies*, and is Editor of *Curriculum Inquiry*.

David K. Wiggins is Professor and Director of the School of Recreation, Health, and Tourism at George Mason University. A specialist in sport history, he has published numerous essays in journals such as the *Journal of Sport History*, *The International Journal of the History of Sport* and the *Research Quarterly for Exercise and Sport*. He is also the author of *Glory Bound: Black Athletes in a White America* (1997), co-author of *The Unlevel Playing Field: A Documentary History of the African American Experience in Sport* (2003); editor of *Sport in America: From Wicked Amusement to National Obsession* (1995) and *African Americans in Sports* (2004); and co-editor of *Ethnicity and Sport in North American History and Culture* (1995) and *Sport and the Color Line: Black Athletes and Race Relations in Twentieth-Century America* (2004).

1

Encountering the Field

Sports Studies and Qualitative Research

Michael L. Silk, David L. Andrews and Daniel S. Mason

The academic discipline known as "sports studies" has evolved over the last few decades into an eclectic mix of research ideologies and viewpoints that seek to critically investigate the role, effects and position of sport within broader society. Contextualizing sport within networks of political, economic and social linkages, the field of sports studies critically interrogates the sporting empirical and attempts to provide comprehension of the dynamism and complexities of cultural life. Such an approach is one that recognizes the creative and contextual character of human interaction (Hammersley, 1989), a position that centers on research designs suited to studying performative human beings in their lived (physical) cultural domains. As the following chapters will show however, the field has developed a number of (at times, conflicting) viewpoints on the nature of research, the types of research questions that are asked, and the manner through which these questions can be explored. In many instances, these views have been taken from broader, parent disciplines, such as history, cultural studies, cultural geography, management, psychology, and/or sociology, and have been held by scholars in traditional kinesiology/physical education/sports studies programs, or by scholars in parent disciplines who have chosen to focus on sport in their research.

Locating sport – as a cultural form within which the production of knowledge and identities takes place – within the material and institutional contexts that structure everyday life provides the underlying site for the critical interrogation of sporting experiences, forms, meanings, structures, and practices. No longer marginalized as a second-rate field of study within academe, and indeed taking a central role in a symbolically oriented, global, entertainment economy, the study of sport must now be taken seriously. Sport provides the site for critical interrogation through a variety of theories or "lenses," a space that has been characterized by a broad spectrum of research approaches, interdisciplinarity, flexibility, and, as Samantha King indicates in the second chapter of this volume, a methodological contingency that can allow the researcher to employ the tools suitable for critical interrogation of the particular sporting phenomena under investigation.

Unfortunately, the diversity of interests, ideologies and methodologies between sports studies scholars has lead to isolation in the evolution of some of the research that has been conducted in this field (see for example, the discussion of the relationship between sport historians and sociologists in Chapter 3). A result has been the development of a strong body of literature that has been fragmented and lacks the unity of interests found in other social disciplines. Thus, students and/or aspiring scholars may find their initial forays into the realm of research in sports studies a daunting task. In this sense, students and scholars are often faced with determining how to conceptualize and analyze the complexities of the "constant battlefield" (Hall, 1981) of the (sporting) world, while at the same time recognizing that they are participating in this world, and thereby shaping it (Slack, 1996). Further, concerns over deciding what questions to ask and how to go about answering them abound, as do issues concerning methodological approaches that would suit an aspiring scholar's ideas about what questions should be asked and how they should be answered.

Typically, students can start to address these issues by taking courses in research design within their respective institutions, which mostly rely on a number of quality, established texts that discuss qualitative research method and design, such as those written by Denzin and Lincoln (2000a), Berg (2001), Creswell (1994), Burton (2000), Denscombe (1998), Silverman (2000) and Yin (1994), or journals that, relatively recently, have treated qualitative research as a field in its own right (e.g. *Qualitative Inquiry*, *Journal of Contemporary Ethnography*, *Cultural Studies ↔ Critical Methodologies*). However, while these texts are critical in providing a foundation, and indeed for teasing out the complexities of the field, for students who seek to use qualitative research methods in their research, there still exists a knowledge gap between the research strategies learned in these and how they have been specifically applied within the sports studies context. This volume thus provides a modest attempt to fill this gap by bringing together a number of varying research approaches to the critical interrogation of the contextually grounded sporting empirical. Given the breadth of research areas within sports studies, and the varying methods used within each, it would be beyond the scope of any book to provide representative examples of all of the strategies used within sports studies. Instead, we have sought to present a small sample of the ways in which certain methods, designs and approaches can illuminate the investigation of physical human beings in their cultural worlds. The contributors offer an array of qualitative approaches that can be used to shed light on the sporting empirical – this volume thus provides a space for the connections between various research strategies, methods, paradigms, histories and communities of those involved in contextual sports studies. In doing so, we hope to provide a supplementary text for courses exploring qualitative research methods and designs that allows students to get a closer look at how some of the varying approaches have been employed in research being done in the field, written by those who have had first-hand experience with a given approach.

Encountering the Field: A Brief Genealogy of Qualitative Research

The emergence and utility of qualitative research were not universally embraced by scholars attuned to the rigor and mechanics of positivism. Denzin and Lincoln's (2000b) genealogy of qualitative research outlines seven moments that have impacted upon the critical analysis of human beings in their contexts. Such a genealogy is, as Denzin and Lincoln (2000b) suggest, socially constructed and quasi-historical; these moments overlap and simultaneously operate within the present. Nonetheless, these moments provide an excellent sketch of the emergence of qualitative research and the nuances, contradictions and increasing sophistication of the field, and provide the underpinning for consideration of a contemporary contextual sports studies. While we cannot do justice to the history of qualitative research, or indeed the genealogy provided by Denzin and Lincoln (1994; 2000a; 2000b), it is important to briefly summarize these moments for they build toward a "conceptual framework" (Denzin & Lincoln, 2000b: 2) for qualitative research within the field of sports studies. This historical field consists of the traditional, the modernist, blurred genres, the crises of representation, the postmodern, post-experimental inquiry and the future. The traditional period, not surprisingly given its specific socio-historical location, was characterized by often misguided attempts to objectively analyze "other" or "exotic" human beings in colonized settings. The modernist phase was dominated by the collection of qualitative data which researchers attempted to fit to the canons of positivism (Denzin & Lincoln, 1994; 2000b). The blurred or interpretive genres phase drew upon a range of often competing theoretical narratives (e.g. symbolic interactionism, ethnomethodology, neo-Marxism, feminism, racial and ethnic theories) that bought into question the "golden age" of social science (Denzin & Lincoln, 2000b). Following from the blurred genres phase, the crisis of representation began to address questions of race, gender and class, making writing more reflexive and rupturing foundational concepts such as validity, reliability and objectivity. The "crisis" referred to the researcher's authority and ability to write the experience of the "other" (and indeed the separation of the researcher/other) and the recognition that this experience is created in the text "written" by the researcher (Richardson, 2000a). Postmodern influences have produced new expressions of qualitative data such as fictional ethnographies, ethnographic poetry, self narratives, performance pieces and multi-media texts (Denzin, 1997; Denzin & Lincoln, 2000b). The sixth moment asks that the social sciences and the humanities become sites for critical conversations about democracy, race, gender, class, nation-states, globalization, freedom and community (Denzin & Lincoln, 2000b), while the "future," according to Denzin and Lincoln (2000b: 3) is the current temporality "concerned with moral discourse and the development of sacred textualities."

The Promise of a Contextual Sports Studies: Paradigms, Potentialities and Pitfalls

Denzin and Lincoln's (1994; 1998; 2000a; 2000b) moments are not necessarily directional, or a purview for *the way* contemporary qualitative research ought to be carried out. Rather, as we indicated above, qualitative research is characterized by all of these overlapping "moments" simultaneously operating in the present (Atkinson et al., 1999; Denzin & Lincoln, 2000b) and pointing towards an increasing sensitivity to the promises of qualitative research within sports studies. A contextual sports studies that places sport within the material contexts of everyday life can become an important site for critical conversations about cultural politics and multiracial, economic, and political democracy – conversations that address the imperatives of consumption, the dynamics of the marketplace, commercial space, the sweeping reach of neo-liberal ideology, power and influence, the production of knowledges and identities, nation-states, globalization, freedom and community (Denzin & Lincoln, 2000b; Giroux, 2001). Further, qualitative research speaks to the varying roles of contextual sports studies researchers, the civic and political responsibilities assumed through their roles as engaged critics and cultural theorists, forms of intervention, and pedagogical practices that are interdisciplinary, transgressive and oppositional (Giroux, 2001). Thus, qualitative researchers in sports studies can engage in concrete steps that will "change situations" and potentially "bring new value to identities and experiences that are marginalized and stigmatized by the larger culture. They will demonstrate how particular commodities or cultural objects negatively affect the lives of specific people. They indicate how particular texts directly and indirectly misrepresent persons and reproduce prejudice and stereotypes" (Denzin, 2002: 486). This is a contextual sports studies that can, and should, "take sides" (Denzin, 2002: 487), revealing through multifarious forms of (re)representation the shifting oppressive structures of global and local capitalism and how the (sporting) media reproduce gender, racial, sexual orientation, and social class stereotypes and even contribute to consumer practices that are harmful to personal health and the environment (Denzin, 2002). In so doing, this is a contextual sports studies that engages in social critique and moral dialogue, identifying the different relations of cultural capital that operate in specific cultural contexts, offers programs and recommendations for change, and holds the researcher accountable for the moral and personal consequences of any particular instance of advocacy (Denzin, 2002).

Given the potential of qualitative research for a contextual sports studies, the chapters in this volume offer a variety of strategies, methods of inquiry and expressions of "data." These contributions reflect a variety of perspectives and suggest that qualitative research in sports studies is shaped, refined and recreated by diversity, controversies and continuities from the past (Atkinson et al., 1999). These rich and turbulent histories provide the (ever changing) parameters for what is currently considered qualitative research. Given that a definition of qualitative research is essentializing and thus grounded within a particular historical conjecture it is somewhat problematic to "define" what is meant by the term. Recognizing that qualitative research will mean different things in the future, as it did in the past, Denzin and Lincoln (2000b: 3) offer the following account:

> Qualitative research is a situated activity that locates the observer in the world. It consists of a set of interpretive, material practices that make the world visible. These practices transform the world. They turn the world into a series of representations, including field notes, interviews, conversations, photographs, recordings and memos to the self. At this level, qualitative research involves an interpretive, naturalistic approach to the world. This means qualitative researchers study things in their natural settings, attempting to make sense of, or to interpret, phenomena in terms of the meanings people bring to them.

This definition of qualitative research is clearly guided by paradigmatic assumptions, values and beliefs that work against (or alongside, or even, at times, within) positivist and post-positivist models (Denzin & Lincoln, 2000a). Indeed, the paradigms that structure qualitative research work within relativist ontologies (multiple constructed realities), interpretive epistemologies (where the knower and the known interact and shape one another) and interpretive, naturalistic (in nature) methods (Denzin & Lincoln, 2000a; Lincoln & Guba, 1985; 2000).

The critical interrogation of the sporting empirical, by its very nature, cannot treat the dynamism and complexities of the physically active human being as a set of static, isolatable, measurable, mechanical, artificial and observable variables (Atkinson & Hammersley, 1994; Hammersley, 1989). Rather, to capture the essence and contexts of the sporting empirical, research needs to recognize the fluid and intricate interactions between people and the socio-historical worlds in which they exist. This recognition speaks to a deeply entrenched, and at times quite bitter, battle within the field of research design – the debate over legitimate, or "valid," research designs and methodologies – often manifested in a crude paradigmatic positivism versus interpretivism.

Of course, methodologies are commensurate with particular paradigmatic stances, thus prior to addressing particular methodologies there is a need to understand how they are interwoven with, and emerge from, the nature of particular disciplines and perspectives (Lincoln & Guba, 2000). It was the work of Thomas Kuhn (1962) which brought the concept of the paradigm into the popular lexicon of research design. Kuhn (1962) suggested that a paradigm is the entire constellation of beliefs, values and techniques shared by the members of a given scientific community. Of course, paradigms are human constructions, yet nonetheless provide the basic set of beliefs that guides the researcher (Denzin & Lincoln, 2000a). In essence, Denzin and Lincoln (2000a) propose that a paradigm encompasses axiology (questions of ethics within the social world), ontology (the nature of reality and the nature of the human being in the world), epistemology (how I know the world and the relationship between the knower and the known) and methodology (the best means for gaining knowledge about the world). The history of research design has been plagued by (an almost redundant) quest by various groups of scientists to "prove" that their way of conducting research is the correct, and thereby only, way to investigate the matter at hand. Technical or physical scientific thought dominated these debates which appropriated a particular dominant approach to studying human beings. This approach, taking place within the positivist paradigm, is based on decontextual, formal and standardized experimentalism that seeks to analytically separate distinct variables in an effort to prove causality – cause and effect. In other words, through formal measurement and conceptualizing the social world as a system of variables, positivism seeks facts or causes of certain phenomena, a truth that can be objectively obtained through the rigorous testing of hypotheses. As such, positivist researchers distance themselves from the particular phenomena under investigation, searching for a reality that is entirely independent of our opinions about certain phenomena. We can term this a positivist ontology – a measurable and objective reality that determines a universal truth. This positivist ontology thus provides the permit for scientists to go about their daily lives, investigating isolated variables in relation to the cornerstones of scientific faith – universal truth, validity, reliability, generalizability. Of course, this perspective lends itself to certain ways of knowledge generation – often termed "epistemology." As such, a positivist epistemology is centered on controlled data collection, objective distance between the researcher and the subject, quantitative measurement, hypothesis testing and statistical analysis to prove causality.

Given that human behavior is not reducible to fixed patterns, and that it is shaped by, and in turn produces (sporting) cultures, positivist science is not well suited to capturing the myriad perspectives of those in the social world, the contextual character of human interaction (Hammersley, 1989) and thereby the network of political, economic and social linkages that produce, and give meaning to, the sporting empirical. Such a position does not reject outright, the important contributions of positivist science to the understanding of our life worlds; however, it does reject the position that for so long dominated the study of human beings, that positivism was the only way to critically interrogate human beings (Atkinson & Hammersley, 1994; Hammersley & Atkinson, 1995; Harding, 1986; Maguire, 1991) – a position that dominated, and perhaps to some degree still does, "sports studies," kinesiology and physical education departments throughout the world.

The recognition of the limitations or pitfalls of positivism frames the rich, and often troubled, history of the emergence of qualitative designs and methods that aim to recognize the central importance of human action and meaning in the construction of the social world (Hollands, 1985). Challenges to the positivist hegemony began to emerge around the beginning of the twentieth century, and centered on a different set of ontological and epistemological propositions that framed the type of research methodologies employed. Rather than a quest for universal truths or laws, and a distinctly artificial and static laboratory environment, there was the belief that the social world should be studied in its natural, as opposed to artificial, state (Hammersley & Atkinson, 1995). This approach was thus rooted, from the outset, in a doctrine that surpasses: "the notion that the world is a value free, objective, experiential realm that can be reduced to neat rows and columns of numbers ... in a very basic sense, qualitative methodology plays with words instead of numbers. It is an intellectual field in which language is stretched, moulded and turned on itself, but where numbers evoke – not without reason – anal, male forms of power" (Lewis, 1997: 86). In this sense, rather than suggesting that "reality" or truth will be the same for everyone (positivist ontology), the interpretive project is founded upon the premise that the social world is complex, that researchers and subjects are fundamentally and subjectively attached to the world, and that people define their own realities. In the quest for knowledge then, the interpretive project – a pursuit in understanding the particular behaviors, meanings and realities of individuals within particular social settings – is distinct from its positivist sibling. As opposed then to strict, laboratory standards, qualitative methodologies centred on observation, texts, conversation, interpretation, narrative, writing, performance, and small-scale and local interaction, tend to dominate – a set of approaches to gathering knowledge of the social world that are more fluid and flexible, and often emerge as the project unfolds.

Lincoln & Guba (2000) suggest that the paradigms that provide the structure for qualitative research take as their primary field of interest subjective and intersubjective social knowledge and recognize that the active construction and co-creation of such knowledge by human agents is produced by human consciousness. As opposed to positivism and post-positivism, the metaphysics of the constructivist paradigm assumes a relativist ontology, a subjectivist epistemology and a naturalistic set of methodological procedures – the orientation is thus to the production of reconstructed understandings of the social world (Denzin & Lincoln, 2000a). In a sense, this epistemological approach towards the social world can be characterized as hermeneutic in that to offer an understanding of a particular action requires an emphasis upon grasping the situation in which human actions make or acquire meaning (Schwandt, 2000). Indeed, a contextual sports studies, in many ways, draws upon the hermeneutic circle that suggests to understand the part (the specific) there needs to be comprehension of the whole (context, beliefs, desires of the text, practices, forms of life, language, beliefs and so on) (Schwandt, 2000). In essence, the hermeneutic circle thus requires a "continuous dialectical tacking between the most local of local detail and the most global of global structure in such a way to bring both into view simultaneously... Hopping back and forth between the whole conceived through the parts that actualize it and the parts conceived through the whole which motivates them, we seek to turn them, by a sort of intellectual perpetual motion, into explications of one another" (Geertz in Schwandt, 2000: 93). "Data" are thus ground in context, while credibility, transferability, dependability, trustworthiness, conformability and reciprocity replace the usual positivist criteria of internal and external validity, reliability and objectivity (Denzin & Lincoln, 2000a; Harrison et al., 2001).

Existing alongside the constructivist paradigm is the participatory paradigm. The participatory paradigm suggests a participative, co-created, subjective–objective reality (ontology), an experiential, propositional, practical epistemology producing co-created findings, and a practical methodology centered on political participation in collaborative action inquiry and a language that is grounded within a shared experiential context (Heron & Reason, 1997; Kemmis & McTaggart, 2000; Lincoln & Guba, 2000). Participatory research is characterized by researchers entering into interactive relations with research participants in some or all phases of the research. Clearly eschewing many of the last vestiges of positivism, the co-participation and co-constriction of knowledge can take place throughout the research process, including: collectively deciding on relevant research questions, determining appropriate data collection methods, collaboratively analyzing the results, and communicating the findings (Frisby et al., 2005; Greenwood et al., 1993; Reid, 2000; Ristock & Pennell, 1996). The participatory paradigm is a relatively new approach in qualitative inquiry generally, and has only recently begun to make an impact within sports studies. In particular, it is in the pioneering work of Wendy Frisby and colleagues (Frisby et al., 1997; Frisby et al., 2005), who have utilized participatory forms of research to ensure relevance (to the community under investigation), trustworthiness of the data, and that research projects in sport are conceptualized and conducted with the aim of improving the human condition.

Existing alongside these paradigms are a series of perspectives – each with its own criteria, assumptions and methodological practices – which are not as well unified or solidified as the paradigms (Denzin & Lincoln, 2000a). Privileging a materialist–realist ontology centered on a recognition that the real world makes a material difference in terms of race and gender, feminist, ethnic, Marxist, cultural studies and queer theory models (all of which are multiple projects) proffer a subjective epistemology and naturalistic (often ethnographic) methodologies (Denzin & Lincoln, 2000a). Under the influence of post-structural and postmodern sensibilities, the social text is itself problematized given the inability to fully represent the world of lived experiences; as such, works that emphasize reflexivity, that are multivocal, that are ground in the experiences of oppressed peoples and that focus on emancipation are produced (Denzin & Lincoln, 2000a).

Doing Contextual Sports Studies

Despite important differences among paradigms and a recent conceptual blurring (Denzin & Lincoln, 2000a; Fine et al., 2000; Lincoln & Guba, 2000) between paradigms, the qualitative researcher cannot afford to be naïve to the axiological, ontological, epistemological and methodological assumptions of each. As research becomes increasingly interdisciplinary, and given the recognition that all truths are "partial" and "incomplete" (Denzin & Lincoln, 2000a), the researcher is being freed from the shackles of a single way of seeing the world. As Lincoln & Guba (2000) suggest, the various paradigms are beginning to interbreed – such that two theorists previously thought to be in irreconcilable conflict may now appear, under a different theoretical rubric, to be informing one another's arguments. As such, it is time to shift the argument away from how different paradigms structure our efforts to "do" qualitative inquiry and which "label" best suits us. Instead, and as Schwandt (2000: 204) proposes, we should focus on the choices about how each of us wants to live the life of a social inquirer in terms of practical and moral knowledge – "how should I be towards these people I am studying?" This question of course raises a number of issues in respect to our differential quests, and indeed the underpinning reasons of our efforts, to critically interrogate the physically active, and socio-historically contextualized, human being. These issues therefore form the balance of this chapter, and indeed, the other chapters in this book.

In the spirit of Denzin and Lincoln's (2000c) call to "get on with it," and in an effort not to get caught in "prescribing" a "right way" to investigate the sporting empirical – every researcher will develop their own axiological, ontological and epistemological stances – we would like to devote some space to consideration of what a qualitative approach to sport might look like. Again, it is important to reiterate that we are not proposing to provide the "correct" or "only" way to address the sporting empirical; rather, the individual researcher will approach the social world with their own political, moral, ethical, ontological and epistemological positions that will inform the particular methodological strategies to be deployed. However, and in an attempt to aid us in recognizing the potential influence of our investigations and, of course, the (re)presentations of such investigations – whether written, performed, poetic, visual, auditory or involving a combination of these or some other forms – we draw on the work of Michelle Fine and colleagues (2001), who provide tentative "guidelines" for the qualitative researcher. These guidelines are useful across, between and beyond approaches to the sporting empirical and offer a lucid starting point for the critical interrogation of the sporting world. Fine and her colleagues propose a set of questions that each researcher may well ask of themselves as they conduct qualitative research. No matter the specific methodological approaches deployed as part of the armory of the qualitative researcher as bricoleur – an interdisciplinary jack of all trades (see Denzin & Lincoln, 2000b; Kincheloe, 2001; Lincoln, 2001) – the following list perhaps provides an idea of the life worlds, and indeed challenges, facing the qualitative researcher. Such a list, far from exclusive, and operating across paradigmatic (or not) boundaries, provides a useful point of departure for the qualitative researcher:

1. Have I connected the voices and stories of individuals back to the set of historic, structural and economic relations in which they are situated? (Is the sporting empirical addressed in context?)

2. Have I deployed multiple methods so that very different kinds of analysis have been constructed?
3. Have I described the mundane (as opposed to the unique or startling)?
4. Have some informants/constituencies/participants reviewed the material with me and interpreted, dissented, challenged my interpretations? And then how do I report these disagreements in perspective?
5. How far do I want to go with respect to theorizing the words of informants?
6. Have I considered how these data could be used for progressive, conservative, repressive social policies?
7. Where have I backed into the passive voice and decoupled my responsibility for my interpretations?
8. Who am I afraid will see these analyses? Who is rendered vulnerable/responsible or exposed by these analyses?
9. What dreams am I having about the material presented? (What issues am I pulling from my own biography and what emphasis have I given these?)
10. To what extent has my analysis offered an alternative to the common-sense or dominant discourse? What challenges might very different audiences pose to the analysis presented?

(Adapted from Fine et al., 2000: 126–7)

Clearly, such a list not only frames qualitative inquiry, but embodies a set of self-reflexive points of critical consciousness around how to "represent responsibility" (Fine et al., 2000: 108) and thereby transform public consciousness and common sense about the sporting empirical. Qualitative inquiry into the sporting empirical then is more than methodology alone; it is bound with a set of questions to do with oppression, marginalization, subordination, politics, the economy, crisis, morality, the status quo, the personal, the public and the private – it is a civic, participatory, collaborative project ensconced in moral dialogue (Denzin & Lincoln, 2000c).

In locating, or articulating, sport as an element of the cultural terrain within a wider cultural politics, qualitative inquiry of the sporting empirical can begin to understand sport as a site through which various discourses are mobilized in regard to the organization and discipline of daily life in the service of particular political agendas (Andrews, 1995; Giroux, 2001; Grossberg, 1992; 1997). Sport, thus becomes a component of a wider ideological critique that critically interrogates a range of sites in which the production of knowledge and identities takes place (Giroux, 2001). In essence then, at a methodological level, whatever the geographies and histories at stake, such an approach to the sporting empirical sets great store on situating (Hebdige, 1988) particular objects for analysis (Frow & Morris, 2000). By this, we mean that to understand the site or object of inquiry (sporting structures, experiences and forms) we need to understand the disparate structures that meet in and flow through sport. To do so, the critical sporting empiricist may not only draw upon, and cross, a number of disciplines and theoretical approaches, but also draw on a number of strategies of inquiry to aid in "situating sport." Somewhat modifying Frow and Morris then, the critical sport researcher may well attempt to:

1. Address the local and global economic context of sport
2. Address the aesthetic context – in relation to architecture, advertising and the interrelations between aesthetics and economies
3. Address the political context that addresses the mundane and the politics of physically active bodies in space
4. Address a gendered context – such as the organization of gender relations by a mythologized spatial structure
5. Address the ethnographic context – to get at the particularities of lived experience
6. Address the historical context – in terms of thinking through change and continuities
7. Address a textual context – allowing for consideration of sporting forms, structures and experiences as a textual construct and as a form of popular culture directly interrelated with other cultural forms and with an economy of representations and practices that make up a way of life.

(Adapted from Frow & Morris, 2000: 326–7)

Clearly, there would be very few qualitative inquiries that would be able to complete such an analysis; rather, the majority of cultural analyses accept their partiality and provide accounts that are openly incomplete and partisan and insist on the political dimensions of knowledge (Frow & Morris, 2000). In this way, critical analyses of the sporting empirical often start with the particular, sport, the "scrap of ordinary or banal existence," and then work outwards, upwards, internally, sideways and across to unpack the density of relations and intersecting social domains that inform it (Frow and Morris, 2000: 327).

The nuances of qualitative research are important for considering the type of impact, in respect to the generation of knowledge, which qualitative research designs can bring to our understanding of the sporting empirical. Indeed, as Maguire (1991) suggested, qualitative research provides a bold, imaginative, multidisciplinary view of sports studies that has the potential to tell us about human beings generally, rather than reducing them to variables within a performance-enhancing research agenda. Embracing the interpretive paradigm in sports studies clearly recognizes the complexity of the social world, the role of the researcher within that world and the meanings that people attribute to everyday life. Furthermore, through rejecting the idea that research can be carried out in some autonomous realm that is insulated from the wider society and from the particular biography of the researcher, the qualitative researcher in sports studies focuses on the qualitative values and meanings in the context of a "whole way of life" – a concern about sporting cultures, life-worlds and identities

– and thereby provides an opportunity for the expression of "other" cultures and indeed those from the margins of our own cultures. In essence, a qualitative approach to the critical interrogation of sport can provide the route by which our own sporting cultures can be made strange to us, allowing for new descriptions of the world to be generated which can offer the possibility of improvement of the human condition (Barker, 2000). This opens up the critical interrogation of sport to a plethora of intimate and previously "taboo" topics in the social sciences and sports studies – friendship, love, sexuality, physical violence, rape, body habitus, sexuality, ethnicity, physicality, misogyny, gender politics, (marginal) sub-identities, power, disempowerment, diaspora, exercise disorder behavior (a far from exhaustive list) – providing space for marginalized voices in important steps towards the democratization of (sporting) knowledge (Tedlock, 2000).

Strategies of Sporting Inquiry

We suggested above that the qualitative researcher is likely to be a bricoleur – a handyman or handywoman who makes use of the tools available to complete a task (Denzin & Lincoln, 1994). This of course can be as problematic as it is exciting for reaching the potentialities of contextual sports studies. Bricoleurs refute the limitations of a single method, the discursive strictures of one disciplinary approach, the historicity of certified modes of knowledge production, and the inseparability of the knower and known (Kincheloe, 2001). However, at the same time, bricolage is critiqued for potential superficiality, a failure to understand the disciplinary fields and knowledge bases from which particular modes of research emanate, and for signifying interdisciplinarity – a daunting concept for a graduate student and tenure track faculty member within the halls of institutionalized disciplinarity (Kincheloe, 2001). Yet, despite these critiques – negotiating the boundaries is never going to be easy – the potential gains and insights from such work can go some way to the development of a "vibrant democratic public culture and society" (Giroux, 2001). The contextual sports studies researcher then is likely to require an expansive and flexible methodological arsenal – not to mention an array of disciplinary knowledge bases. In terms of method, this point has been clearly made by Lawrence Grossberg, who noted:

> I believe that one can and should use any and every kind of empirical method, whatever seems useful to the particular project. Use them as rigorously and as suspiciously as you can ... I do not think that ethnography, or any other methodology, has a privileged status... Nor do I think that any one methodology has a greater claim to being somehow more empirical than another. Use anything, including surveys and statistics, if it seems useful, but consider how they are themselves rearticulated (and their practice changed) by the theoretical and political commitments ... of one's own project. I am in favor of anything that helps you gather more and better information, descriptions, resources, and interpretations. (Wright, 2001: 145)

Within this text then, we provide an array of strategies of inquiry that the critical sport researcher may choose from, and across, to locate sport within context – what we would essentially term as a contextual sports studies informed by a critical hermeneutics.[1] We have deliberately steered away from crudely splitting the process of gathering data (engaging the field) from the process of expressing data to an audience given they are highly interrelated, simultaneous and continuous processes (Burgess, 1984). Further, and in line with the latest "moments" addressed in the work of Denzin and Lincoln (2000b), there has been a recent shift towards a concern with various different ways of describing, inscribing and interpreting reality (Denzin, 1994; Richardson, 2000a; 2000b) in qualitative research, a concern that derived from recognition that qualitative written accounts have been the products of asymmetrical power relations. As such, we asked each of our contributors to think about how the particular methodological strategies that they explicate engage with newer forms of (re)presentation, including the multiple voices of those being represented and a rejection of the authoritative, realist and objectivist style of scientific writing (James, Hockey & Dawson, 1997). As such, the purview of the contributions is to provide the reader with a deeper comprehension of the types of questions that can be addressed by various approaches, the types of knowledge gained thus far from engagement with particular methodologies within the realm of sports studies, the nuances and techniques of the particular methodologies and the opportunities to be derived from utilizing the approaches within sports studies that have yet to be addressed, and critical reflection on "exemplar studies," providing the reader with (often personal) accounts of the actual research experience.

Given the above call to locate, or articulate, sport within the wider cultural context, and in an effort to avoid reducing "complex connections into simple catchwords" (Gottdiener, 2000: 7) we open this anthology with an explication of cultural studies that draws on the nuances of engaging and expressing the sporting empirical. Samantha King's contribution not only points to the ways in which cultural theorists in sports studies conceptualize, analyze and participate in the varied sites of the sporting empirical but highlights the ways in which "data" is weaved or articulated with political, economic and social contexts. In sum, King's contribution suggests a way for scholars to attune the sporting empirical to the methodological, epistemological and ontological debates that run throughout this text, yet at the same time negotiate praxis in linking the lived experience of human actors, and cultural texts and representations, with the broader political and economic structures of contemporary societies. This chapter sets the scene as it were for the deployment of qualitative strategies that can unearth and reconstruct the context within which a sporting practice, product or institution becomes understandable (Andrews, 2002).

In their chapter, "The Socio-Historical Process in Sports Studies," David Wiggins and Daniel Mason speak to the developments in sport history in recent decades – developments that have emerged from a recent self-referential examination of the discipline. Through epistemological and ontological transformations within the field, Wiggins and Mason point towards the insights that can be gained from a critical, interpretive sport history, distanced from objectivity, that can yield rich knowledges on social change and (dis)continuities with the present. In Chapter 4, "Sporting Ethnography – Philosophy, Methodology and Reflection," Michael Silk discusses the rich and troubled histories of ethnography and proposes that the variety of often contradictory approaches and epistemologies classified under the umbrella term "ethnography" provides an exciting space for the acceptance of competing ontologies and for the production of knowledge of the sporting empirical. Following discussion of the varied ethnographic approaches, Silk highlights how these have been taken up within the field of sports studies, pointing to the utility of ethnography in provision of space for marginalized voices in interrogation of dominant and subordinate power struggles, and in (re)connection of the field to the inexorable questions and tensions between praxis, politics and power. Finally, Silk provides a critical and personal reflection on his own work, a "confessional tale" (Sparkes, 1995) that offers the reader a first-hand account of an ethnographic experience.

Often bound with the multiple tools of the ethnographer, the techniques, philosophies and power relations in the practices of interviewing are worthy of academic consideration in their own right – a contention taken up by John Amis in Chapter 5 "Interviewing for Case Study Research." Amis proposes that to understand the various interpretations of social life requires a position of relativism, a realization underpinned by the logic that talking to people will provide access to the multiple realities, complexities, inconsistencies, contradictions and paradoxes of everyday lives. The chapter provides the reader with a trace of the different types of individual and group interview that have been used within sports studies and an account of the ethics of the research interview, the nuances of, and protocols inherent within, the interview process, and the political decisions made in interpretation, analysis, and expression of interview data. Finally, Amis points towards a number of exemplar studies that provide pointers towards good interviewing practice.

Given sport's embeddedness within the symbolic regimes of late capitalism, Darcy Plymire, in Chapter 6 "Qualitative Methods in Sport-Media Studies," highlights the recent boom in sport-media studies. Although media research has a long and established history, Plymire contends that due to its relatively recent entry into the field of sports studies, those studies centered on the relationships between the sport and the media have tended to be, for the most part, qualitative in nature and heavily influenced by the epistemological turn towards cultural studies within the academic study of sport. This influence has meant that the majority of sport-media studies have focused on (1) observations of production, (2) the text and (3) consumption. Plymire discusses the key researchers in each of these three areas, the epistemological, ontological and methodological approaches to each area and the rhetorical strategies that can be employed in expressing media research and points towards exemplar studies that have employed a multilayered approach to sport-media studies in an effort to provide a robust analytical framework.

As highlighted in a number of these chapters, the ways in which qualitative data is analyzed, interpreted and presented, have been the subject of a fundamental debate within the field of qualitative research design. Initially centered around the concern over the author's place in the text and over voice, who speaks, who is excluded, how individuals are given weight and how they are interpreted, debate emerged around the decisions made in, and the style of, qualitative writing (see Altheide & Johnson, 1994; Atkinson, 1992; Clifford & Marcus, 1986; Clough, 2001; Denzin, 1989; 1994; James et al., 1997; Sparkes, 1992; 1995; Richardson, 2000a; 2000b). The central concern was the realization that the qualitative account was often written in the language of science and that the researcher was a politically bound conduit for the decoding and recoding of the data. The concern with writing culture, and the emergence of differential styles of data presentation are essentially attempts to break down the misleading distinctions between science and rhetoric (Atkinson and Hammersley, 1994). These concerns have heralded a new age for qualitative research, one in which "messy," uncertain, multivoiced texts, cultural criticism and new alternative works have become more common (and in many ways displaced classic forms of representation as the "only" legitimate form) alongside reflexive forms of fieldwork, analysis and intertextual representation (Tedlock, 2000). These expressions of qualitative data are clearly more than just questions of semantics or aesthetics; rather such accounts clearly contribute to our understanding of social life (Denison & Rinehart, 2000; Richardson, 2000a), can create voices for previously silenced groups, and are thus at the center, according to Denzin and Lincoln (2000c) and Tedlock (2000), of qualitative practice. The final contributions to this volume speak in different ways to the philosophical and political strategies of expression.

Markula and Denison reveal the transformations in the expression of data in recent years, pointing towards the theoretical, methodological and interpretive convergences inherent in hailing writing as a method of inquiry and praxis. The particular focus for Chapter 7, "Sport and the Personal Narrative," is the insights to be gained from crafting stories from people's experiences, showing how lives are lived and understood as complete wholes from the inside and recognizing the role of the researcher in the reconstruction of the narrative text. From this juncture, Markula and Denison discuss the various steps and procedures in the conduct of storied research, the strategies involved in representation, and provide examples of different storied genres that have appeared within sports studies. Finally, the chapter deals with an oft-raised concern over "experimental" representations, the judgment of multiple, or relaxed, ways of representation.

While the borders between the "institution" and the "street," the (private) "intellectual" and the "public" are becoming increasingly crossed (Giroux, 2001) within a number of parent disciplines that inform sports studies – manifest for example through participatory research, intervention, art, image, film, performance, multiple voicing and stylized representations – there has been little movement within sports studies away from "scientific writing" as the form of expression (there are of course, a few notable exceptions which surface in a number of chapters within this volume). To remove the last vestiges of objectivity, yet sustain voice, an increasing number of scholars are moving towards performance as a mode of research/presentation (Carlson, 1996; Gergen & Gergen, 2000). In the final chapter in this volume, Heather Sykes, Jennifer Chapman and Anne Swedberg show how intellectual work can be both theoretical and performative in a personal account of the construction of a performance ethnography, based on life history interviews of physical education teachers, titled *Wearing the Secret Out*. Sykes et al. details the ontological, epistemological methodological issues inherent in life history interviewing and the potentialities of a "public pedagogy" and "performative politics" (Giroux, 2001), and offer a detailed account of the creation of a performance ethnography prior to reflecting on a number of important issues that emerged from the project.

Both of these final two chapters straddle a key issue in qualitative research – the intersection of epistemology and the dilemma of practice and politics. While there has been profound and dramatic transformation in the short histories of qualitative research in sports studies, concerns over self-reflexivity need not be barriers to the political and practical orientations of the qualitative researcher in sports studies. The key appears to be an almost contradictory ability to recognize and embody the insights from reflexive and deconstructive critiques of expression, yet maintain a "residual" need for political action, mis-representation, an historical pervasiveness and theoretical abstraction (Bourdieu, 1977; Quigley, 1997). In this way, writing, performance and as yet unimagined ways of expressing our research are never simply a narrative or a life story; rather they are wider projects that proffer a space for disputing conventional academic borders and expanding the range of cultural sites and locations across which knowledges, values, identities and social practices are produced and disseminated (Giroux, 2001). Such expressions not only embrace the tensions between the scientific and interpretive inquiry, between impersonal and experimental texts, and between realist and experiential analyses – the very struggles that will hopefully allow for the continued discussion of the litany of social, personal and ethical dilemmas and for the expansion of qualitative horizons within sports studies – but speak to the potential for a contextual sports studies to interrogate, critique, oppose and intervene in the most pressing social problems of our time.

Note

1. We acknowledge the existence and utility of an array of methodological approaches available to the sports studies researcher. For example, ground within a psychological perspective, are projective methods (e.g. laddering and the Zaltman technique) seeking to identify the cognitions and/or affect of people in sport. There also exists an array of other qualitative methods that take an avowedly positivistic stance which

have been used in sports studies (most notably, the Delphi technique in focus group research – see Fontana & Frey, 2000). However, given that these approaches lie outside the purview of the ontological and epistemological positions forwarded in our conceptualization of a contextual sports studies, and indeed are marginal to the potentialities we envision for the political and transformative agenda of the field, we have chosen not to incorporate such approaches in this text (although, for an excellent account of how focus groups have been rediscovered by postmodern feminist ethnographers given this utility in fostering the free expression of ideas in a collective forum, see Madriz, 2000; Amis, this volume).

References

Altheide, D. & Johnson, J. (1994). Criteria for Assessing Interpretive Validity in Qualitative Research. In N. Denzin & Y. Lincoln (eds). *Handbook of Qualitative Research*. London: Sage.

Andrews, D. (1995). Excavating Michael Jordan: Notes on a Critical Pedagogy of Sporting Representation. In G. Rail and J. Harvey (eds). *Sport and Postmodern Times: Culture, Gender, Sexuality, the Body and Sport*. Albany, NY: State University of New York Press.

—— (2002). Coming to Terms with Cultural Studies. *Journal of Sport and Social Issues*, 26, 1, 110–17.

Atkinson, P. (1992). *Understanding Ethnographic Texts*. London: Sage.

Atkinson, P., Coffey, A. & Delamont, S. (1999). Ethnography: Post, Past and Present. *Journal of Contemporary Ethnography*, 28, 5, 460–71.

Atkinson, P. & Hammersley, M. (1994). Ethnography and Participant Observation. In N. Denzin & Y. Lincoln (eds). *Handbook of Qualitative Research*. London: Sage.

Barker, C. (2000). *Cultural Studies: Theory and Practice*. London: Sage

Berg, B. (2001). *Qualitative Research Methods for the Social Sciences* (4th edition). Boston: Allen & Bacon.

Bourdieu, P. (1977). *Outline of a Theory of Practice*, trans. R. Nice. Cambridge: Cambridge University Press.

Burgess, R. (1984). *In the Field: An Introduction to Qualitative Research*. London: Allen & Unwin.

Burton, D. (ed.) (2000). *Research Training for Social Scientists: A Handbook for Graduate Students*. London: Sage.

Carlson, M. (1996). *Performance: A Critical Introduction*. London: Routledge.

Clifford, J. & Marcus, G. (eds) (1986). *Writing Culture: The Poetics and Politics of Ethnography*. Berkeley: University of California Press.

Clough, P. (2001). On the Relationship of the Criticism of Ethnographic Writing and the Cultural Studies of Science. *Cultural Studies ↔ Critical Methodologies*, 1, 2, 240–70.

Creswell, J. (1994). *Research Design: Qualitative and Quantitative Approaches*. London: Sage.

Denison, J. & Rinehart, R. (2000). Introduction: Imagining Sociological Narratives. *Sociology of Sport Journal*, 17, 1, 1–5.

Denscombe, M. (1998). *The Good Research Guide*. Buckingham, UK: Open University Press.

Denzin, N. (1989). *The Research Act: A Theoretical Introduction to Sociological Methods* (3rd edition). Englewood Cliffs, NJ: Prentice Hall.
—— (1994). The Art and Politics of Interpretation. In N. Denzin & Y. Lincoln (eds). *Handbook of Qualitative Research.* London: Sage
—— (1997). *Interpretive Ethnography.* London: Sage.
—— (2002). Confronting Ethnography's Crisis of Representation. *Journal of Contemporary Ethnography*, 31, 4, 482–90.
Denzin, N. & Lincoln, Y. (1994). Introduction: Entering the Field of Qualitative Research. In N. Denzin & Y. Lincoln (eds). *Handbook of Qualitative Research.* London: Sage.
—— (eds) (1998). *Strategies of Qualitative Inquiry.* London: Sage.
—— (eds) (2000a). *Handbook of Qualitative Research* (2nd edition). London: Sage.
—— (2000b). Introduction: The Discipline and Practice of Qualitative Research. In N. Denzin & Y. Lincoln (eds). *Handbook of Qualitative Research* (2nd edition). London: Sage.
—— (2000c). The Seventh Moment: Out of the Past. In N. Denzin & Y. Lincoln (eds). *Handbook of Qualitative Research* (2nd edition). London: Sage.
Fine, M., Weis, L., Weseen, S. & Wong, L. (2000). For Whom? Qualitative Research, Representations and Social Responsibilities. In N. Denzin & Y. Lincoln (eds). *Handbook of Qualitative Research* (2nd edition). London: Sage.
Fontana, A. & Frey, J. (2000). The Interview: From Structured Questions to Negotiated Text. In N. Denzin & Y. Lincoln (eds). *Handbook of Qualitative Research* (2nd edition). London: Sage.
Frisby, W., Crawford, S. & Dorer, T. (1997). Reflections in Participatory Action Research: The Case of Law-Income Women Accessing Local Physical Activity Services. *Journal of Sport Management*, 11, 1, 8–28.
Frisby, W., Reid, C., Millar, S. & Hoebnar, L. (2005, forthcoming). Putting "Participatory" into Participatory Forms of Action Research. *Journal of Sport Management*, Special Issue: Expanding Disciplinary Horizons (eds J. Amis and M. Silk).
Frow, J. & Morris, M. (2000). Cultural Studies. In N. Denzin & Y. Lincoln (eds). *Handbook of Qualitative Research* (2nd edition). London: Sage.
Gergen, M. & Gergen, K. (2000). Qualitative Inquiry: Tensions and Transformations. In N. Denzin & Y. Lincoln (eds). *Handbook of Qualitative Research* (2nd edition). London: Sage.
Giroux, H. (2001). Cultural Studies as Performative Politics. *Cultural Studies ↔ Critical Methodologies*, 1, 1, 5–23.
Gottdiener, M. (2000). Approaches to Consumption: Classical and Contemporary Perspectives. In M. Gottdiener (ed.). *New Forms of Consumption: Consumers, Culture, and Commodification.* Lanham, MD: Rowman & Littlefield.
Greenwood, D. J., Whytes, W. F. & Harkavy, I. (1993). Participatory Action Research as a Process and as a Goal. *Human Relations*, 46, 2, 175–92.
Grossberg, L. (1992). *We Gotta Get Out of this Place: Popular Conservatism and Postmodern Culture.* London: Routledge.
—— (1997). *Bringing it all Back Home: Essays on Cultural Studies.* Durham, NC: Duke University Press.
Hall, S. (1981). Notes on deconstructing "the popular." In R. Samuel (ed.). *People's History and Socialist Theory.* London: Routledge & Kegan Paul.
Hammersley, M. (1989). *The Dilemma of Qualitative Methods: Herbert Blumer and the Chicago Tradition.* London: Routledge.

Hammersley, M. & Atkinson, P. (1995). *Ethnography: Principles in Practice* (2nd edition). London: Routledge.
Harding, S. (1986). *The Science Question in Feminism.* Buckingham, UK: Open University Press.
Harrison, J., MacGibbon, L. & Morton, M. (2001). Regimes of Trustworthiness in Qualitative Research: The rigors of Reciprocity. *Qualitative Inquiry*, 7, 3, 323–45.
Hebdige, D. (1988). *Hiding in the Light: On Images and Things.* London: Comedia.
Heron, J. & Reason, P. (1997). A Participatory Inquiry Paradigm. *Qualitative Inquiry*, 3, 274–94.
Hollands, R. (1985). *Working for the Best Ethnography.* Birmingham: Centre for Contemporary Cultural Studies.
James, A. Hockey, J. & Dawson, A. (eds) (1997). *After Writing Culture: Epistemology and Praxis in Contemporary Anthropology.* London: Routledge.
Kemmis, S. & McTaggart, R. (2000). Participatory Action Research. In N. Denzin & Y. Lincoln (eds). *Handbook of Qualitative Research* (2nd edition). London: Sage.
Kincheloe, J. (2001). Describing the Bricolage: Conceptualizing a New Rigor in Qualitative Research. *Qualitative Inquiry*, 7, 6, 679–92.
Kuhn, T. (1962). *The Structure of Scientific Revolutions.* Chicago: University of Chicago Press.
Lewis, J. (1997). What Counts in Cultural Studies. *Media, Culture and Society*, 19, 83–97
Lincoln, Y. (2001). An Emerging New Bricoleur: Promises and Possiblities – A Reaction to Joe Kincheloe's "Describing the Bricoleur." *Qualitative Inquiry*, 7, 6, 693–705.
Lincoln, Y. & Guba, E. (1985). *Naturalistic Inquiry.* London: Sage.
—— (2000). Paradigmatic Controversies, Contradictions, and Emerging Confluences. In N. Denzin & Y. Lincoln (eds). *Handbook of Qualitative Research* (2nd edition). London: Sage.
Madiz, E. (2000). Focus Groups in Feminist Research. In N. Denzin & Y. Lincoln (eds). *Handbook of Qualitative Research* (2nd edition). London: Sage.
Maguire, J. (1991). Human Sciences, Sport Sciences, and the Need to Study people "In the Round." *Quest*, 43, 190–206.
Quigely, D. (1997). Deconstructing Colonial Fictions? Some Conjuring Tricks in the Recent Sociology of India. In A. James, J. Hockey & A. Dawson (eds). *After Writing Culture: Epistemology and Praxis in Contemporary Anthropology.* London: Routledge.
Reid, C. (2000). Seduction and Enlightenment in Feminist Action Research. *Resources for Feminist Research*, 28, 1/2, 169–88.
Richardson, L. (2000a). Writing: A Method of Inquiry. In N. Denzin & Y. Lincoln (eds). *Handbook of Qualitative Research* (2nd edition). London: Sage.
—— (2000b). Evaluating Ethnography. *Qualitative Inquiry*, 6, 2, 253–5.
Ristock, J. L. and Pennell, J. (1996), *Community Research as Empowerment: Feminist Links, Postmodern Interruptions.* Oxford: Oxford University Press.
Schwandt, T. (2000). Three Epistemological Stances for Qualitative Inquiry: Interpretivism, Hermeneutics, and Social Constructionism. In N. Denzin & Y. Lincoln (eds). *Handbook of Qualitative Research* (2nd edition). London: Sage.
Silverman, D. (2000). *Doing Qualitative Research: A Practical Handbook.* London: Sage
Slack, J. D. (1996). The Theory and Method of Articulation in Cultural Studies. In D. Morley & K.H. Chen (eds). *Stuart Hall: Critical Dialogues in Cultural Studies.* London: Routledge.

Sparkes, A. (1992). Writing and the Textual Construction of Realities: Some Challenges for Alternative Paradigms in Physical Education. In A. Sparkes (ed.). *Research in Physical Education and Sport: Exploring Alternative Visions.* London: Falmer Press.
—— (1995). Writing People: Reflections on the Dual Crises of Representation and Legitimation in Qualitative Inquiry. *Quest,* 45, 188–95.
Tedlock, B. (2000). Ethnography and Ethnographic Representation. In N. Denzin & Y. Lincoln. *Handbook of Qualitative Research* (2nd edition). London: Sage.
Wright, K.H. (2001). "What's going on?" Larry Grossberg on the Status Quo of Cultural Studies: An Interview. *Cultural Values,* 5, 2, 133–62.
Yin, R. (1994). *Case Study Research: Design and Methods.* London: Sage.

2

Methodological Contingencies in Sports Studies

Samantha J. King

In the face of what has come to be viewed as the widespread misuse of the signifier "cultural studies," scholars in the field have devoted considerable energy to defining and delineating the criteria for effective cultural studies research (Andrews, 2002; Bennett, 1992; Grossberg, 1989a; 1989b; 1997a; 1997b; Grossberg et al., 1992; Hall, 1980a; 1980b; Johnson 1986/7; Nelson, 1994).[1] A claim common to most of these expositions is that the field of cultural studies is characterized by a refusal either to endorse a singular method, or to conceive of and apply methodological tools as rigid, formal templates. Indeed, the usefulness of cultural studies as a critical approach for understanding cultural phenomena is said by these scholars to lie in its interdisciplinarity, anti-formalism, and flexibility – particularly in its sensitivity to changing economic, political, and social conditions.

Taking these claims seriously, this chapter is less of a "how to" guide to cultural studies, and more of an exploration of the ways that the different methods discussed in the remainder of this volume have been taken up within cultural studies analyses of sport (i.e., in "sports studies"). In drawing attention to the enormously diverse range of methods deployed in the field, it is particularly concerned with elaborating upon the assertion that cultural studies research is "sensitive" to its economic, political, and social context. In so doing, the chapter characterizes sports studies as a practice that is most useful when it is characterized by *methodological contingency*. As is the case with other research traditions, effective work in sports studies employs the methodological tools that will best enable the researcher to answer her or his research questions. Cultural studies approaches to sport are distinctive, however, in that the assembled sources are always analyzed within the context of a network of economic, political, and social linkages that produce and give meaning to them. Called "contextual analysis" or "articulation" by scholars in the field, and strongly embedded in neo-Marxist theories of culture and society, these approaches provide both a methodological framework "for understanding how cultural theorists conceptualize the world, analyze it, and participate in shaping it" (Slack, 1996: 112) as well as a strategy for mapping the complexity of the "constant battlefield" that is cultural life (Hall, 1981: 233).

What is Cultural Studies and What is it Good For?

In vastly oversimplified terms, cultural studies draws on elements of sociology, anthropology, political science and theory, literary and media studies, history, semiotics, and philosophy to analyze cultural experiences, practices, texts, and institutions. Cultural studies is therefore "not so much a discipline, but an area where different disciplines intersect in the study of the cultural aspects of society" (Hall et al., 1980: 7).

Most histories of the field point to its formation in post-war Britain and the contribution of scholars Richard Hoggart, Raymond Williams and E.P. Thompson to the radical rethinking of what cultural forms constitute legitimate objects of study (Hoggart, 1957; Williams, 1958; Thompson, 1963). Instead of reducing culture to canonical literary texts and works of art ("high culture"), these authors argued for an understanding of culture as a "whole way of life" (Williams, 1958: 310). This opened the way for analyses of working-class and popular culture, for explorations of the mundane and the marginal, and for discussions of the variously oppressive and liberatory potential of cultural relations. Although early work in cultural studies tended to focus on white, male, working-class culture, the 1980s witnessed the widespread recognition that research in the field must take seriously the intersection of relations of class with race, gender, sexuality, and nation in shaping the experience and organization of everyday life.

Given the concern of cultural studies with the everyday and the ordinary, it should come as no surprise that in addition to cultural forms such as clothing, music, and popular media, sport emerged early on as a key site of analysis within the field. Mirroring broader debates about how best to theorize the relationship between "culture" and "society," the connection between "sport" and "society" represented a central problematic in initial work in sports studies.

Writing in 1982, for example, Paul Willis noted that much contemporary physiological and sociological research on women in sport exhibited "the clearest aspects of positivism in contemporary social research" (1993: 33). The research to which Willis was referring centered on the ability of women to achieve in sport and attempted to isolate a range of variables – physical and/or cultural – that might explain particular levels of athletic achievement. Such "linear determinism," Willis noted, does not get us very far in understanding the social meaning of a phenomenon. He wrote: "[T]o know, more exactly, why it is a women can muster only 90 per cent of a man's strength cannot help us comprehend, explain, or change the massive feeling in our society that a woman has no business flexing her muscles anyway" (Willis, 1993: 33). Even if it *were* possible to identify all the relevant variables shaping the relationship of women with sport, moreover, the number would be so large as to make plotting co-variation and determination impossible. Beyond this, Willis noted, there is no way to quantify cultural meaning as it is circulates through ideological systems, social attitudes, and cultural values and, furthermore, cultural processes do not operate in a unidirectional manner: "It is not the case," he wrote, "that there is a culture over here that affects sport over there, in a simple, one-way relationship" (Willis, 1993: 33).

To acknowledge that sporting practices, texts, subcultures, institutions, and events (hereinafter referred to as "sport") are shaped by "society" and in turn shape "society" goes someway towards a more useful conceptualization of the sport and society problematic in that it moves us away from linear determinism and towards a more dynamic sense of the relationship between the two. But it still assumes an analytically imposed separation between these realms such that "society" appears as a "great monolithic entity, with a protuberance – sport – stuck on the outside" (Willis, 1993: 33): "The understanding of interrelationship and interconnection is of the essence," Willis argued, "if we are even to ask the right questions" (1993: 33) (Figure 2.1). Here Willis advocated a contextual, cultural studies approach to the study of women and sport. In doing so, he joined a growing number of sport scholars who at that time were drawing on the cultural studies tradition to understand the place of sport in society (Cantelon & Gruneau, 1982; Gruneau, 1983; J. E Hargreaves, 1982; J. A. Hargreaves, 1982a; Hollands, 1984).

The particular contribution of cultural studies to research on sport, according to Robert Hollands (1984), has been to link up the lived experience of human actors, and cultural texts and representations, with the broader political and economic structures of modern industrial societies. In other words, cultural studies research conceives sport *relationally*. To paraphrase Cary Nelson, the analysis of a sporting text, discourse, behavior, ritual, style, genre or subculture does not constitute cultural studies – despite claims often made to the contrary – unless the thing being analyzed is considered in terms of its "competitive, reinforcing, and determining relations" with other objects and forces (1994: 199).

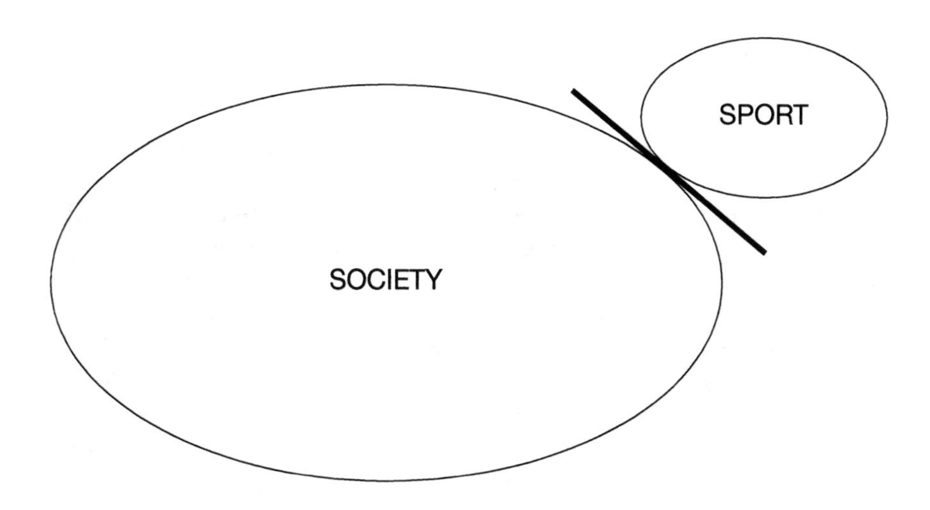

Figure 2.1 *The "sport as a reflection of society" approach*

Contextual Analysis/Articulation: Theoretical and Methodological Contingencies

Thus, although as the introduction to this chapter made clear, cultural studies has never been dominated by a single theoretical or methodological position – according to Stuart Hall (1992), its growth has been characterized by an ongoing "unity-in-difference" – it can be distinguished by an orientation to research and writing processes that seeks to capture the relationality of culture. The term "articulation" has been used most often to describe this orientation. In its manifestation as a theoretical sensibility, articulation offers for scholars in sports studies a model of society as a "layered complex of elements" – including sporting phenomena in all their variety – "all intricately and dialectically interrelated with one another" (Willis, 1993: 33). As a methodological ethos, articulation provides strategies for undertaking a cultural study of sport, that is, for contextualizing one's object of analysis.

It seems important to recognize here – via a rather lengthy detour – that articulation is referred to variously as a concept, a theory, a method, a political strategy, and sometimes as a combination thereof (Andrews, 2002; Grossberg, 1997a; Slack, 1996). How articulation might be best categorized is a difficult question to settle given that theory and method are conceived of as mutually constitutive in cultural studies research on sport (Andrews, 2002; Grossberg 1997a). This difficulty is compounded, moreover, by the fact that articulation has more explanatory power than a concept (it is in part an attempt to reconfigure the perceived economic determinism of classical Marxism and the relativism of cultural humanism, both of which were key influences in the emergence of cultural studies), but at the same time does not pretend to offer an overarching explanation of social structure and social change. This is typical of theoretical approaches deployed within cultural studies because although the field is theoretical, it does not "apply" pre-existing theory as an objective, formal tool that can be attached with "exact theoretical fit" to a given empirical field (Morris, 1997; Slack, 1996). Nor does cultural studies "do theory" as a literary genre – it would be hard to imagine, for instance, a self-described cultural studies scholar whose oeuvre is devoted to theoretical exegesis of articulation or any other central line of thought (Morris, 1997: 43). Rather, theory within cultural studies is developed in relation to changing epistemological and political conditions and thus is itself radically contextualized. In Cary Nelson's (1994) words: "Cultural studies accepts the notion that the work of theorizing its enterprise is inescapably grounded in contemporary life and current politics. New social and political realities require fresh reflection and debate on the cultural studies enterprise, no matter what historical period one is studying" (1994: 202). So, while contextual analysis is committed to a "detour through theory," it is not "theory-driven." The detour it takes is used to "help ground our engagement with what newly confronts us and to let that engagement provide the ground for retheorizing" (Slack, 1996: 115).

To illustrate this point with reference to the field of sports studies, in the early 1980s, when the field was relatively young, and the history of modern sport was inadequately theorized, scholars working in the cultural studies tradition (particularly those located in Britain and Canada) produced a plethora of Gramscian-inspired work (Cantelon & Gruneau, 1982; Gruneau, 1983; 1988; J. A. Hargreaves, 1982a; 1982b; 1987; Ingham & Hardy, 1984). For Italian theorist, socialist activist, and political prisoner Antonio Gramsci (1971), hegemony was the consent given by the great masses of the population to the ideological leadership exercised by the dominant group through the state as well as civic and cultural institutions and processes. In this way, his writing challenged those strains of Marxist thought that viewed the mode of production or the economic base as producing and shaping all other elements in a social formation – including culture – and in which there was little room for understanding culture as at moments productive of economic relations as a potential site for resistance to capitalist relations. Gramsci used hegemony to refer not simply to political and economic control, moreover, but also to the success on the part of the dominant group in projecting its own particular way of seeing the world so that this becomes accepted as "common sense." Because hegemony relies on the consent of the dominated it was always, he argued, subject to contestation, negotiation, and redefinition. Gramsci's aim was to understand these complex processes and the ways that culture was related to domination and resistance in the service of change towards socialism (Hargreaves & McDonald, 2000).

Gramsci's ideas enabled scholars to conceptualize the emergence of modern sport in terms of a process of ongoing struggle, rather than either a "cultural by-product of the technological and social changes associated with the development of an urban and industrial society" à la modernization theory (Gruneau, 1988: 9), or a superstructural effect determined by capitalist relations of production – the dominant approach among Marxist scholars of sport up until that point (Brohm, 1978; Hoch, 1972; Vinnai, 1973). More specifically, Gramsci's writings held particular appeal for British scholars of this era because they helped challenge orthodox Marxist theories – the inadequacies of which had become apparent in the failure of the left to predict or forestall the popular appeal of Thatcherism – while maintaining ideology, class analysis and political economy as core concerns.

As the 1980s proceeded and the Reaganite/Thatcherite ideologies of self-responsibility gained the status of hegemony, the body became the site of condensation for a whole range of social anxieties. Fat bodies, crack bodies and HIV-positive bodies all became symbols of failed self-discipline and what Susan Willis terms the "hard body" emerged as the ideal against which these abject bodies were measured (Cole, 1993). As this new social, political, and economic formation took shape, many scholars in the cultural studies of sport and the body turned to the writings of French philosopher Michel Foucault (particularly *Discipline and Punish* [1979] and *The History of Sexuality* [1980]) to help "ground their engagement" with this new set of conditions (Andrews, 1993; Bartky, 1988;

Bordo, 1993; Cole, 1993; Hargreaves, 1987). While Gramsci's insights into cultural struggle remained key for understanding how one particular set of beliefs about the body and sport gained dominance during late capitalism, Foucault's writings on normalizing power provided insight into the micro-level practices through which individuals take up social norms in ongoing processes of bodily management. Moreover, in articulating the pivotal place that the body occupies in social relations, Foucault's work proved indispensable to scholars in sports studies who in the face of the emergence of the fit body as a primary emblem of neoconservative ideologies of the period were faced with the realization that the body had been neglected, if not erased, from research on sport (Andrews, 1993; Cole, 1993; Hargreaves, 1987).

As this discussion makes clear, "from a cultural studies perspective ... one never imagines that it is possible to theorize for all times and places" (Nelson, 1994: 202). While work in cultural studies is theoretically contingent, however, it has been consistent, as Stuart Hall argues, in conceiving of the cultural realm as a "constant battlefield" in which the constraining forces of social structures vie with the creative impulses of human actors (1981: 233). As such, sports studies research reflects the broader field and particularly the work of Stuart Hall in attempting to move beyond more reductionist Marxist understandings of the relationship between culture and society as economically determined and cultural humanist approaches which, at the other end of the spectrum, argue that there exists no necessary correspondence between different elements in a society, or between the social structure/economic base and the cultural realm.

It would be beyond the scope of this chapter to explore questions about the relationship of base to superstructure in any more detail, and at the risk of caricaturing both orthodox Marxism and cultural humanism, suffice it to say that the contextual bent of cultural studies assumes that while there are no necessary correspondences, there are always real or effective correspondences between lines of force in a social formation.[2] Thus, the meanings, effects and politics of particular practices, texts and structures are never guaranteed and alternative configurations of social relations are always possible.

More specifically, it is through articulation (the joining of two parts) that social forces are connected and through disarticulation that social forces are disconnected. Hall, drawing on Althusser, defines articulation as follows:

> [T]he form of the connection that *can* make a unity of two different elements, under certain conditions. It is a linkage which is not necessary, determined, absolute and essential for all time. You have to ask, under what circumstances *can* a connection be forged or made? So the so-called "unity" of a discourse is really the articulation of different, distinct elements which can be rearticulated in different ways because they have no necessary "belongingness." The "unity" which matters is a linkage between the articulated discourse and the social forces with which it can, under certain historical conditions, but need not necessarily, be connected. Thus, a theory of articulation is both a way of understanding how ideological elements come, under certain conditions, to cohere together within a discourse, and a way of

> asking how they do or do not become articulated at specific conjunctures, to certain political subjects. (1986: 141–2)

What makes articulation particularly useful is that it presents a way out of what Meghan Morris calls "paralyzing debates" about the relative status of different practices conceptualized as though they were mutually exclusive realities (e.g., the "discursive" and the "real") and a way to ask, instead, how these practices connect and interact in specific instances (1997: 47).

This, in very broad strokes, is how articulation works as a "'*process*' in the world around us" (Morris, 1997: 48), but, as I have already emphasized, articulation is also a methodological practice – in order to "do" articulation, it is necessary to reconstruct or fabricate the network of social, political, economic, and cultural articulations, or linkages, that produce any particular cultural phenomenon and trace, in turn, how the phenomenon (re)shapes the formation of which it is a part. Indeed, as Sugden and Tomlinson suggest, theoretical models are ideal-typical and society as lived out is a "much more fluid enterprise" (2002: 9). Drawing on Michael Mann (1986), they argue that it is only through empirical research, not theory, that we can understand how particular social forces are articulated to one another or what these articulations might mean to those engaged with them.

This fluid understanding of social relations also means that articulation as a methodological sensibility cannot be deployed as a rigid template or offered up as a set of clearly defined practical techniques for undertaking research as is the case with research methods traditionally defined (Slack 1996). The outline that follows should therefore be read with two general insights, put forth by Slack (1996), in mind: first, articulation is not a completely "sewn-up" method but rather a complex, unfinished perspective that continues to emerge geneaologically. Second, articulation should not be understood as "simply one thing" (Slack, 1996: 115). It has been discussed and developed in ways that variously background and foreground certain theoretical, methodological, political and strategic forces, interests and issues. It has thus emerged unevenly within a configuration of those forces and carries with it "traces" of forces from one piece of scholarly interpretation to another.

Doing Contextual Analysis

The process and procedures through which contextual analysts gather and analyze their data or sources, the research ethics that must be considered, the question of the relationship between the researcher and the "researched," and concerns about validity, all vary according to the research questions under exploration and the methodological tools borrowed, combined, worked and reworked in any particular project. These issues are best adddressed, therefore, in the context of discussions about particular methods in the chapters that follow.

Having said this, the understanding of sport as an element of the cultural terrain through which disparate forces flow and coalesce, and the emphasis on situating particular objects for analysis, require that researchers draw on at least some of the possible strategies outlined by Silk, Andrews and Mason in Chapter 1 (Frow and Morris, 2000; Hebdige, 1988; Silk, Andrews & Mason, this volume). These might include critically analyzing the research object's economic, political, gendered, racial, historical, ethnographic, or textual contexts, among many possible others. Although, as Silk et al. note, there would be very few inquiries that would be able to explore all of these realms, the most successful research in cultural studies tends to be the most complex and intricate in its analysis of context – even as its practitioners acknowledge its inevitable partiality and incompleteness.

Instead of presenting a step-by-step guide, then, I explore the ways that the six different qualitative methods described in the remaining chapters of this volume might be deployed in contextual analyses of the sporting world and in so doing aim to highlight the strengths of articulation as a mode of analysis for advancing the field of sports studies. Inspired by Toby Miller's (2001) introductory essay in *A Companion to Cultural Studies*, the analysis is presented in the form of a table. The left side of the table highlights key features of contextual methodology – "what it is and how it works" – and the right side highlights "what it isn't and how it doesn't work." As Miller acknowledges, attempts to draw lists like the one below, especially when they engage in binarization, are inevitably fraught since demonstrating the linguistic and thus material interdependence of supposed opposites has been at the core of much work in cultural studies, and such lists depend on oversimplification and generalizations about the methods under analysis. In the present case, by necessity, both sides of the table, but especially the right side, are ideal types, or caricatures, of what are in reality are extraordinarily diverse approaches to scholarship. Nevertheless, I have tried to compile some central and recognizable features of contextual and "acontextual" research because binaries are, in Miller's words, "good to think with and good to tinker with" (2001: 7) and it is in this spirit of openness and incompleteness that the table is presented.

A Note on Objectivity

As the table makes clear, contextual cultural studies analysis makes no pretensions to scientific objectivity or political disinvestment. It assumes that all scholarship is partial (that is, incomplete and partisan) and that our research methods and theories cannot be usefully distinguished from their social origins and institutional locations. However, research in cultural studies goes further than other methodologies that refuse claims to objectivity in that it is always undertaken – explicitly – as a response to and intervention in political and social conditions. To take some examples from recent work, Kent Ono's (1997) essay "'America's' Apple Pie: Baseball, Japan-Bashing, and the Sexual Threat of Economic Miscegenation" is explicitly positioned as a response to what Ono demonstrates to be the racist ideologies motivating anxieties about Japanese investment in major league baseball in the United States. For scholars and activists struggling to end the use of Native American team names, logos, and

Table 2.1 *Contextual Sports Studies*

	What it is/how it works	*What it isn't/how it doesn't work*
History	Premised on the understanding that social practices, not nature, genius, or individuality make a way of life and change over time; sometimes known as "cultural materialism."	Highlights the role of individual failures and accomplishments in the creation of cultural forms and change over time.
	Rather than focusing on individual people, dates, and events as representative of cultural dynamics and change, focuses on the products of culture and their circumstances of creation and circulation (Williams, 1977).	A documentarian approach that records the facts of the sporting world in order to preserve specific insights into the time period in question; does not "read" products or consider their circumstances of creation and circulation.
	Focuses on marginal, ordinary, everyday, and grass-roots sport experiences as well as those of the dominant culture; demonstrates how sport is produced by ordinary people and repackaged and sold back to them.	Often privileges the actions and experiences of dominant groups (e.g., sport leaders, elite athletes, organized sport).
	Focuses on power relations, conflict and struggle. As Miller writes, "The relations of culture, their twists and turns, the often violent and volatile way in which they change, are part of the material life of society" (2001: 5).	Utilizes a one-dimensional approach focused on linear "marches of progress," such that power dynamics are often invisible.
	Examples: Adams, 2004; Cahn, 1994; Farred, 1999; Gillick, 1984; Gruneau & Whitson, 1994; Staurowsky, 2001.	
Ethnography	Recognizes spaces of fieldwork as already thoroughly mediated through other projects of representation.	Through thick description provided by the ethnographic reporter, conceives of and recreates the object of ethnography as an "unmediated site of discovery" (Marcus, 2001: 182).
	Involves reflexive, contextual fieldwork which interprets and maps the experiences of subjects within layers and competing sectors of those representations (Marcus, 2001).	

Table 2.1 *Contextual Sports Studies (continued)*

	What it is/how it works	*What it isn't/how it doesn't work*
	An approach known as "writing culture," as opposed to recording an objective reality that is "out there" (Clifford and Marcus, 1986).	
	Conceptualizes mediated experiences as articulations of broader social forces, which must be mapped in their complexity in order to understand the ethnographic lifeworld under investigation; that is, ethnographic lifeworlds are considered to develop in specific historical contexts.	Focuses on the "internal" dynamics of the ethnographic setting rather than broader social forces and patterns of development; as Silk suggests in this volume, this has been an observation made, in particular, about symbolic interactionist ethnography.
	The effort to connect ethnographic interpretations to wider social processes is linked to the political commitment of cultural studies research, particularly the struggle to overcome social oppressions of class, race, and gender.	Eschews politicized forms of ethnography as subjective, unscientific, and hence invalid.
	Examples: Crossett & Beal, 1997; Donnelly, 1985; Gruneau, 1989; MacNeil, 1996; Silk, 2001; Wheaton, 2002; Zwick & Andrews, 1999.	
Interviewing	In cultural studies, has primarily been used to explore how audiences interact with media texts ranging from news programming, to soap operas, to television commercials; although contextual media studies is discussed above, here the focus is specifically on audience research.	Experimental or survey methods focused on the attitudinal and behavioral consequences of media tests on viewers while ignoring their active, interpretive capacities.
	Key assumption of contextual audience research is that the influences of the media cannot be "read" simply from the message of any media text and that interviews with consumers are necessary to understand what audiences do with what they consume.	
	Understands responses to interviews to be negotiated within structural constraints.	
	Examples: Wilson & Sparks, 1996.	

	What it is/how it works	*What it isn't/how it doesn't work*
Media Studies	Interpretive and political approach to analyzing media institutions, practices, and products.	Deploys an apolitical conception of communication with functional and practical research objectives.
	Rather than claiming objectivity or an ability to record and measure truth, concerned with how positivist, objectivist research might collude with dominant political and economic systems.	Positivist and objectivist.
	Draws on a structural and historical model of ideology. For example, the "criminal male athlete" – the subject of numerous analyses in sports studies – is not treated as a "fact" consumed in the circuit of public communication, but as a *relation* "in terms of the social forces and contradictions accumulating within it . . . or in terms of the wider historical context in which it occurs" (Hall et al., 1978: 185); that is, the historical context is precisely what *produces* the "criminal athlete."	Acontextual reading of texts with transactional conceptualization of ideology in which the "criminal male athlete," for instance, is treated as a fact that remains as such "underneath" whatever representations of it are circulated through the public sphere.
	Examples: Cole, 1997; Cole and Hribar, 1995; Hartmann, 2001; Howell, 1991; King, 2000; King & Springwood, 2000; Maharaj, 1999; McDonald, 2005; McDonald & Andrews, 2001; Miller, 1998; Ono, 1997; Rowe, 1999; Sandell, 1995.	
Personal Narrative	Recognizes that narratives always exist in tension with various other accounts; that is, stories are not stories in their own right – they don't claim to show a real, valid culture underneath the official version waiting to be revealed – but only exist in tension with other stories (Steedman, 1987).	According to Joan Scott, accounts that use experience as an authenticating source deploy a "referential notion of evidence which denies that it [evidence] is anything but a reflection of the real" (1992: 24); that is, acontextual personal narratives often fail to question the truth of veracity of memory and therefore of the account itself; experience in this context becomes incontestable evidence and the foundation upon which analyses are based.

Table 2.1 *Contextual Sports Studies (continued)*

	What it is/how it works	*What it isn't/how it doesn't work*
	Shares in common with contextual critical ethnography a concern with the practice of writing and representation (see Markula, this volume)	
	Recognizes the dynamic relationship between competing accounts of the world and thus allows the possibility that a critical examination of personal experience can contribute to a reworking of existing theories and paradigms.	
	Assumes that personal experience is the process by which subjectivity is constructed. In de Lauretis's words, "Through that process one places oneself or is placed in social reality and so perceives and comprehends as subjective ... those relations –material, economic, and inter-personal – which are in fact social, and, in a larger perspective, historical" (de Laurentis, 1984: 159); thus, by analyzing experience in the broader context of the social world, it is possible to trace how subjectivities are constructed and in turn how we help shape, as active agents, the world around us.	When personal narratives are decontextualized, questions about the constructed nature of experience, how subjects are constituted, and how their vision is structured, are erased; the evidence of personal experience then becomes evidence for the fact of difference, rather than a way of exploring how difference is established, how it operates, and how it constitutes subjects who see and act in the world.
	Examples: *Sociology of Sport Journal Special Issue*, 17, 1, 2000; Sparkes (1996; 2002).	
Performance Ethnography	Like ethnography and personal narrative, shares a concern with the politics of representation both within and beyond academic writing.	
	In particular, seeks to find new ways of presenting scholarly work so that it moves beyond the confines of the academic world and becomes more immediately politically and socially useful and engaged.	A purely artistic/scholarly exercise.

	What it is/how it works	*What it isn't/how it doesn't work*
	Experimental, artistic, public political, interdisciplinary, collaborative, inter-textual, multi-vocal, participatory, interactive, and always in progress.	Mainstream, scientific, private, apolitical, disciplinary, individualist, non-collaborative, unitextual, univocal, unidirectional, complete.
	Seeks to open the meanings of research to the informants/research subjects and to wide audiences; the emphasis is on speaking "with informants and audiences rather than speaking for or about them" (Mienczakowski, 1998: 117).	Dictatorial, purely academic, objectifying.

mascots in the world of college and professional sports, Rosemary Coombe's (1999) "Sports Trademarks and Somatic Politics: Locating the Law in a Critical Cultural Studies" highlights the vulnerability of such trademarks to political critique and the claims of those they (mis)represent (i.e. Native Americans). As such, her essay cautions us to consider the politically generative capacities of sports trademarks (be they the Washington Redskins or the Nike swoosh) as we might also struggle to abolish them.

Although these analyses demonstrate unambiguous political commitments, we should be clear that to undertake cultural analysis and commentary is not tantamount to undertaking political action. As Ian McDonald argues in an essay on critical social research on sport and political intervention, to identify and critically analyze dominant power relations can help create the possibility for transformation, but it is not the same as "securing practical changes" (2002: 108). Describing his involvement with an anti-racism campaign in which he was both an activist and researcher, he highlights the dangers that involvement in activism can pose to academic integrity, but also the benefits that a symbiotic relationship between the two can bring. He writes: "As an activist I knew that academically sound research could be used as powerful evidence to pressurize the ECB [English Cricket Board] into action. As a social researcher I was committed to the production of knowledge that would expose and explain injustice and unequal relations of power, and thus provide the possibility for social change" (McDonald 2002: 114). Cultural studies, since its inception, has been distinguished by its commitment to exposing dominant configurations of power and it has done so by tracing the articulation of economic, political and social forces in the cultural field. Cultural studies researchers should be aware, however, that doing contextual analysis is not equivalent to rearticulating, in a practical sense, those conjunctures of forces that produce the conditions under analysis.

Potential Pitfalls

Like any approach to scholarly production, contextually contingent research has its potential pitfalls. Because there is no template for contextual analysis, no clearly identifiable place at which a particular study should begin or end, there is a danger that radical contextualization becomes random contextualization. There is a tendency within cultural studies research, for instance, for scholars to assert connections without doing the careful work that it takes to reconstruct the connection and to show it actually exists. When this occurs, the context begins to appear as a mere backdrop to the object of study and to exist independently of it, rather than as a set of productive social forces that represents the conditions of *possibility* for the appearance of that object in its current form and that is therefore a constitutive part of it. So while contextual analysis asks how economic, political, social and cultural forces shape and produce the phenomenon being analyzed, it is not sufficient to merely identify the context into which a particular text is inserted. Indeed, Grossberg (1992) has argued that the context is in some sense the goal and end product of any cultural studies analysis and that as such it will only be defined more fully at its conclusion. It could be argued, of course, that this potential weakness in contextual research is not evidence of the limitations of the approach itself, but of bad scholarship. While this might be so, contextual analysis does lend itself to this possibility.

While contextual analysis tries to move us away from a concern with sport "for its own sake" or sport as a practice isolated from broader social forces, there is also a danger that the object of analysis, the thing we are trying to understand, might get "lost" in the context. While the study of sport *in itself* is a rather limited intellectual and political enterprise, it is nonetheless necessary to carefully excavate the nature, meaning and organization of the phenomenon under analysis, for it is at this level that the articulation of social forces is experienced and at which they might also be transformed or rearticulated.

Notes

1. This chapter is heavily indebted to David Andrews' essay "Coming to Terms with Cultural Studies," which appeared in the February 2002 edition of the *Journal of Sport and Social Issues*. Andrews' piece issued a call for intellectual specificity on the part of scholars claiming to do cultural studies work on sport, but also outlined some primary methodological tenets of cultural studies research. My chapter can be read as an attempt to elaborate on the latter. I am also grateful to Ben Carrington for his comments on an earlier draft of this chapter.
2. In a recent essay on post-Marxism and the sociology of sport, for example, Ian McDonald argues that "within the broad Marxist tradition, only the most fatalistically naive Second Internationalist, or the most ideologically driven Stalinist, would insist on the 'absolute predictability of particular outcomes'" (2004: 4).

References

Adams, M. L. (2004). Freezing Social Relations: Ice, Rinks and the Development of Figure Skating. In P. Vertinsky & J. Bale (eds). *Sites of Sport: Space, Place, Experience*. London: Routledge.

Andrews, D. (1993). Desperately Seeking Michel. *Sociology of Sport Journal*, 10, 2, 148–67.

—— (2002). Coming to Terms with Cultural Studies. *Journal of Sport and Social Issues*, 26,1, 110–17.

Bartky, S. (1988). Foucault, Femininity, and Patriarchal Power. In I. Diamond & L. Quinby (eds). *Feminism and Foucault: Reflections on Resistance*. Boston: Northeastern University Press.

Bordo, S. (1993). *Unbearable Weight*. Berkeley: University of California Press.

Bennett, T. (1992). Putting Policy into Cultural Studies. In L. Grossberg, C. Nelson, & P. Treichler (eds). *Cultural Studies*. London: Routledge.

Brohm, J. (1978). *Sport: A Prison of Measured Time*. London: Inks Links.

Cahn. S. (1994). *Coming on Strong: Gender and Sexuality in Twentieth-Century Women's Sport*. New York: The Free Press.

Cantelon, H. & Gruneau, R. (1982). *Sport, Culture and the Modern State*. Toronto: University of Toronto Press.

Clarke, J. & Critcher, C. (1985). *The Devil Makes Work: Leisure in Capitalist Britain*. London: Macmillan.

Clifford, J. & Marcus, G. (eds) (1986). *Writing Culture: The Poetics and Politics of Ethnography*. Berkeley: University of California Press.

Cole, C. (1993). Resisting The Canon: Feminist Cultural Studies, Sport, and Technologies of the Body. In S. Birrell & C. Cole (eds). *Women, Sport and Culture*. Champaign, IL: Human Kinetics.

—— (1997). American Jordan: P.L.A.Y., Consensus and Punishment. *Sociology of Sport Journal*, 13, 366–97.

Cole, C. & Hribar, A. (1995). Celebrity Feminism: Nike Style (Post-Fordism, Transcendence, and Consumer Power). *Sociology of Sport Journal*, 12, 347–60.

Coombe, R. (1999). Sports Trademarks and Somatic Politics: Locating the Law in a Critical Cultural Studies. In R. Martin and T. Miller (eds). *SportCult*. Minneapolis: University of Minnesota Press.

Crossett, T. & Beal, B. (1997). The Uses of "Subculture" and "Subworld" in Ethnographic Works on Sport. A Discussion of Definitional Distinctions. *Sociology of Sport Journal*, 14, 73–85.

De Lauretis, T. (1984). *Alice Doesn't*. Bloomington, IN: Indiana University Press.

Donnelly, P. (1985). Sport Subcultures. *Exercise and Sport Sciences Review*, 13, 539–78.

Farred, G. (1999). The Nation in White: Cricket in a Postapartheid South Africa. In R. Martin and T. Miller (eds). *Sportcult*. Minneapolis: University of Minnesota Press.

Foucault, M. (1979). *Discipline and Punish: The Birth of The Prison*. New York: Vintage.

—— (1980). *The History of Sexuality. Vol. 1: An Introduction*. New York: Vintage.

Frow, J. & Morris, M. (2000). Cultural Studies. In N. Denzin and Y. Lincoln (eds). *Handbook of Qualitative Research*. London: Sage.

Gillick, M. (1984). Health Promotion, Jogging, and the Pursuit of The Moral Life. *Journal of Health Politics, Policy, and Law*, 9, 3, 369–87.

Gramsci, A. (1971). *Selections from the Prison Notebooks*. New York: International Publishers.

Grossberg, L. (1989a). The Formation of Cultural Studies: An American In Birmingham. *Strategies*, 2, 114–49.
—— (1989b). The Circulation of Cultural Studies. *Critical Studies in Mass Communication*, 6, 4, 413–20.
—— (1992). *We Gotta Get Out of this Place: Popular Conservatism and Postmodern Culture*. London: Routledge.
—— (1997a). *Bringing it all Back Home: Essays on Cultural Studies*. Durham, NC: Duke University Press.
—— (1997b). Cultural Studies, Modern Logics, and Theories of Globalization. In A. McRobbie (ed.). *Back to Reality? Social Experience and Cultural Studies*. Manchester: Manchester University Press.
Grossberg, L., Nelson, C., & Treichler, P. (1992). Cultural Studies: An Introduction. In L. Grossberg, C. Nelson & P. Treichler (eds). *Cultural Studies*. London: Routledge.
Gruneau, R. (1983). *Class, Sports, and Social Development*. Amherst, MA: University of Massachusetts Press.
—— (1988). Modernization or Hegemony: Two Views on Sport and Social Development. In J. Harvey & H. Cantelon (eds). *Not Just a Game: Essays in Canadian Sport Sociology*. Ottawa: University of Ottawa Press.
—— (1989). Making Spectacle: A Case Study in Televised Sport Production. In L. Wenner (ed.). *Media, Sport and Society*. London: Sage.
—— (1999). *Class, Sports, and Social Development* (2nd edition). Amherst, MA: University of Massachusetts Press.
Gruneau, R. & Whitson, D. (1994). *Hockey Night in Canada: Sport, Identity, and Cultural Politics*. Toronto: Garamond Press.
Hall, S. (1980a). Cultural Studies: Two Paradigms. *Media, Culture, and Society*, 2, 57–72.
—— (1980b). Cultural Studies and the Center: Some Problematics and Problems. In S. Hall et al. (eds). *Culture, Media, Language*. London: Hutchinson.
—— (1981). Notes On Deconstructing "The Popular." In R. Samuel (ed.). *People's History and Socialist Theory*. London: Routledge & Kegan Paul.
—— (1986). The Problem of Ideology: Marxism Without Guarantees. *Journal of Communication Inquiry*, 10, 2, 28–44.
——, Critcher, C., Jefferson, T., Clarke, J. & Roberts, B. (1978). *Policing the Crisis: Mugging, the State, and Law and Order*. London: Macmillan.
Hargreaves, J. A. (1982a). Sport and Hegemony: Some Theoretical Problems. In H. Cantelon & R. Gruneau (eds). *Sport, Culture, and the Modern State*. Toronto: University of Toronto Press.
—— (1982b). Sport, Culture, and Ideology. In J. A. Hargreaves (ed.). *Sport, Culture, and Ideology*. London: Routledge & Kegan Paul.
—— (1987). The Body, Sport, and Power Relations. In J. Horne, D. Jary, & A. Tomlinson (eds). *Sport, Leisure, and Social Relations*. London: Routledge & Kegan Paul.
Hargreaves, J. E. (1982). Theorizing Sport – An Introduction. In J. A. Hargreaves (ed.). *Sport, Culture, and Ideology*. London: Routledge & Kegan Paul.
Hargreaves, J. E. & Mcdonald, I. (2000). Cultural Studies and the Sociology of Sport. In J. Coakley & E. Dunning (eds). *Handbook of Sport Studies*. London: Sage.
Hartmann, D. (2001). Notes on Midnight Basketball and the Cultural Politics of Recreation, Race and At-Risk Urban Youth. *Journal of Sport and Social Issues*, 25, 4, 339–72.
Hebdige, R. (1988). *Hiding in the Light: On Images and Things*. London: Routledge.

Hoch, P. (1972). *Rip Off the Big Game: The Exploitation of Sports by the Power Elite*. New York: Doubleday.
Hoggart, R. (1957). *The Uses of Literacy*. London: Chatto and Windus.
Hollands, R. (1984). The Role of Cultural Studies and Social Criticism in the Sociological Study of Sport. *Quest*, 36, 1, 66–79.
Howell, J. (1991). A Revolution in Motion: Advertising and the Politics of Nostalgia. *Sociology of Sport Journal*, 8, 258–71.
Ingham, A. & Hardy, I. (1984). Sport: Structuration, Subjugation, and Hegemony. *Theory, Culture, and Society*, 2, 2, 85–103.
Jarvie, G. & Maguire, J. (1994). *Sport and Leisure in Social Thought*. London: Routledge.
Johnson, R. (1986/7). What Is Cultural Studies Anyway? *Social Text*, 16, 38–80.
King, C.R. & Springwood, C.F. (2000). Fighting Spirits: The Racial Politics of Sports Mascots. *Journal of Sport and Social Issues*, 24, 282–304.
King, S. (2000). Consuming Compassion: AIDS, Figure Skating, and Canadian Identity. *Journal of Sport and Social Issues*, 24, 2, 148–75.
MacNeil, M. (1996). Networks: An ethnography of CTV's Production of 1988 Winter Olympic Ice Hockey Tournament. *Sociology of Sport Journal*, 13, 103–24.
Maharaj, G. (1999). Talking Trash: Late Capitalism, Black (Re)Productivity, and Professional Basketball. In R. Martin and T. Miller (eds). *Sportcult*. Minneapolis: University of Minnesota Press.
Mann, M. (1986). *The Sources of Social Power: Vol. 1: A History of Power from the Beginning to A.D. 1760*. Cambridge: Cambridge University Press.
Marcus, G. (2001). The Unbalanced Reciprocity Between Cultural Studies and Anthropology. In T. Miller (ed.). *A Companion to Cultural Studies*. Oxford: Blackwell.
McDonald, I. (2002). Critical Social Research and Political Intervention: Moralistic Versus Radical Approaches. In J. Sugden & A. Tomlinson (eds). *Power Games: A Critical Sociology of Sport*. London: Routledge.
—— (2004). The Deleterious Impact of Post-Marxism on the Marxist Sociology of Sport. Paper presented at the annual meetings of the North American Society for the Sociology of Sport, Tucson, Arizona.
McDonald, M. (2005). Imagining Benevolence, Masculinity and Nation. Tragedy, Sport and the Transnational Marketplace. In M. Silk, D. Andrews, & C. Cole (eds). *Sport and Corporate Nationalisms*. Oxford: Berg.
McDonald, M. & Andrews, D. (2001). Michael Jordan: Corporate Sport and Postmodern Celebrityhood. In D. Andrews & S. Jackson (eds). *Sport Stars: The Cultural Politics of Celebrity*. London: Routledge.
Mienczakowski, J. (1998). Theatre of Change. *Research in Drama Education*, 2, 2, 159–72.
Miller, T. (1998). *Technologies of Truth: Cultural Citizenship and the Popular Media*. Minneapolis: University of Minnesota Press.
—— (2001). What Is It and What Isn't It: Introducing ... Cultural Studies. In T. Miller (ed.). *A Companion to Cultural Studies*. Oxford: Blackwell.
Morris, M. (1997). A Question of Cultural Studies. In A. Mcrobbie (ed.). *Back to Reality? Social Experience and Cultural Studies*. Manchester: Manchester University Press.
Nelson, C. (1994). Always Already Cultural Studies: Academic Conferences and a Manifesto. In I. Smithson & N. Ruff (eds.). *English Studies/Cultural Studies: Institutionalizing Dissent*. Champaign, IL: University of Illinois Press.

Ono, K. (1997). "America's" Apple Pie: Baseball, Japan-Bashing and the Sexual Threat of Economic Miscegenation. In A. Baker & T. Boyd (eds.). *Sport, Media, and the Politics of Identity*. Bloomington, IN: Indiana University Press.

Rowe, D. (1999). *Sport, Culture and the Media: The Unruly Trinity*. Buckingham, UK: Open University Press.

Sandell, J. (1995). Out of the Ghetto and Into the Marketplace. *Socialist Review*, 95, 2, 57–82.

Scott, J. (1992). Experience. In J. Butler & J. Scott (eds). *Feminists Theorize the Political*. London: Routledge.

Silk, M. (2001). The Conditions of Practice: Television Production Practices at Kuala Lumpur 98. *Sociology of Sport Journal*, 18, 3, 277–301.

Slack, J. (1996). The Theory and Method of Articulation in Cultural Studies. In D. Morley & K. Chen (eds). *Stuart Hall: Critical Dialogues*. London: Routledge.

Sparkes, A. (1996). The Fatal Flaw: A Narrative of the Fragile Body-Self. *Qualitative Inquiry*, 2, 463–94.

—— (2002). *Telling Tales in Sport and Physical Education: A Qualitative Journey*. Champaign, IL: Human Kinetics Press.

Staurowsky, E. (2001). Sockalexis and the Making of the Myth at the Core of Cleveland's "Indian" Image. In C.R. King & C.F. Springwood (eds). *Team Spirits: The Native American Mascot Debate*. Lincoln: University of Nebraska Press.

Steedman, C. (1987). *Landscape for a Good Woman: A Story of Two Lives*. Rutgers, NJ: Rutgers University Press.

Sugden, J. & Tomlinson, A. (2002). Theory and Method for a Critical Sociology of Sport. *Power Games: Towards a Critical Sociology of Sport*. London: Routledge.

Thompson, E. P. (1963). *The Making of the English Working Class*. London: Victor Gollancz.

Vinnai, G. (1973). *Football Mania*. London: Ocean Books.

Wheaton, B. (2002). Babes on the Beach, Women in the Surf: Researching Gender, Power and Difference in the Windsurfing Culture. In J. Sugden & A. Tomlinson (eds). *Power Games: A Critical Sociology of Sport*. London: Routledge.

Williams, R. (1958). *Culture and Scoiety*. London: Chatto and Windus.

—— (1977). *Marxism and Literature*. Oxford: Oxford University Press.

Willis, P. (1993). Women in Sport in Ideology. In S. Birrell & C. Cole (eds). *Women, Sport, and Culture*. Champaign, IL: Human Kinetics Press.

Wilson, B. & Sparks, R. (1996). "It's Gotta Be the Shoes": Youth, Race, and Sneaker Commercials. *Sociology of Sport Journal*, 13, 4, 398–427.

Zwick, D. & Andrews, A. (1999). The Suburban Soccer Field: Sport and the Culture of Privilege in Contemporary America. In G. Armstrong & R. Guilianotti (eds). *Football Cultures and Identities*. London: Macmillan.

3

The Socio-Historical Process in Sports Studies

David K. Wiggins and Daniel S. Mason

In 1974 Marvin H. Eyler, one of the founders of the academic subdiscipline of sport history and long-time Dean of what is now the University of Maryland's College of Health and Human Performance, published an article in the inaugural issue of the *Journal of Sport History* titled "Objectivity and Selectivity in Historical Inquiry" (Eyler, 1974). The article, which appeared alongside three others written by well-known sport historians David Voigt, Eugene Murdock and Steven Riess, discusses the problem of communicating truth in historical research. Utilizing the works of historians Sidney Hook, William Von Humboldt and Charles Beard among others, Eyler speculated as to whether truth about the past was ever attainable, if historians could escape personal bias, and if the necessary method of historical reconstruction precluded objectivity. In the end, Eyler contended that "the past can never be precisely replicated," but must be "reconstructed on the basis of evidence which has been selected from pre-suppositions" (1974: 45). Furthermore, he noted that history uses a "different standard of objectivity," to science and is concerned with knowledge that is "inferential and indirect" (Eyler, 1974: 45).

According to Berg "historical research attempts to systematically recapture the complex nuances, the people, meanings, events and even ideas of the past that have influenced and shaped the present" (2001: 210–11). Another definition, offered by Burke, is that history is "the study of human societies in the plural, placing the emphasis on the differences between them and also on the changes which have taken place in each one over time" (1992: 2). Quite simply, a history is an account of some event or series of events that has taken place in the past (Berg, 2001). To put historical research within the broader context of this book, perhaps the best way to justify the use of historical methods is through the following statement by Peter Burke: "If we want to understand *why* social change takes place, it may be a good strategy to begin by examining *how* it takes place" (1992: 139). Thus the role of the historian is then to uncover the evidence and analyze it in a way that lends new insights into social change over time.

This chapter draws on Eyler's article and subsequent historiographical works to examine the status of sport history as an academic subdiscipline and the major issues and methodological approaches associated with sport history, identify exemplary research studies in sport history, and discuss future avenues of inquiry in the field. The underlying contention of the chapter is that a great deal of progress has been made in sport history since the 1970s with regards to the expansion of knowledge and the quality of publication outlets, but as an academic subdiscipline sport history has only very recently engaged in self-examination and reflection. It is hoped that this review will provide a greater awareness of sport history as an academic subdiscipline and, more specifically, the strengths and weaknesses of the research process in this field.

The Development of the Discipline

Returning to the time of Eyler's article, it is important for aspiring sport historians to understand this period in the evolution of the field of sport history. First of all, the article was written at a time when there was unbridled optimism about the future of sport history as an academic subdiscipline. The first four years of the 1970s alone would witness the creation of two organizations, two journals, and three symposiums devoted to sport history (Berryman, 1973; Pope, 1997b; Struna, 1997). Second, the article was one of the first attempts by a sport historian to reflect on the historical process and discuss both methodological and epistemological issues related to the subdiscipline. Although covering debates waged for years by those in the parent discipline of history, Eyler's article provides an initial blueprint for sport historians concerned with the meaning of their work, and methods for recovering information from the past and seeking historical truth. Last, the article provides, albeit very briefly, an analysis of the early models utilized by sport historians. These were models "emanating particularly from the social sciences" (Eyler 1974) and used in efforts toward a greater understanding of the development of sport.

Much of the momentum established in sport history during the early 1970s would be maintained over the next twenty-five years. Courses in various aspects of sport history at both the undergraduate and graduate levels of instruction were added to university curriculums, and a number of research studies on sport history proliferated. Utilizing different methodologies and approaches, scholars examined what seemed to be every conceivable topic (Adelman, 1983; Baker, 1983; Guttmann, 1983; Hill, 1996; Kruger, 1990; Morrow, 1983; Park, 1983; Pope, 1997b; Struna, 1985; 1997; 2000; Walvin, 1984; Wiggins, 1986; 2000). Perhaps most important, the number and quality of research outlets increased significantly. Besides *Sport History Review*, the *Journal of Sport History*, and *International Journal of the History of Sport,* scholars could choose to publish their work in one of the journals from the parent discipline or in such sports studies-related journals as *Sport, Education and Society, Sporting Traditions* and *Olympika.* In addition to academic journals, both university and commercial presses added sport history titles to their publication lists. A real boon to the subdiscipline was the establishment of the "Sport and Society" series by the University of Illinois Press in 1986, and the production of similar types of series by such publication houses as Syracuse University Press and the State University of New York Press.

Jack Berryman, Nancy Struna, Steven Pope and others have pointed out that a number of important articles and books on various aspects of sport history were published during the first half of the twentieth century, including Frederic L. Paxson's "The Rise of Sport" in the *Mississippi Valley Historical Review* (1917), John A. Krout's *Annals of American Sport* (1929), Jennie Holliman's *American Sports, 1783–1835* (1931), Herbert Manchester's *Four Centuries of Sport in America, 1490–1890* (1931) and John R. Betts' "Organized Sport in Industrial America" (1951). The watershed for sport history, however, in regards to organizational structure and institutional support, occurred during the 1960s and early 1970s. Buoyed by the era's new-found interest in the history of the common person and everyday life (often called "histories from below"), a group of individuals, largely from departments of physical education, held symposiums, founded organizations and began publishing academic journals devoted to sport history. In 1962 in the United States, a section on sport history was included for the first time within the college Physical Education Association. This occurred largely through the efforts of Marvin H. Eyler, who had been the first doctoral student of Seward Staley, the University of Illinois professor who had initiated the idea of sport history courses in the academic curriculum at his university. In 1968, the First International Seminar on The History of Physical Education and Sports was held in Israel, and a year later a section on the history of physical education was established within the American Association for Health, Physical Education and Recreation. The inauguration of sport history as an academic subdiscipline was finalized during the early 1970s with the founding of the North American Society for Sport History, the holding of the first Canadian Symposium on the History of Sport and Physical Education, the Big Ten Symposium on the History of Physical Education and Sport, and the establishment of both the *Canadian Journal of History of Sport and Physical Education* (now the *Sport History Review*) and the *Journal of Sport History* (Berryman, 1973; Pope, 1997b; Struna, 1997).

Unfortunately, much of the enthusiasm for sport history has seemingly abated over the last few years (Booth, 1997; 1999; Phillips, 1999; 2001; Nauright, 1999). Although research studies in sport history continue to be produced and both individual and institutional memberships remain steady in sport history organizations, the field has gradually been marginalized as an academic subdiscipline. Evidence of this marginalization is plentiful. History departments, which have never been overly enthusiastic about the field, view sport history more as a "cash cow" than a legitimate subdiscipline. They offer undergraduate, and sometimes even graduate, courses in sport history in order to increase enrollment figures and allow students to conduct sport-related research projects. However, these programs typically do not offer major concentrations in the field or hire faculty on tenure track lines who identify primarily with sport history. As a group, historians generally view sport as frivolous and unimportant in the grand scheme of things. The reasons for this attitude are impossible to explain with any certainty. Elliott Gorn and Michael Oriard, in their appropriately titled and frequently cited essay "Taking Sports Seriously," note that "athletes' bodies remain curiously off-limits" in cultural studies, history, and other disciplines and speculate that intellectuals are simply "uncomfortable with physicality" or are "playing out the long-standing faculty antagonism to the distorted priorities of universities with multimillion-dollar athletics programs" (1995: A52).

The status of sport history is not much different in departments of physical education, human movement or kinesiology. Only on rare occasions do these departments advertise for positions in sport history; if these departments do offer courses in sport history they are sometimes taught by faculty trained in other subdisciplines, and typically these departments do not offer sport history as a major area of concentration or make it a requirement for any students in their degree programs. The reasons for sport history's lowly position in these departments are many and complex, but certainly one of the major factors has to do with the renewed emphasis these departments are placing on health, exercise, and the hard sciences. Academicians in biomechanics or exercise physiology, or even what is termed the pedagogical sciences do not see the relevance of sport history (Booth, 1997; 1999). An interesting, but not all that surprising, response by some sport historians to this transformation in these fields has been to change their own emphasis and focus more directly on the history of the body and exercise rather than the institution of sport. There is now a group of sport historians, like there is now a group of sport sociologists, who are more interested in examining the development of physical culture, representations of the human body, the interconnections between health, exercise, and medicine, and other such topics (Berryman & Park, 1992; Todd, 1998; Vertinsky, 1990; Whorton, 1982).

However, the marginalization of sport history in departments of physical education, human movement, or kinesiology is not simply a result of the kinds of topics and phenomena that are explored. In fact, the relatively low status granted sport history in these departments is as much a result of the perceived limitations of its research techniques and methodological approaches as anything else (Booth, 1997). Scholars from various subdisciplines, either out of ignorance or due to deep philosophical differences, have been highly critical of the approaches taken by many sport historians. No group has been more critical of the subdiscipline than sport sociologists, a group that in many ways has faced the same challenges within its own parent discipline and within physical education and kinesiology programs. Generally recognizing how important an understanding of the past is to their own work, some sport sociologists have railed against sport historians for their refusal to utilize models and adequately conceptualize their research data. In response, sport historians have criticized sport sociologists for their technical jargon, overemphasis on theory, and inability to grasp the complexities of the past (Phillips, 2001). In reality, there are elements of truth in the criticisms of both groups. Unfortunately, both groups, but particularly sport historians, generally pay little attention to these criticisms and have been reluctant to reflect on methodological approaches and the meaning of their work. Several scholars have surmised that historians avoid self-reflection because they are simply too busy collecting data and adding to the body of knowledge. It is hoped that this chapter provides a model for conducting sport history research that can at least partially reconcile some of the divisiveness within the field of sports studies.

Theory and Sport History

Despite the issues identified above, the field of sport history has much to offer to the realm of sports studies. In many respects the problems within the discipline largely reflect a marginalization on the part of some other areas of sports studies and kinesiology/physical education programs. However, there are a number of very competent scholars who have used a variety of approaches to study the history of sport, and the role sport has had within a broader social context. As noted earlier, one of the roles that sport historians play is in discovering and uncovering evidence that allows one to have a better understanding of how our world works today. Peter Burke (1992) identified two basic approaches to historical knowledge, which seem to work as ends of a continuum. He has called these two approaches *particularizing and generalizing*, *historical and theoretical*, and *splitting and lumping*. The difference between them lies in the level and type of analysis used by the historian. For example, *particularizers* are interested in minute details related to the past, whereas *generalizers* are more interested in how things "fit" into a bigger picture. Similarly, many traditional historians have been interested in simply uncovering the events of the past, while others are more keen on the broader theoretical implications of their research. *Splitting* can be described as chipping away at a theory like a sculptor, by examining how it holds against empirical data uncovered by the historian. In contrast, *lumping* consists of a complementary process of lumping together seemingly disparate facts, "working outwards from the particular to the general" (Burke, 1992: 130). With these two basic approaches in mind, there has been a movement within the history literature away from traditional histories that sought to examine the deeds of elite individuals (typically male), and a greater emphasis on understanding the social structures and processes of change that affected a given time period (Iggers, 1997). This can be described simply as a movement away from studying the limited and myopic realm of "the great deeds of great men" to more inclusive studies of what can be called "histories from below." An example of this can be seen in the various histories of Muhammad Ali. It could be argued that his athletic accomplishments (the great deeds of a great man) were not as important as the impact that he had on millions of people from his generation (how his deeds impacted those "from below"). In other words, how society was affected by his outspokenness and exploits during the turbulent period of the late 1960s could be considered of greater interest and importance than the number of knockouts that he had in his career.

The Relationship Between Theory and Method

It is important to note that, in the example above, Ali would not have been able to have such an impact were it not for his boxing ability. Thus, it is critical for historians to be aware of both *splitting* and *lumping* – a sport historian needs to be able to obtain evidence, critically ascertain its trustworthiness and then understand how it adds to our greater understanding of whatever phenomenon the historian has sought to investigate. As this section will reveal, the manner through which historians have sought to gain a greater understanding is directly related to the theoretical perspective taken by the researcher. As will be described below, sport historians have chosen a number of different ways in which to undertake this process, and they have been criticized for relying on several popular approaches. For the purposes of this chapter, we have identified three analytical paradigms: structural-functionalism, Marxism, and postmodernism. However, before we examine them in more detail, it is important to note that "theory can never be 'applied' to the past. What theory can do, on the other hand, is to suggest new questions for historians to ask about 'their' period, or new answers to familiar questions" (Burke, 1992: 165). In this manner the types of questions that are asked by sport historians, and the types of conclusions that they come to, are to a large degree influenced by the theories that they use to draw broader inferences about the past. The more dominant approaches that have emerged in the field of sport history are outlined below.

One of the earliest and most enduring approaches utilized by sport historians is related to social structures. Functionalism is characterized by an interest in social systems, institutionalization, specific periodization, and urbanization. Structural-functionalism has been an especially popular approach among sport historians, particularly in the United States. Many historians during World War II and immediately thereafter adopted this approach assuming that sport reflected America's superior way of life, democratic institutions and unabated progress. Works of this genre include Foster Rhea Dulles' *A History of Recreation: America Learns to Play* (1965), Frederick W. Cozens and Florence Scovil Stumpf's *Sports in American Life* (1953), and John R. Betts' *America's Sporting Heritage, 1850–1950* (1974). Of these three works, Betts' survey is the most recognized and influential. Published posthumously, the book was reconstructed from Betts' 1951 dissertation "Organized Sport in Industrial America" by noted sport sociologist John Loy with assistance from Betts's son Richard and prominent sport historian Guy Lewis. The book, wonderfully researched and characterized by a nice combination of social and business history, provides a framework and organizational structure utilized in subsequent monographs and sport history surveys. Betts discussed such topics as the technological revolution and the rise of sport, the "Golden Age of Sport" in the 1920s, the influence of the Great Depression and World War II on organized sport and the interrelationships between sport and such institutions as education, religion, and art. The structural-functionalist approach to the study of sport continues to dominate much of the work in the subdiscipline. According to Peter Burke, the appeal of functionalism to historians lies in the fact that is has compensated for the long-standing tendency of historians to explain too much of the past in terms of the actions and intentions of specific individuals (1992: 106). Instead, according to structural-functionalists, the past is best explained by the broader social structures and forces exerted during a given time period. The structural-functionalist approach does have its critics, however. Sports studies scholar Doug Booth, for one, believes the system has serious flaws. "Functionalist explanations in sport history," notes Booth, "typically gloss over disparities in sporting interests between different social and economic groups, exaggerate social stability and harmony, and ignore the inevitable losers and outsiders in local (community, regional, national) consensus building activities" (2003: 11).

Certainly one of the most influential analytical designs in sport history is the modernization paradigm popularized by Allen Guttmann in his classic study *From Ritual to Record: The Nature of Modern Sports* (1978). According to Steven Pope, modernization theory has developed as a way of investigating the means through which society has evolved from a rural agrarian society to an urban and industrial society, at different times and in different places throughout the world (1997b: 4). *From Ritual to Record* charts the formal-structural characteristics of modern sports and the extent to which these characteristics were evident in sport during earlier periods in history, and was considered so influential that an entire issue of *Sport History Review* was recently devoted to "A Retrospective Critique" of the book (Booth, 2001; Brownell, 2001; Guttmann, 2001; Howell, 2001; Von der Lippe, 2001). Utilizing an impressive list of diverse sources, continually making astute historical and statistical comparisons, and full of cogent analysis and thoughtful questions, Guttmann's book is essentially a structural-functional analysis that outlines seven characteristics of modern sport: secularism, equality, rationalization, specialization, bureaucratization, quantification, and an obsession with records.

The modernization paradigm was also utilized with much success by Melvin Adelman in his pathbreaking study *A Sporting Time: New York City and the Rise of Modern Athletics, 1820–70* (1986). The first book in the University of Illinois Press's sport and society series, *A Sporting Time* is one of the most frequently cited and important studies in sport history. Adelman, through painstaking research and perceptive analysis, examined the transformation of American sport from its premodern to modern forms by exploring early baseball, horse and harness racing, boxing, and such traditionally neglected activities as cricket, rowing, yachting and billiards. Adelman challenged previous research by arguing that sport, particularly in New York City, evolved from an informal, unorganized activity to a more highly structured and organized phenomenon between 1820 and 1870 rather than during the late stages of the nineteenth century. The 1820 to 1870 time period witnessed the growth of commercialized athletics and evidence of a fledgling sports information system, standardization of records and equipment, specialized player roles and philosophical rationales for sport participation.

The modernization paradigm adopted by Guttmann and Adelman has received some criticism. In fact, in the aforementioned "A Retrospective Critique" of *From Ritual to Record*, several prominent scholars took turns poking holes in Guttmann's approach. Colin Howell is critical of the book for its sweeping approach to history, arguing that the book assisted in identifying the "process of change" in sport over time, but was less successful in "explaining" the transformation of sport; "while many processes are identifiable in history," writes Howell, "it is another thing altogether to understand history itself as a process. *From Ritual to Record* was written at a time of grand theorizing, when the grand narratives of development that postmodernist scholars now disdain were clearly in vogue" (2001: 13). Doug Booth generally has high praise for the book, but claims that Guttmann's work provides a "limited conceptualization of the process of modernization and the nature of modernity" and "lacks adequate political and dialectical analyses" (2001: 22). Steven Pope also weighs in on the debate, noting that critics of modernization theory have "exposed modernization as an ahistorical construct that distorted the past by emphasizing structure at the expense of human agency" (1997b: 5). In some ways, this criticism is similar to that leveled against supporters of structuralism.

Guttmann counters these criticisms and others with his usual aplomb and erudition. He acknowledges that his modernization paradigm has limitations, including the fact that it can be "too abstract to account for every detail in history's vast panorama," "can easily be misinterpreted to mean that the observed changes occurred as part of some uniform and inevitable process," and "can be misused as a facile instrument of ethical judgment – as if modern ways were somehow a moral advance as well as a technological advance beyond traditional customs" (Guttmann, 2001: 5). He argues, however, that in spite of the obvious limitations of the modernization paradigm, no alternative model has been postulated that does a better job in chronicling the changes in sport over time and marking the differences between sport of yesteryear and that of today. "Despite the manifest possibility that the concept of modernization can be misunderstood and misrepresented" writes Guttmann, "I continue to find it more useful than the postmodernism [to be described in more detail below, and throughout this book] that is currently fashionable in what once were called the social sciences. An imperfect and admittedly selective account of the historical facts seems preferable to the startled discovery that there is no such thing as absolute truth" (2001: 6).

The last three decades, however, have witnessed the adoption of new and varied theoretical approaches and paradigms in sport history. Taking their cues from the vast changes taking place in historical scholarship during the 1970s and 1980s, sport historians increasingly have turned to the analytical frameworks utilized in such fields as anthropology, cultural studies and sociology to examine the development of sport. Although it is not always easy to discern specific patterns of inquiry, there seems to have been an emphasis in the subdiscipline on concepts such as community formation and power and how socially constructed notions of race, ethnicity, gender, class and religion impacted sport and vice versa. Increasingly, sport historians have adopted the works of Max Weber, Norbert Elias, Clifford Geertz and the like to frame their analyses and interpretations (Pope, 1997b).

Many sport historians have employed different versions of Marxism to analyze the development of sport. Interested in the mode of production and the use of political and social power, Marxist sport historians have focused on sport in regards to social-class aspirations and the manner in which sport has been redefined by blacks, women, workers and various other groups in society. Richard Gruneau (1983), the noted Canadian sociologist, has had a profound effect on the work of sport historians through his many publications on sport and Marxist cultural studies. Equally significant to sport historians have been the theoretical insights provided by such cultural Marxists as E.P. Thompson, Raymond Williams, Eric Hobsbawn and Antonio Gramsci. Historian Colin Howell correctly observes that "over the past few years it has been difficult to pick up an issue of one of the major sport history journals and not find any article employing Gramsci's notion of hegemony or referring to notions of human agency" (1998: 101).

Howell might also have added that the theoretical approaches of Gramsci as well as other cultural Marxists have found their way in one form or another into some of the most important sport history monographs. One example of this is Steven Pope's *Patriotic Games: Sporting Traditions in the American Imagination, 1876–1926* (1997a). Utilizing Eric Hobsbawn's concept of invented traditions, Pope examines the national sporting culture that was established in the United States between the 1876 centennial and the 1926 sesquicentennial. He illustrates how sport becomes a cultural transmitter of patriotic meaning, intertwined with Thanksgiving and Fourth-of-July holiday celebrations and military preparedness. Perhaps most important, Pope makes clear that sport served as both a metaphorical activity and class drama and helped define public discourse on American hopes and dreams.

Pope's book is significant in that it is reflective of what Jeffrey Hill (1996) and Richard Holt (1998) refer to as the subtle shift in sport history from causation to meaning. Since the 1980s scholars have been less concerned about the determinants of sport participation and more interested in the multiple and complex meanings sport has had for athletes, spectators and various other individuals, groups and communities. Examples of this scholarship are numerous. John MacAloon focuses on rituals and cultural symbols in his book *This Great Symbol: Pierre de Coubertin and the Origins of the Modern Olympic Games* (1981). Peter Levine argues in his *Ellis Island to Ebbetts Field: Sport and the American Jewish Experience* (1992) that sport served as a middle ground for American Jews who were striving to become full participants in American society while at the same time attempting to maintain their sense of ethnic pride and identity. Utilizing an impressive list of source materials and wonderful stories of individual athletes and teams, Levine makes clear that for East European Jewish immigrants and their children during the first half of the twentieth century, sport was seen as an avenue of assimilation and a means to pursue the American dream. Elliott Gorn provides a fascinating analysis of the meaning of prizefighting in nineteenth-century America in his *The Manly Art: Bare-Knuckle Prizefighting in America* (1986). Integrating the work of anthropologists, sociologists, folklorists, labor and social historians and American and gender studies specialists, Gorn examines how prizefighting was transformed from a working-class ritual that symbolized physical prowess and toughness to a middle-class sport that illustrated dominant ideas of social mobility and meritocracy.

Finally, it is important to recognize the presence of postmodern approaches to sport history. It is probably safe to say that most sport historians reject many of the basic tenets of the postmodernist approach, believing that it only results in a "dazzling kaleidoscope of impressions where anything can be construed to mean anything" and ultimately anarchic nihilism (Holt, 1998). As explained by historian Georg Iggers, "the basic idea of postmodern theory of historiography is the denial that historical writing actually refers to an actual historical past" (1997: 118). There have been, however, a few brave and adventurous souls in the field who have employed different versions of this approach in their research. Two studies that depend to some extent on postmodernist theory are Patricia Vertinsky's *The Eternally Wounded Woman: Women, Exercise, and Doctors in the Late Nineteenth Century* (1990) and Susan Cahn's *Coming on Strong: Gender and Sexuality in Twentieth-Century Women's Sport* (1994). Tina Parratt (1998) is absolutely correct in noting that both of these works are indebted to post-modernism, particularly the notion that power and knowledge are the result of discursive practices. The first and perhaps only genuine postmodernist study in sport history, however, is Synthia Sydnor's "A History of Synchronized Swimming" (1998). Published in a special issue of the *Journal of Sport History* titled *Sport History: Into the Twenty-First Century*, Sydnor's essay follows in the path of Marxist theorist Walter Benjamin in that it avoids such standard historical practices as recording facts and periodization to "ponder" synchronized swimming through an assemblage of symbols, images and spectacles. Sydnor, designating her "essay as a modern text with postmodern concerns" does not analyze or explain or contextualize; rather she provides a number of evocative ideas through an "exhibition or performance" presented in a poetic and literary form (1998: 260). However, works such as Sydnor's remain very much in the minority within the field of sport history.

An approach that is, in the words of Genevieve Rail, "an amalgam of often purposely ambiguous and fluid ideas," postmodernism is variously thought of as a revolt against modernism and structuralism, a radical break from the past that leans towards a deconstruction of linguistic systems, a distaste for disciplinary boundaries and a belief that the world is fragmented into many isolated and autonomous discourses that cannot be explained by any grand theory (Rail, 1998: x). Michel Foucault, one of the most prominent postmodernist thinkers, argues that truth is only a partial, localized version of reality and that power relations and meaning are the function of language and discourse (Rail, 1998).

All of the approaches described above have been shown to be viable ways to study the history of sport. However, as we have tried to show, each has its shortcomings with regards to an ability to better understand the past. In a recent article, historian Colin Howell critiqued the use of the concept of hegemony in sport history. Although his criticisms were directed at one specific lens for historical research, in some respects similar criticisms could also be leveled at the other approaches we have discussed:

> Unfortunately, the idea of hegemony is often employed by the unimaginative as a formula to lend a patina of academic respectability to an academic paper or journal article. In turn, its overuse has made the concept appear hackneyed, especially when it is misconstrued as a more academically credible form of social-control analysis. One should keep in mind that the end of historical inquiry is not to confirm Gramsci, but rather to use his theoretical insights to better understand what happened. (Howell, 1998: 101)

Perhaps the lesson to be taken for aspiring sport historians is to make sure that one uses an appropriate approach that will help the researcher to more capably investigate the question at hand. In the meantime, as Howell warns, researchers must not get too caught up in an approach and use it simply to justify their own research.

To end this section, it is important to revisit perhaps the most important issue at hand with regard to the theoretical approaches to the study of sport history – sporting activities, like social practices in general, have always tended to be indicative of, and at times reinforced by, class distinctions (Booth and Loy, 1999: 6). Within these class distinctions, it is also critical to identify issues and differences concerning gender, race and other social concerns. For this reason, the sport historian must try to gain a greater understanding of the broader social context of the period which he/she chooses to study, particularly as it relates to the relationships between classes. Thus, sport history must be informed by social theories that seek to draw inferences from a number of different contexts and time periods to better explain and understand the role of sport in society.

Research Goals and Questions

Sport historians generally adhere to a specific and recognizable historical method. The first and, in some ways, most important task of the sport historian is to become conversant with the secondary literature. According to historians, there are two basic types of sources – primary and secondary. Primary sources are those that are directly associated with the topic that is being investigated. For example, imagine if one were to explore an Olympic boxing match that took place in 1988. A primary source would be a person who was involved in the match itself, or a first-hand witness to the event. There are a number of different ways in which primary source material could be obtained. One might be to interview a spectator, a participant, a judge, etc. Another would be to read a newspaper account written by someone who was at the event (such as a sports reporter who covered the event and wrote an article that appeared in the next day's paper). Another way might be to watch video footage of the event. Primary sources are critical for the sport historian because they allow the researcher to get as close as possible to the event. On the other hand, secondary sources are distinguished from primary sources in that they are usually comprised of books or articles written by others who were not directly associated with an event. In many cases, they are written by researchers who have done their own primary source-based research. However, they involve a degree of filtering that makes them less valuable to the historian, in the sense that someone else has already analyzed the sources and come to his/her own independent conclusions.

However, at the outset of doing research, secondary sources are extremely important for the sport historian, as they allow the researcher to obtain background information on a topic and have an understanding of what is known with regards to a given topic. Thus, when starting out, the historian usually explores the secondary literature. To locate the secondary literature, sport historians traditionally turn first to the library catalogue to find entries for book titles, subjects and names of authors. They also depend on such resource aids as historical dictionaries, large general histories, specialized academic journals, biographical dictionaries, periodical indexes, bibliography of bibliographies and current national bibliographies. Times have changed, however. In addition to the aforementioned tools, sport historians now conduct computer searches to locate secondary sources or contact colleagues on various list serves to find secondary material (Atkinson, 1978; Gottschalk, 1969; Porter, 1981; Shafer, 1980). Search engines such as SPORT Discus also provide opportunities to search online for topics using keywords. In addition, other athletic bodies, such as the Amateur Athletic Federation of Los Angeles (AAFLA.org) have made journal and other sport sources available in full text through their websites.

Collecting and Identifying Historical Data

According to Berg, "the major impetus in historical research, as with other data-collection strategies, is the collection of information and the interpretation or analysis of the data" (2001: 213). Sport historians are fortunate in that the improvement of finding aids has coincided with a dramatic increase in both the quality and quantity of secondary works dealing with various aspects of sport history. Thought provoking, creative and imaginatively designed studies have been completed on such topics as the pattern of sport in both rural and urban settings (Adelman, 1986; Berryman, 1982; Borish, 1996; Gems, 1997; Hardy, 1981; 1982; Riess, 1989; Roberts, 2000; Somers, 1972; Uminowicz, 1984), the history of baseball and other team and individual sports (Goldstein, 1989; Kirsch, 1989; Oriard, 1993; 2001; Riess, 1980; Sammons, 1988), the sport participation patterns of African Americans and other racial and ethnic groups (Cahn 1994; Festle, 1996; Guttmann, 1991; Mangan & Park, 1987), the interconnections between organized sport, physical culture and the medical profession (Berryman & Park, 1992; Fair, 1999; Green, 1986; Todd, 1998; Verbrugge, 1988; Vertinsky, 1990; Whorton, 1982), the origin and evolution of the modern Olympic movement (Dyreson, 1998; Guttmann, 1984; 1992; MacAloon, 1981; Senn, 1999; Young, 1996), the role of women in sport at the national and international levels of competition (Bass, 2002; Bloom, 2000; Eisen

& Wiggins, 1994; Hoberman, 1997; Levine, 1992; Regalado, 1998; Riess, 1998; Shropshire, 1996; Wiggins, 1997; Wiggins & Miller, 2003), and the conception of leisure and transformation of public recreation and organized sport at different times in history and among different classes and geographical locations (Cavello, 1981; Hardy, 1990; Rosenzweig, 1983; Rosenzweig & Blackmar, 1992).

The responsibility of sport historians is not simply to familiarize themselves with this literature, but to assess and analyze it in regards to the types of evidence used, generalizations drawn and historical frameworks employed. A thorough and detailed understanding of the secondary literature assists scholars in formulating paradigms and asking good questions which are at the heart of the historical process. It is precisely for this reason that the more experienced scholar has little difficulty in selecting a topic and delimiting that topic to manageable proportions, while the fledgling scholar usually struggles to find a topic that will contribute to the body of knowledge and add to the research literature. Armed with a firm grasp of the secondary literature, the more experienced sport historian can usually establish appropriate themes and set parameters conducive to consistent and logical arguments. On the other hand, the less experienced members of the subdiscipline, equipped with a limited understanding of the secondary literature, often pick topics that are too broad in scope, underestimating rather than overestimating the amount of source material available on a given subject.

One reason for a tendency on the part of novice sport historians to choose topics too broad in scope might be that, in an effort to make their "mark," they are worried about choosing a topic that might seem too narrow and insignificant to be worthy of study. According to Peter Burke (1992), historical examinations on a small, local scale are called *micro histories*. Perhaps one thing to keep in mind when formulating a topic is that, if using good primary resources, an examination of a small, obscure topic can truly shed light on broader social phenomena and should not be trivialized. As explained by Burke: "One might begin with the charge that the micro historians trivialize history by studying the biographies of unimportant people or the difficulties of small communities... However, the aim of the micro historian is generally more intellectually ambitious than that. If they do not aspire to show the world in a grain of sand, these historians do claim to draw general conclusions from local data" (1992: 41).

For sport historians, then, a thorough grounding in the secondary literature is essential in formulating good questions, and these questions need not be on a grand scale. Scholars in the subdiscipline know full well, however, that good questions are also those of interest to the researcher, those that are answerable and those that are tied to the primary evidence. It is wise for sport historians to listen to the advice of advisors and colleagues, but ultimately they must address those questions that are of interest to them and not particularly anyone else. A traditional but still very valuable strategy to adopt is for the sport historian to consider some basic kinds of questions. The first have to do with the phenomenon to be studied. Is the researcher most interested in examining sport? Athletics? Exercise? Leisure? Recreation? Other questions have to do with chronology. Is the researcher interested in a particular year? The Renaissance period? The late nineteenth century? The 1920s? Post World War II Period? Further questions have to do with geography. Is the researcher interested in Great Britain? Canada? The United States? Latin America? China? Finally, the researcher needs to ask questions about the individuals or groups to be studied. Is the researcher interested in elite athletes? Particular racial and ethnic groups? Ancient Greeks? Physical culturists? Health reformers?

In reality, of course, these questions are not mutually exclusive and the sport historian must arrive at a final set of manageable questions that beg answers gleaned from primary sources. Once the questions have been finalized, the sport historian then puts together a research design. Although they do not construct experiments or have the ability to manipulate and control data, sport historians are similar to all scholars in that they map strategy and develop a research design characterized by a systematic arrangement of questions and the approach necessary to answer those questions. The two most commonly cited designs in sport history are termed descriptive history and analytical history. Descriptive history is primarily concerned with what happened in sport while analytical history is more interested in the complexity of relationships and drawing connections to determine how and why sport developed the way it did and what role it served in the lives of participants and spectators alike. Notwithstanding the fact that differences between the two basic research designs are not always discernable, it is analytical history that most sport historians strive to complete and has been most evident (although some scholars in the subdiscipline would certainly disagree) from the very beginning. As our earlier discussion of the need to link theory and method in historical research would suggest, a reliance upon descriptive histories may simply reinforce and rationalize the lack of respectability the field has within both sports studies and in the parent discipline of history. As a result, we would encourage aspiring sport historians to employ more analytical approaches to their own research.

Irrespective of the paradigm chosen, all sport historians must be concerned with the collection of evidence. In order to seek answers to their questions, sport historians seek to locate as many primary sources or first-hand accounts as possible. Although recognizing the impossibility of locating all documents, and the inevitable incompleteness of the historical process, sport historians search archives, libraries, private collections and a host of other repositories to find the primary sources necessary to gain an understanding of the sporting past. One consideration that bodes well for the sport historian is the greater ease of access to primary sources created by new technologies. As explained by Cox and Salter, "technology will release the sport historian from unskilled, repetitive, time-consuming tasks, allow him or her to concentrate on the core activities of a sport historian – analysis, synthesizing, theorizing, and communicating information" (1998: 294). For example many newspapers, which historians typically research in microform format in libraries, are now available in PDF format through online databases. In many cases, these databases can be searched using keywords. So, rather than reading pages and pages of old newspapers on a microform reader, looking for articles concerned with a topic, one can now have a database "pull up" the appropriate newspaper pages reporting on a given issue. An example of these types of databases is the Toronto Star newspaper's "Pages of the Past" database http://micromedia.pagesofthepast.ca/default.asp.

In other instances, primary source materials may be obtained through sources that are not necessarily considered first when doing primary source-based data collection. For example, Iacovetta and Mitchinson (1998) suggest exploring case files as a source of information on a topic. This could include employment records, court proceedings, patient records, psychiatrists' case histories, and so forth. They explain that "historians have turned to case files because they offer us a rare window on human interaction and conflict... These records can illuminate the ways in which dominant class, gender and racial ideologies shaped official discourses and actions and relations between experts and clients" (Iacovetta & Mitchinson, 1998: 6). Thus, the aspiring sport historian in many ways has an opportunity to start doing historical research without many of the traditional impediments or restrictions to access to primary sources faced by sport historians of earlier years.

Data Analysis and Interpretation

Once the primary sources have been identified and located, the sport historian then exposes the sources to a rigorous two-step evaluative process known as external and internal criticism (Atkinson, 1978; Gottschalk, 1969; Porter, 1981; Shafer, 1980). External criticism involves establishing the authenticity of the primary source. The sport historian, using tests similar to those employed by lawyers or detectives, must determine if the chosen documents either are forged or have been tampered with since the time the event being examined took place. To differentiate between a forgery or misrepresentation and an authentic document, the sport historian is largely concerned with examining sources to determine whether events, objects, persons or customs are correctly placed chronologically. Was a particular type of paper being used at the time the purported document was supposedly being written? Could the alleged author of the document possibly have been at the location where it was supposedly written? Were the punctuation, spelling, proper names and signatures utilized in the document consistent with other contemporary writings? Does the alleged author of the document refer to events about which he/she could not possibly have known? Another common issue relates to authorship. For example, a book or article may be credited to a person who might be considered a primary source (such as an autobiography written by the participant of a certain event). However, these types of books are often "ghostwritten" and therefore less reliable as a result.

Once authenticity has been established, the sport historian then assesses the credibility of documents through a process known as internal criticism (Atkinson, 1978; Gottschalk, 1969; Porter, 1981; Shafer, 1980). A time-consuming and extremely important part of the historical method, internal criticism is concerned with determining who left documents and the relationship of the source of those documents to the event or events being described. In other words, what interests or biases might the author of the document have with regards to the event in question? Internal criticism is also concerned with the wording of documents, particularly how the words employed were defined and used during the historical period being studied. Moreover, internal criticism is concerned with both the information included in and the information omitted from historical documents. Historians must be cognizant of the fact that all historical documents are only partial glimpses into the past and that some information is often either intentionally or unintentionally left out of written and oral accounts. This is precisely why scholars in sport history always seek corroboration by searching for the independent testimonies of two or more trustworthy witnesses. If only one witness of an event is known to exist, scholars must seek other forms of corroboration, including the reputation of the author of the document, the absence of contradictions within the document and among other sources, and the lack of anachronisms.

A good example of where internal criticism is critical occurs when sport historians rely upon newspapers as sources of data. According to Danuta Reah (1998), newspaper reports are simply accounts of *selected* information on recent events. In other words, the reporter will, subconsciously or not, put an ideological "spin" on events, providing a skewed viewpoint (Reah, 1998: 9). An example of this occurs in McNeil's (2001) study of a worker's riot in Britain, where he found that newspaper coverage was biased toward management. Similarly, Mason and Duquette (2004) reported that newspaper coverage of the first professional hockey league was very different in major cities in Canada where hockey was popular than in the cities in the United States where the teams from the league played. Thus, newspaper reports must be viewed with some skepticism, as reports tend to present the reader with aspects of news offered in a way that will tend to guide the stance of the reader toward the issue or event that is being investigated (Reah, 1998: 50). Thus "journalists are actors and creators as well as reporters. They collect, select, and color the information they dispense to their customers; they frame the issues and assumptions from which cultural debates arise. Reporters thus shape opinion just as surely as do newspaper editors and columnists" (Baker, 1994: 530). With this in mind, the sport historian must try to gain an understanding of the potential biases that might influence the reporter. For example, it is likely that early coverage of professional sports teams in local newspapers favored the home team. This was due to civic boosterism and also to the very close ties that early newspaper reporters had with their local sporting clubs. Thus, the historian cannot rely solely on information on an event from such a source, as it represents only one viewpoint. The sport historian then needs to seek out other sources to corroborate facts or identify biases in the coverage. Perhaps the easiest way of doing this would be to compare coverage in other newspapers (such as that of the visiting team), or to find other accounts from other sources (interviews with spectators, etc.).

Every sport historian can probably relate personal stories about establishing the credibility of documents. David Wiggins, one of the authors of this chapter, found that his most challenging struggle with the problem of internal criticism took place while he was doing research on the role of leisure and recreation in the lives of slaves on plantations in the antebellum South – a very sensitive and controversial subject (Wiggins, 1983a; 1983b). He was faced with the problem of how to reconcile the differing conceptions of slave leisure and recreation expressed by an enormously diverse group of witnesses with their own biases and vantage points. He had access to British travel accounts located in the Library of Congress. British travelers, who visited the South in fairly large numbers between 1780 and 1860, varied greatly in their observational skills and represented such diverse professions and occupations as land scouts, missionaries, scientists, politicians, educators and actors. White planters provided another vantage point in which to view the institution. Wiggins' used letters and plantation diaries from such repositories as The Southern Historical Collection (Chapel Hill, NC) and the Library of Congress to analyze a group who obviously had a strong allegiance to the institution of slavery and reluctance to point out its many cruelties and horrors. The final group of witnesses to the cruel institution were the slaves themselves who typically did not know how to read or write, and frequently could recount their lives on Southern plantations only after realizing their freedom. For their view of the institution, Wiggins turned to both published slave narratives and interviews conducted by the Works Progress Administration (WPA) during the great depression of the 1930s.

To assess the credibility of these divergent sources, Wiggins was forced to call upon everything he had ever learned about the historical method. First of all, he had to constantly remind himself that what was most important was the credibility of particular statements made by authors rather than their overall credibility as witnesses. For example, planters and their families, while generally providing a rather romantic view of slavery and refusing to acknowledge the insidiousness of the institution, were able to detail with some accuracy the types of play activities and games participated in by slaves because of their frequent contact and close proximity with them. Second, Wiggins had to constantly remind himself that there was a great deal of variability among witnesses in regards to the degree of attention they paid to the phenomenon being studied and the literary style they employed. For example, British travelers, many of whom were searching for large audiences and obviously seeking to appear omniscient, often recounted the leisure patterns and recreation of slaves based on nothing more than hearsay or tradition. Last, Wiggins had to remind himself that many witnesses were far removed in time from the events they were describing. For example, many former slaves were at an advanced age when they recounted their days in slavery, a fact that obviously tested their memory and begged the question as to whether their longevity was due to better treatment than their fellow slaves. In addition, former slaves were often describing their childhood days, a time when their lives were typically more carefree and devoid of the intense labor and horrors more characteristic of the institution of slavery as a whole.

In addition to establishing the credibility of documents, sport historians must carefully read the evidence to ascertain the information being imparted while at once keeping in mind the close interrelationship between empirical particulars and theory formation. Wiggins certainly discovered this in a recent study he conducted on Muhammad Ali's relationship to the Nation of Islam (Wiggins, 1995). *Muhammad Speaks*, the official organ of the Nation of Islam, provided important details of Ali's membership in the organization, but not a comprehensive view of the champion's religious beliefs. Ali's autobiography, *The Greatest: My Own Story*, provides insights into the champion's involvement with the Nation of Islam, but virtually nothing about his strained and sometimes acrimonious relationship with both Elijah Muhammad and Malcolm X. Black newspapers only covered Ali's relationship to the Nation of Islam in a cursory fashion, seemingly either disinterested or unwillingly to discuss the champion's involvement with the politically active and, some would say, racist organization. In order to piece together these seemingly incomplete sources and craft as accurate a portrayal of Ali's relationship to the Nation of Islam as possible, Wiggins had to pay particular attention to content, meaning and historical context. This necessitated a close examination and comparison of written documents and a constant search for the biases that inevitably pervaded any discussion and analysis of Ali's involvement in and influence on the Nation of Islam. Wiggins had to be speculative on occasion and draw historical generalizations that helped explain not only Ali's connection to the Nation of Islam but how the great heavyweight champion fit into the larger black power movement and came to symbolize the tumultuous Vietnam Era.

As evidenced by the discussion above, the sport historian's job is not as simple as having a good research topic grounded in the secondary literature:

> The historian is still bound by his or her sources, and the critical apparatus with which he or she approaches them remains in many ways the same. Nevertheless we view these sources more cautiously. We have become more aware of the extent to which they do not directly convey reality but are themselves narrative constructs that reconstruct these realities, not willy-nilly, but guided by scholarly findings and by a scholarly discourse. (Iggers, 1997: 10)

In other words, today's sport historian is not so bold as to think that he/she can know exactly what happened in the past. Instead, an attempt is made to better understand what happened, and how this fits into our broader understanding of the conditions that shaped both that time and the present. It is assumed that the researcher's understanding will be influenced by her/his own experiences, the availability of sources, the potential biases of the resources, the underlying social dynamics of the time period studied (and the present as it affects the researcher), and the general epistemological and theoretical frameworks that guide the researcher and his/her subsequent research questions.

Writing up the Findings

The limited information provided by each source is exactly why all sport historians seek to find as much evidence as possible about their chosen topic. Once all the available evidence is collected, and the sport historian has attempted to determine "what it all means," the next job is to disseminate their findings to colleagues and hopefully a larger public. There is no specific formula for accomplishing this task, but there are certain principles to which all good sport historians adhere when writing up their final product. They present their evidence in as logical a fashion as possible, careful to discuss as well as to analyze and interpret the primary material within an overall theme. They are careful to present their evidence within the proper historical context, providing a meaningful framework for the data they have assembled on the chosen topic. They are also careful to consider the arrangement of historical data, recognizing the importance of establishing at least some form of framework that both reveals and clarifies the progression of events. And last, but certainly not least, they pay special attention to writing style and composition. Sport historians recognize, as do other scholars involved in qualitative approaches to the study of sport, that how one says something is just as crucial as the information being imparted. Thus, the narrative, or the way in which the researcher pieces together the data and results into a story, is absolutely critical. It is essential to use words that convey exact meanings, to avoid vague generalities and typification when possible, and to refrain from using artificial rhetoric. In many respects, by adhering to this practice, writing in the field of sport history has remained one of the most accessible bodies of literature in the field of sports studies.

Exemplary Studies in Sport History

Now that we have reviewed the field of sport history, and given an overview of how to go about doing research in this area, we turn to reviewing several works that we feel exemplify the type of quality research that is being done in this subdiscipline. Two pathbreaking studies that address the complex meaning of sport and stand as outstanding examples are Michael Oriard's *Reading Football: How the Popular Press Created an American Spectacle* (1993) and *King Football: Sport and Spectacle in the Golden Age of Radio and Newsreels, Movies and Magazines, the Weekly and the Daily Press* (2001). Oriard's books are significant in that they are two of only a handful of works in the subdiscipline of sport history to employ the narrative form so popular in some recent historical studies. According to Phillips, "Oriard's book is pioneering in the context of sport history because it typifies a wider trend, identified by Peter Burke as the inventive use of alternative forms of narrative to portray the past" (2001: 336). Thus, as explained by Phillips (2001), in *Reading Football*, Oriard utilizes Clifford Geertz' classic work on the Balinese cockfight to read early American football as a cultural text. Although providing empirical data on the history of the game, Oriard's book is more concerned with how football at the turn of the twentieth century is best understood as a textual narrative, an open-ended story of mediated interpretations. Oriard melds sport history with narrative theory and popular cultural studies to illustrate that football emerged as a multivalent story through a process of reading, and that process implicated such key cultural themes as violence, immigration, race, masculinity and power. Thus, "his book is a remarkable attempt to critically engage with narrative by exploring football as a cultural text through multiple voices and perspectives" (Phillips, 2001: 336). In *King Football*, Oriard continues his story by exploring football through the media from the 1920s through the 1950s. Through an analysis of "conventional, formulaic narratives and images" portrayed in newspapers, magazines, movies and other powerful communications media, Oriard traces what football meant to an American middle class that was as diverse as it was homogeneous (Oriard, 2001: 16). Most importantly, Oriard does something remarkable for a historian. He moves "freely between fact and fiction: between the local newspaper's account of last Saturday's game, a magazine profile of a prominent coach, the magazine's cover painting of a lovely lady ministering to her wounded football hero, and a short story or film about the son of a coal miner subsidized to play football at Ivy College or State U" (Oriard, 2001: 17). This approach is important, says Oriard, because an understanding of the "fantasies concocted by magazine covers and short stories" provide insights into "how people thought about football" (Oriard, 2001: 17).

Conclusions

This chapter has sought to give a brief overview of the subdiscipline of sport history and the theories underpinning research in this field, and to assist readers in gaining a basic understanding of the process that sport historians undergo in order to explore their research questions. We have brought to light some of the issues facing the field of sport history as a field of study within the broader context of sports studies. We hope that we have been able to identify the issues in a way that allows aspiring sport historians to continue undertaking interesting and worthwhile research projects that can contribute to this relevant and rewarding area of study.

While it could be argued that the field of sport history has been marginalized to a certain degree, we feel that sport history can and should continue to be an integral component of sports studies. As explained by Briesach, "Once we accept that human life is marked both by change as that which makes past, present and future different from each other and continuity as that which links them together, we begin to understand why historians have played so central a role in Western civilization" (1994: 3). Thus, we can only understand our present (and begin to ponder our futures) with a greater understanding and appreciation of that which has occurred in the past.

As this chapter has shown, the process whereby sport historians have gone about achieving this understanding is, to a large degree, affected by a number of different influences, including one's epistemological and theoretical approaches, the context in which the event in the past occurred and the context in which the researcher is investigating his/her research questions. Thus, it can be argued that "historians are practitioners of an imperfect craft" (Iacovetta & Mitchinson, 1998: 13), and an awareness of this fact can only help sport historians with their own research endeavors.

To conclude, we would like to end this chapter with two comments from two prominent sport historians, Colin Howell and Steven Pope. According to Howell: "Any of you who know my work will be aware of my attempt to nudge sport historians away from their preoccupations with elite, urban, or metropolitan sporting experiences, away from sport at the national and international levels, to a study of hinterland localities and borderland regions" (Howell, 2001: 16). This comment in some ways reflects a desire to move away from exploring the traditional "great deeds of great men" to a more inclusive historical paradigm. Similarly, Steven Pope noted that: "Sport historians can no longer conceive of their works in a specialized, narrowly-focused fashion and expect to receive wide institutional approval. Historical case studies cannot be written in a scholarly vacuum; they must be relevant to contemporary issues and problems" (1998: vii). With this in mind, we would argue that the field of sport history remains an interesting and rewarding field of study. By adhering to this advice and following some of the basic research tools outlined in this chapter, researchers might be able to carve a significant niche in this foundational area of sports studies, and produce work that continues to show the relevance of this field within the academy.

References

Adelman, M.L. (1983). Academicians and American Athletics: A Decade of Progress. *Journal of Sport History*, 10, 80–106.

—— (1986). *A Sporting Time: New York City and the Rise of Modern Athletics, 1820–70.* Champaign, IL: University of Illinois Press.

Atkinson, R.F. (1978). *Knowledge and Explanation in History*. Ithaca, NY: Cornell University Press.

Baker, W.J. (1983). The State of British Sport History. *Journal of Sport History*, 10, 53–66.

—— (1994). Press Games: Sportswriters and the Making of American Football. *Reviews in American History*, 22, 530–7.

Bass, A. (2002). *Not the Triumph but the Struggle: The 1968 Olympics and the Making of the Black Athlete*, Minneapolis: University of Minnesota Press.

Berg, B.L. (2001). *Qualitative Research Methods for the Social Sciences* (4th edition). Boston, MA: Allyn & Bacon.

Berryman, J.W. (1973). Sport History as Social History? *Quest*, 20, 65–73.

—— (1982). Sport, Health, and the Rural–Urban Conflict: Baltimore and John Stuart Skinner's American Farmer 1819–1820. *Conspectus of History*, 1, 43–61.

—— & Park, R.J. (eds) (1992). *Sport and Exercise Science: Essays in the History of Sports Medicine*, IL: University of Illinois Press.

Betts, J.R. (1951). Organized Sport In Industrial America. Doctoral presentation, Columbia University.

—— (1974). *America's Sporting Heritage, 1850–1950*, Reading, MA: Addison Wesley.

Bloom, J. (2000). *To Show what an Indian can Do: Sports at Native American Boarding Schools*. Minneapolis: University of Minnesota Press.

Booth, D. (1997). Sports History: What Can Be Done?, *Sport, Education and Society*, 2, 191–204.

—— (1999). Sport History. In D. Booth & A. Jutel (eds). *Sporting Traditions*, 16, 5–15.

—— (2001). From Ritual to Record: Allen Guttmanns' Insights into Modernization and Modernity, *Sport History Review*, 32, 19–27.

—— (2003). Theory: Distorting or Enriching Sport History?, *Sport History Review*, 34, 1–32.

—— & Loy, J. (1999). Sport, Status, and Style, *Sport History Review*, 30, 1–26.

Borish, L.J. (1996). Do not Neglect Exercise nor Recreation: Rural New Englanders, Sport and Health Concerns, *Colby Quarterly*, 32, 25–35.

Briesach, E. (1994). *Historiography: Ancient, Medieval, and Modern* (2nd edition). Chicago: University of Chicago Press.

Brownell, S. (2001). The Problems with Ritual and Modernization Theory, and Why We Need Marx: A Commentary on *From Ritual to Record. Sport History Review*, 32, 28–41.

Burke, P. (1992). *History and Social Theory*, Ithaca, NY: Cornell University Press.

Cahn, S. (1994). *Coming on Strong: Gender and Sexuality in Twentieth-Century Women's Sport*. New York: The Free Press.

Cavello, D. (1981). *Muscles and Morals: Organized Playgrounds and Urban Reform*. Philadelphia, PA: University of Pennsylvania Press.

Cox, R.W. & Salter, M.A. (1998). The IT Revolution and the Practice of Sport History: An Overview and Reflection on Internet Research and Teaching Resources. *Journal of Sport History*, 25, 283–302.

Cozens, F. & Stumpf, F. (1953). *Sports in American Life*. Chicago: University of Chicago Press.

Dulles, F.R. (1965). *A History of Recreation: America Learns to Play*. Englewood Cliffs, NJ: Prentice Hall.

Dyreson, M. (1998). *Making the American Team: Sport, Culture and the Olympic Experience*. Champaign, IL: University of Illinois Press.

Eisen, G. & Wiggins, D.K. (1994). *Ethnicity and Sport in North American History and Culture*, Westport, CT: Greenwood Press.

Eyler, M.H. (1974). Objectivity and Selectivity in Historical Inquiry, *Journal of Sport History*, 1, 63–76

Fair, J.D. (1999). *Muscletown USA: Bob Hoffman and the Manly Culture of York Barbell*. University Park, PA: Pennsylvania State University Press.

Festle, M.J. (1996). *Playing Nice: Politics and Apologies in Women's Sports*. New York: Columbia University Press.

Gems, G.R. (1997). *Windy City Wars: Labor, Leisure, and Sport in the Making of Chicago*. Lanham, MD: The Scarecrow Press, Inc.

—— (2001). Welfare Capitalism and Blue-Collar Sport, *Rethinking History*, 5, 43–58.

Goldstein, W. (1989). *Playing for Keeps: A History of Early Baseball.* Ithaca, NY: Cornell University Press.

Gorn, E.J. (1986). *The Manly Art: Bare-Knuckle Prize Fighting in America.* Ithaca, NY: Cornell University Press.

—— & Oriard, M. (1995, March 24). Taking Sports Seriously. *Chronicle of Higher Education*, p. A52.

Gottschalk, L. (1969). *Understanding History: A Primer of Historical Method.* New York: Alfred A. Knopf, Inc.

Green, H. (1986). *Fit for America: Health, Fitness and Sport in American Society*. Baltimore, MD: Johns Hopkins University Press.

Gruneau, R. (1983). *Class, Sports, and Social Development.* Amherst, MA: University of Massachusetts Press.

—— (2001). From Ritual to Record: A Retrospective Critique. *Sport History Review*, 32, 2–11.

Guttmann, A. (1978). *From Ritual to Record: The Nature of Modern Sports*. New York: Columbia University Press.

—— (1983). Recent Work in European Sport History. *Journal of Sport History*, 10, 35–52.

—— (1984). *The Games Must Go On: Avery Brundage and the Olympic Movement.* New York: Columbia University Press.

—— (1991). *Women's Sport: A History*. New York: Columbia University Press.

—— (1992). *The Olympics: A History of the Modern Games*. Champaign, IL: University of Illinois Press.

Hardy, S. (1981). The City and the Rise of American Sport, 1820–1920. *Exercise and Sports Sciences Reviews*, 9, 183–229.

—— (1982). *How Boston Played: Sport, Recreation and Community, 1865–1915*. Boston: Northeastern University Press.

—— (1990). Adopted by all the Leading Clubs: Sporting Goods and the Shaping of Leisure. In R. Butsch (ed.). *For Fun and Profit: The Transformation of Leisure into Consumption*. Philadelphia, PA: Temple University Press.

Hill, J. (1996). British Sports History: A Post-Modern Future. *Journal of Sport History*, 23, 1–19.

Hoberman, J. (1997). *Darwin's Athletes: How Sport Has Damaged Black America and Preserved the Myth of Race*. Boston, MA: Houghton Mifflin.

Holliman, J. (1931). *American Sports*. Durham, NC: Seeman Press.

Holt, R. (1998). Sport and History: British and European Traditions. In L. Allison (ed.). *Taking Sport Seriously*. Aachen: Meyer and Meyer.

Howell, C. (1998). On Metcalfe, Marx, and Materialism: Reflections on the Writing of Sport History in the Postmodern Age. *Sport History Review*, 29, 96–102.

—— (2001) Of Remembering and Forgetting: From Ritual to Record and Beyond. *Sport History Review*, 32, 12–18.

Iacovetta, F. & Mitchinson, W. (1998). Social History and Case Files Research. In F. Iacovetta and W. Mitchinson (eds). *On the Case: Explorations in Social History*. Toronto: University of Toronto Press.

Iggers, G.G. (1997). *Historiography in the Twentieth Century: From Scientific Objectivity to Postmodern Challenge*. Middletown, CT: Wesleyan University Press.

Kirsch, G.B. (1989). *The Creation of American Team Sports: Baseball and Cricket, 1838–72*. Champaign, IL: University of Illinois Press.

Krout, J.A. (1929). *Annals of American Sport.* New Haven, CT: Yale University Press.
Kruger, A. (1990). Puzzle Solving: German Sport Historiography of the Eighties. *Journal of Sport History*, 17, 261–77.
Levine, P. (1992). *Ellis Island to Ebbetts Field: Sport and the American Jewish Experience.* Oxford: Oxford University Press.
Lippe von der, G. (2001). Sportification Processes: Whose Logic? Whose Rationality? *Sport History Review*, 32, 42–55.
MacAloon, J. (1981). *This Great Symbol: Pierre de Coubertin and the Origins of the Modern Olympic Games.* Chicago: University of Chicago Press.
Manchester, H. (1931). *Four Centuries of Sport in America, 1490–1890.* New York: The Derrydale Press.
Mangan, J.A. & Park, R. (eds) (1987). *From "Fair Sex to Feminism:" Sport and the Socialization of Women in the Industrial and Post-Industrial Eras.* London: Frank Cass.
Mason, D.S. & Duquette, G.H. (2004). Newspaper Coverage of Early Professional Ice Hockey: The Discourses of Class and Control. *Media History*, 10, 157–73.
McNeil, D. (2001). The Spectacle of Protest and Punishment: Newspaper Coverage of the Melksham Weaver's Riot of 1738. *Media History*, 7, 71–86.
Morrow, D. (1983). Canadian Sport History: A Critical Essay. *Journal of Sport History*, 10, 67–79.
Nauright, J. (1999). The End of Sports History? From Sports History to Sport Studies. In D. Booth & A. Jutel (eds). *Sporting Traditions*, 16, 5–15.
Oriard, M. (1993). *Reading Football: How the Popular Press Created an American Spectacle*, Chapel Hill, NC: University of North Carolina Press.
—— (2001). *King Football: Sport and Spectacle in the Golden Age of Radio and Newsreels, Movies and Magazines, the Weekly and the Daily Press.* Chapel Hill, NC: University of North Carolina Press.
Park, R. (1983). Research and Scholarship in the History of Physical Education and Sport: The Current State of Affairs. *Research Quarterly for Exercise and Sport*, 54, 93–103.
Parratt, C.M. (1998). About Turns: Reflecting on Sport History in the 1990s. *Sport History Review*, 29, 4–17.
Paxson, F.L. (1917). The Rise of Sport. *Mississippi Valley Historical Review*, 4, 143–68.
Phillips, M.G. (1999). Navigating Uncharted Waters: The Death of Sports History? In D. Booth and A. Jutel (eds). *Sporting Traditions*, 16, 5–15.
—— (2001). Deconstructing Sport History: The Postmodern Challenge. *Journal of Sport History*, 28, 327–43.
Pope, S.W. (1993). Negotiating the "Folk Highway" of the Nation: Sport, Public Culture and American Identity. *Journal of Social History*, 27, 327–40.
—— (1997a). *Patriotic Games: Sporting Traditions in the American Imagination, 1876–1926.* Oxford: Oxford University Press.
—— (1997b). *The New American Sport History: Recent Approaches and Perspectives.* Champaign, IL: University of Illinois Press.
—— (1998). Sport History: Into the Twenty-First Century. *Journal of Sport History*, 25, i–x.
Porter, D.H. (1981). *The Emergence of the Past: A Theory of Historical Explanation.* Chicago: University of Chicago Press.
Rail, G. (ed.) (1998). *Sport and Postmodern Times.* Albany, NY: State University of New York Press.

Reah, D. (1998). *The Language of Newspapers*. London: Routledge.
Regalado, S. (1998). *Viva Baseball! Latin Major Leaguers and their Special Hunger*. Champaign, IL: University of Illinois Press.
Riess, S.A. (1980). *Touching Base: Professional Baseball and American Culture in the Progressive Era*. Westport, CT: Greenwood Press.
—— (1989). *City Games: The Evolution of American Urban Society and the Rise of Sports*, Champaign, IL: University of Illinois Press.
—— (ed.) (1998). *Sports and the American Jew*. Syracuse, NY: Syracuse University Press.
Roberts, R. (ed.) (2000). *Pittsburgh Sports: Stories from the Steel City*. Pittsburgh, PA: University of Pittsburgh Press.
Rosenzweig, R. (1983). *Eight Hours for What We Will: Workers and Leisure in an Industrial City, 1870–1920*. Cambridge: Cambridge University Press.
Rosenzweig, R. & Blackmar, E. (1992). *The Park and the People: A History of Central Park*. Ithaca, NY: Cornell University Press.
Sammons, J.T. (1988). *Beyond the Ring: The Role of Boxing in American Society*. Champaign, IL: University of Illinois Press.
Senn, A.E. (1999). *Power, Politics, and the Olympic Games: A History of the Power Brokers, Events, and Controversies that Shaped the Games*. Champaign, IL: Human Kinetics.
Shafer, R. (1980). *A Guide to Historical Method* (3rd edition). Homewood, IL: Dorsey Press.
Shropshire, K.L. (1996). *In Black and White: Race and Sports in America*. New York: New York University Press.
Somers, D.A. (1972). *The Rise of Sports in New Orleans, 1850–1900*. Baton Rouge, LA: Louisiana State University Press.
Struna, N.L. (1985). In Glorious Disarray: The Literature of American Sport History. *Research Quarterly for Exercise and Sport*, 56, 151–60.
—— (1997). Sport History. In J.D. Massengale & R.A. Swanson (eds). *The History of Exercise and Sport Science*. Champaign, IL: Human Kinetics.
—— (2000). Social History in Sport. In J. Coakley & E. Dunning (eds). *Handbook of Sport Studies*. London: Sage.
Sydnor, S. (1998). A History of Synchronized Swimming. *Journal of Sport History*, 25, 252–67.
Todd, J. (1998). *Physical Culture and the Body Beautiful: Purposive Exercise in the Lives of American Women, 1800–1870*. Macon, GA: Mercer University Press.
Uminowicz, G. (1984). Sport in a Middle-Class Utopia: Asbury Park, New Jersey, 1871–1895. *Journal of Sport History*, 11, 51–73.
Verbrugge, M.H. (1988). *Able-Bodied Womanhood: Personal Health and Social Change in Nineteenth-Century Boston*. Oxford: Oxford University Press.
Vertinsky, P. (1990). *The Eternally Wounded Woman: Women, Exercise, and Doctors in the Late Nineteenth Century*. Manchester: Manchester University Press.
Walvin, J. (1984). Sport, Social History and the Historian. *The British Journal of Sports History*, 1, 5–13.
Whorton, J.C. (1982). *Crusaders for Fitness: The History of American Health Reformers*. Princeton, NJ: Princeton University Press.
Wiggins, D.K. (1983a). Sport and Popular Pastimes: Shadow of the Slavequarter. *Canadian Journal of the History of Sport and Physical Education*, X, 61–88.
—— (1983b). The Play of Slave Children in the Plantation Communities of the Old South, 1820–1860. *Journal of Sport History*, 7, 21–39.

—— (1986). From Plantation to Playing Field: Historical Writing on the Black Athlete in American Sport. *Research Quarterly for Exercise and Sport*, 57, 101–16.
—— (1995). Victory for Allah: Muhammad Ali, the Nation of Islam, and American Society. In E.J. Gorn (ed.). *Muhammad Ali, The People's Champ*. Champaign, IL: University of Illinois Press.
—— (1997). *Glory Bound: Black Athletes in a White America*. Syracuse, NY: Syracuse University Press.
—— (2000). The African American Athlete Experience. In A.E. Strickland & R.E. Weems, Jr. *The African American Experience: An Historiographical and Bibliographical Guide*. Westport, CT: Greenwood Press.
Wiggins, D.K. & Miller, P.B. (2003). *The Unlevel Playing Field: A Documentary History of the African American Experience In Sport*. Champaign, IL: University of Illinois Press.
Young, D.C. (1996). *The Modern Olympics: A Struggle for Revival*. Baltimore, MD: Johns Hopkins University Press.

4

Sporting Ethnography

Philosophy, Methodology and Reflection

Michael L. Silk

> Numbers do not protect against bias, they merely disguise it. All statistical data are based on someone's definition of what to measure and how to measure it. An "objective" statistic is really made up of very subjective decisions.
>
> Patton, *Qualitative Evaluation and Research Methods*

This paper discusses ethnographic approaches within sports studies – approaches that are qualitatively oriented given the general effort to account for the complex nature of social settings (Maguire, 1991). Under the term ethnography there exists a variety of different approaches, schools or sub-types. Not surprisingly then ethnography has a rich, varied and troublesome history within the social sciences (see Berg, 2001; Denzin & Lincoln, 1994a; 2000; Lofland & Lofland, 1995), a genealogy that perhaps best allows us to view contemporary ethnographic research as a constant "process of oppositions" (Atkinson & Hammersley, 1994). Early ethnographic work took place within a scientific world dominated by a positivistic research paradigm. Although they have quite different, and at times problematic, histories, contemporary ethnographic practices within sports studies pay a great debt to the discipline of anthropology and to the study of human lived experience in symbolic interactionism (Prus, 1996). The groundbreaking work of Herbert Blumer, and others at the Chicago School interested in understanding different patterns of life within Chicago – from the high society of the "gold coast" to the slum ghettos of "Little Sicily" – and the classic works of Whyte (1943) and Becker, Geer, Hughes and Strauss (1961) developed, transformed and transcended the accepted boundaries of social science (see Hammersley, 1989; Prus, 1996; Vidich & Stanford, 1994).

To different degrees, these initial attempts at "understanding" culture found it hard to grapple with the complexities of social life under a scientific regime centered on validity, reliability and objectivity (see also Hallet and Fine, 2000). These frustrations have perhaps most famously been narrated by Malinowski (1967) who, in the early part of the twentieth century, attempted to "enter the field," find out about New Guinea and the Trobriand Island natives and return with stories about strange people. As Malinowski recorded:

> Nothing whatever draws me to ethnographic studies. On the whole the village struck me unfavorably. There is a certain disorganization... The rowdiness and persistence of the people who laugh and stare and lie discouraged me somewhat... Went to the village hoping to photograph a few stages of the Bara dance. I handed out half sticks of tobacco, then watched a few dances, then took pictures, but the results were poor... They would not pose long enough for time exposures. At moments I was furious with them, particularly because after I gave them their portions of tobacco they all went away: (Malinowski, 1967: 73–74 in Denzin & Lincoln, 1994a)

Malinowski's work is provocative, couched in the positivistic language of science and indicative of social research that reflected positivism and provided a colonizing account of an "alien" other (Denzin & Lincoln, 1994a). Such accounts immediately raise concerns in respect to the presence of a researcher in a natural social world, the power relations between the researched and the researcher, colonizing anthropological subject matter and the objectivity of researchers involved in real life or natural situations. Malinowski should perhaps not be too harshly judged given the historical period within which he was operating and the dominant mode of science of which he was a part. Yet, the question remains: how much has changed? Do those who practice ethnography maintain a legitimate place within the "scientific" community? What counts as knowledge? How do the grant bearing institutions view the so-called "soft" sciences? Equally appropriate, how are research methods such as ethnography perceived within the department in which you are based, your faculty, your institution and within the realm of sports studies as a whole? Despite the significant advances and refinement of ethnography – referred to by Ellen (1984 in Berg, 2001), for example, as a quiet revolution – in the twentieth century (see Denzin & Lincoln, 1994a; 2000), there have been pleas for the sports studies community to widen its research boundaries. Specifically, Maguire proposed:

> A bolder and more imaginative view of the sport sciences would centre on its potential to tell us something about human beings generally, not solely relating to their performance in elite sporting events. A multidisciplinary synthesis, eschewing the canons of positivism would focus the sport sciences on a human-development, not a performance-enhancing, research agenda ... the existing tendency however is to treat individual elite athletes as machines or as though they ought to be machines. (1991: 191)

Maguire's (1991) call to arms recognizes the complexities of social life that tend to be overlooked within a positivistic paradigm that relies on artificial settings (in the case of experiments) and/or on what people say rather than what they do (in the case of survey research) (Atkinson & Hammersley, 1994). As such, the quantitative methodology that tends to be tied to a positivistic research paradigm "seeks to reduce meanings to what is 'observable'; and it treats social phenomena as more clearly defined and static than they are, and as mechanical products of social and psychological factors" (Atkinson & Hammersley, 1994: 251). Such an approach clearly and mistakenly treats complex and dynamic factors of social life as if they were well-defined and measurable variables, neglects the creative character of human interaction and decontextualizes variables from their various contexts (Hammersley, 1989). This chapter, and indeed this book, therefore center upon discussion of research tools and paradigms that are more suited to studying human beings within their natural social worlds – for this chapter ethnographic approaches form the focus, a particularly important focus given the potential of various forms of ethnographic inquiry and (re)presentation in relation to the moral obligation to confront the corporate, neo-liberal globalization project, to make visible, and speak to, the death of lives, culture and truth, to undo the official pedagogies that circulate in the media, and to take sides, intervene and proffer a pedagogical academic insurgency, a politics of liberation, against the injustices of capitalism (Denzin, 2002; 2004).

Ethnographic Variants and Challenges: *Verstehen* through "Vectors"

The meaning of ethnography, like that of so many academic terms, is a contested terrain; there are different types of ethnography, different ways of practice, different philosophical underpinnings and researcher commitments, as well as the utilization of different methodological tools that fall under the general umbrella of the term (see Berg, 2001; Gubrium & Holstein, 1997). Ethnographic practice operates in a complex historical field that has at various times throughout its turbulent history been influenced, challenged and celebrated by, among others, foundationalism, positivism, post-positivism, post-structuralism and post-modernism. All of these overlapping "moments" simultaneously operate in the present (Denzin & Lincoln, 2000) and thus impact upon contemporary ethnographic practice to various degrees.

As indicated in the introduction to this volume, the historical "moments" of qualitative research (Denzin & Lincoln, 1994a; 2000) highlight the dominant paradigms at various historical junctures that have shaped the practice of ethnography. These "moments," while not universally accepted (see Atkinson et al., 1999), do provide a sense of the considerable developments, and indeed, tensions, that surround contemporary ethnographic practices. Indeed, the seventh moment, the future, will be carved out by operating in the spaces between the previous moments, will learn from the ontological, epistemological, methodological and representational mistakes of the past, and will likely be dominated by work that addresses the most serious problems of our time – an exciting opportunity for those scholars attuned to the critical interrogation of sport. While there has been, and will likely continue to be, dramatic and profound change within ethnographic circles, challenges and debates are signs of vitality that force those operating under the ethnographic rubric to be reflexive and recognize limitations. Rather than decrying the scepticism of postmodernism and negating the hyper-reflexivity that has questioned the veracity of empirical data and the authority of the ethnographer and being the profit of doom, it is perhaps better to reflect upon the strong continuities in ethnographic research (see Anderson, 1999; Atkinson et al. 1999; Flaherty, 2002; Manning, 2002; Snow, 2002).

Atkinson and colleagues (1999) suggest that accounts such as those of Denzin and Lincoln (1994a; 2000) capture the current sense of diversity and fragmentation in ethnography, but in ascribing too great a degree of novelty to, and perhaps a blind celebration of, the posts, the intellectual field can be mislead or distorted (see also Sanders, 1999; Stoller, 1999). This is not to deny the clear insights provided by critique and reflection on a positivistic totalizing gaze or indeed by newer forms of (re)presentation influenced by postmodern and post-structural critique. Clearly, Denzin and Lincoln (1994a; 1998; 2000) are only able to present a caricature of history, yet their narrative does "neglect the ambiguities and nuances of ethnographies that have extended over many years" (Atkinson et al., 1999: 460). As such, it is important to highlight that contemporary ethnographic practices are not dominated by any one "moment"; instead Atkinson et al. (1999) propose the metaphor of the vector to imply the directionality of forces that influence ethnographic practice. Through use of this metaphor, it can be stated that ethnographies do not take place within the temporality of a moment but reflect a variety of perspectives. In this sense, it would be misleading to propose that all ethnographic work takes place under the dominant orthodoxies of postmodernism or post-experimentalism. Rather, contemporary ethnography is characterized by diversity, controversies and tensions, as well as continuities from the past, which continue to shape, refine and create practice. Indeed, Atkinson et al's (1999) inspection of the field suggests that classical modes of field research (that reflect Denzin and Lincoln's (1994a; 1998a; 2000) modernist moment) continue to flourish. Atkinson and colleagues (1999) do not deny the proliferation of styles, texts and influences that have gathered urgency in recent years; rather they highlight the increasing influence of the "rhetorical" or literary turn and struggle with the tensions, struggles and contradictions this brings. It is this far more blurred and fuzzy account of ethnography that characterizes the contemporary field of sporting ethnography.

Sporting Ethnographies: Work in the "Field"

Ethnographic research holds much promise for the sociology of sport. Through a focus on the qualitative values and meanings in the context of a "whole way of life," that is a concern with questions about cultures, life-worlds and identities, ethnography provides an opportunity for the expression of "other" cultures and indeed those from the margins of our own cultures. As Barker (2000) suggests, ethnography can be the route by which our own culture can be made strange to us, allowing new descriptions of the world to be generated. In this way the continued redescription of our world can offer the possibility of improvement of the human condition. Since the imperialist other provided explanations of the "other," ethnographies have been offered from lower and middle classes, from women, from openly gay and lesbian scholars, from minority, hybrid as well as Third and Fourth World scholars (Tedlock, 2000). This not only has resulted in a critique of western ethnocentric practices in social science but has given voice and space to marginalized peoples, providing the basis for epistemologies from previously silent groups that can (re)connect social science to the "needs of a free democratic society" (Denzin & Lincoln, 2000).

Despite its promise, within sports studies there has been a small, yet growing, number of accounts that have utilized ethnographic research. It is not my aim here to provide a detailed history of the field and the various "hegemonic" theoretical approaches allied to the sociology of sport. This has been superbly dealt with elsewhere by scholars far more qualified to do so (see the 1997, Volume 14, 4, *Sociology of Sport Journal* for a Special Issue on this topic). What is important, however, is to suggest that the sociology of sport has undergone an "epistemological revolution" (Ingham & Donnelley, 1997) that has seen the field move, in its relatively short history, through various theoretical engagements with structural functionalism, symbolic interactionism, Marxism (or perhaps more accurately, various forms of conflict theory), Millsian sociology, the Frankfurt school, Gramsci, Williams and the Centre for Contemporary Cultural Studies (CCCS), feminism, post-structuralism and postmodernism (Ingham & Donnelly, 1997). This list is certainly not exhaustive and it would be fallacious to present such a list as a linear or progressive model or indeed to suggest there is a hegemonic moment that can currently define the field. Rather, much like the previous discussion of the contemporary ethnographic "moment," it is probably best to see the field as a series of intersecting "vectors" that, to differing degrees, impact upon practice and praxis. Ingham and Donnelly (1997) thus describe the field as "disunity in unity." It is perhaps, though, the field's engagement with the CCCS (at least in so far as recognizing the British/Canadian theoretical influence upon the field [see Ingham & Donnelly, 1997] and the shortcomings of a symbolic interactionism that fails to connect wider social processes [see Donnelly, 1985; Crossett & Beal, 1997]) that provided the base for more politicized forms of ethnography that focused on the thick description (Geertz, 1973) of subcultures. In this vein, Gruneau proposed the field could begin to show how "Subcultures, with their various 'establishment' and 'countercultural' emphases, have been constitutively inserted into the struggles, the forms of compliance and opposition, social reproduction and transformation, associated with changing patterns of social development" (1981 in Ingham & Donnelly, 1997: 379–80).

Opening the discipline to social inequalities and the amelioration of the human condition provides a place for the redescription of the sporting world, for scholars from previously silent groups and for the (re)connection of the sociology of sport to the "needs of a free democratic society." These very concerns are the lifeblood of ethnographic practices. Perhaps this is what inspired Janet Harris (1987), in the early pages of the *Sociology of Sport Journal*, to argue for a more flexible approach to research that would transcend the structural functionalist paradigm (and the allied standardized quantitative methodology) and eschew what we have been taught to value in our research training. Scholars who have employed ethnographic methodology have generally produced engaging in-depth accounts of human actions, organizations, (sub)cultures and marginalized groups that have, if nothing else, provided a voice for the previously silenced – even if "providing" voice has been little more than an exercise in ethnographic ventriloquy (see Fine, 1992; Harrison et al., 2001).

Given the broadness of the term ethnography, there is perhaps a danger in attributing the term ethnographic to research in sports studies – nearly all qualitative work could actually fit under such a label. Indeed, although many authors have employed the tools and paradigmatic concerns of ethnography, there will be those who may well take exception to being termed ethnographers. My intention then is not to categorize colleagues within the field as ethnographers; rather I highlight the types of questions that have been dealt with "ethnographically" in the sociology of sport. Research rooted in symbolic interactionism, perhaps most famously the work of Fine (1979, 1987), has been informative in providing critical commentary on pre-adolescent culture in little league baseball, particularly on the use of homosexual images. Michael Atkinson's (2000) work addresses deviance and criminality among ticket scalpers, providing insight into a neglected area of study. However, Fine and other symbolic interactionists can be criticized for failing to place findings within a broader social and historical context (Donnelly, 1985; Crossett & Beal, 1997). Deviance, though, has tended to be an important site for ethnographers. Marsh's work (1978) was perhaps the catalyst for the ethnographic studies on football cultures in Europe and South America (Archetti & Romero, 1994; Armstrong & Guilianotti, 1997; Armstrong & Harris, 1991; Dal Lago & De Biasi, 1994; Dunning et al., 1991; Giulianotti, 1995; 1996; Sugden & Tomlinson, 1994; 1995; 1998; 1999). Although there are considerable disagreements among the various researchers in regard to method, focus and theoretical orientation, there is nonetheless a considerable body of literature that addresses the demonstration and performance of masculinities through soccer hooliganism (see also Young, 1988 on deviant behavior in rugby).

Perhaps most fruitfully, and not denying the important insights of symbolic interactionism, ethnography can be used to provide voices within the academy for those who have not had them in the past and to explain the prevailing systems of domination and oppression within contemporary (sporting) cultures. Peter Donnelly's (1985) studies, particularly those centered on boxing, climbing and rugby subcultures, have explored the incorporation or suppression of alternative ways of "being" in the dominant culture. Beal's (1995) analysis of social resistance in skateboarding addresses how a subordinate group draws strength from marginalization, while Wheaton's (2000) account provides insight into the creation and performance of (sub)cultural identities through consumption of the sport of windsurfing and its attendant lifestyles. Like Beal (1995) and Wheaton (2000), Loland (2000) utilized a combination of observation and interview tools. In so doing, Loland (2000) was able to address gender differences in the use of aerobics for bodily empowerment. Research also flourishes (see, for example, the work of Robert Sands (2000) on surfing subculture) that is based within a more positivistic, anthropological framework (an anthropology devoid of ethnographic innocence that has been recuperated and reordered in a deterritorialized world that focuses more on the fallacies of living in a global village [see Auge, 1997; Stacey, 1999; Stoller, 1999]). Perhaps less clearly defined as ethnographic, Paraschak's (1997) account of the practices of everyday life in sporting events by native peoples in Canada is able to provide voice to a previously silenced group and a critical commentary upon how practices which a particular marginalized group has control of tended to reproduce activities of dominant groups.

While recognizing the utility of the analysis of historically marginalized groups, perhaps especially women, gays, lesbians, minorities, and non-western "others," the sporting ethnographer has cast their gaze upon dominant groups within society. In particular, and perhaps not surprisingly given the prevalence of the sport media, the focus has tended to be on the construction of subject positions and the encoding of preferred meanings. To different degrees, those who have ethnographically analyzed the sport media have addressed the institutionalized practices among the media (Lowes 1997; MacNeill, 1996; Silk et al., 2000; Silk & Amis, 2000), issues of craft pride (Stoddart, 1994), the marginalization of certain sporting practices (Lowes, 1997), the gendered, national or transnational nature of production (MacNeill, 1996; Silk, 1999b; 2001; 2002) and the production of meaning in line with the logic of capital accumulation (Gruneau, 1989; MacNeill, 1996; Silk, 2001). While important, much of this work has tended to be centered upon the west and, within the sport literature, there are few ethnographic accounts that provide voice from the "other."

It can be argued that the most exciting possibility for this – at least in respect to ethnography as a civic, participatory, collaborative project, a project that joins the researcher with the researched in an ongoing moral dialogue and which inscribes and performs utopian dreams where people are free to be who they choose to be, free of gender, class, race, religious, or ethnic prejudice or discrimination (Denzin, 2002) – is through engagement with fictional and storied representations. Denison and Rinehart (2000), with a huge debt to Norman Denzin, co-edited a special edition of the *Sociology of Sport Journal* (17, 1) that formed the basis for a reflection on the practice of writing in the field. With fictional and autobiographical contributions from, among others, Margaret Carlisle-Duncan (2000), Toni Bruce (2000), and David Rowe (2000), the special edition is an attempt to provide an accepted place for such ethnographic representations. Richardson, who terms this class of ethnographies "creative analytical practice," suggests that the "ethnographic genre has been blurred, enlarged and altered to include an accepted place for poetry, drama, conversations, readers' theater and so on" (2000b: 9). Such work in the sociology of sport (although far from common and under-represented in the field) mirrors recent innovations in qualitative methodology and provides voice for (auto)ethnographic accounts (or narratives of the self) and fictional accounts of: knowing oneself through elite sport as a woman, as an academic and as a heterosexual Anglo-Chinese feminist

(Tsang, 2000); moments of physicality for a young female (Carlisle-Duncan, 2000); male only gatherings, sexuality, misogyny and power in the locker room (Bruce, 2000); disempowerment through physical activity for small children (Miller, 2000); exploration of marginal sub-identities (Klein, 2000); learning masculinity (Bethanis, 2000); sporting misogyny (Rowe, 2000); and eating- and exercise-disordered behavior (Wood, 2000). Further, at the recent (2001) NASSS meetings in San Antonio, Heather Sykes (2001; see also Chapter 8 in this volume) presented and discussed an engaging dramatic performance based around life history research about homoeroticism and homophobia. Performative and creative accounts are clearly more than just a question of semantics or aesthetics; rather such accounts can contribute to our understanding of social life (Denison & Rinehart, 2000; Richardson, 2000b) and create epistemologies for previously silenced groups, and are thus at the forefront of innovative ethnographic practice – yet it is important to reiterate that innovation does not have to mean wholesale rejection of the past (Atkinson et al., 1999).

This brief, and partial, account of work within sports studies clearly straddles the tensions implicit within ethnographic practice and indeed encapsulates the "directionality of forces" that influences ethnographic practices. These accounts embrace the tensions between the scientific and interpretive inquiry, between impersonal and experimental texts and between realist and experiential analyses – the very struggles that will hopefully allow for the continued discussion of the litany of social, personal and ethical dilemmas and for the expansion of ethnographic horizons. There is a considerable need for ethnographic work within the field of sports studies that can truly provide voice to previously silenced and marginalized groups and co-produce knowledge, that is targeted towards the development of specific communities (especially the poor and racially oppressed, see hooks, 1990) and grounded within human rights activism, and that promotes a civic conciousness – an approach to ethnographic research that can clearly speak to the political potentialities of sports studies.

There are clearly differences within ethnography, some of which are essentially rooted in terminology and in ontological and epistemological stance. Given the above, it is crucial to highlight that the remainder of the chapter is far from a "hegemonic view of how to do ethnography." Rather, I offer the reader a brief account of the philosophical underpinnings of the approach and the actual "mechanics" and "dynamics" (Hollands, 1985) of the practices of ethnography (a potentially thankless task, given the diversity of the term), and discuss issues over ethnographic representation and voice, thereby tackling some of the tensions implicit within the field of study defined. Finally, in an attempt to provide an example of a sporting ethnography, I reflect, through a "confessional tale" (Sparkes, 1995) of sorts, on a piece of ethnographic research that I undertook (Silk, 1999a) in New Zealand and Malaysia. This tale from the field discusses the ethnographic issues, problematics and processes that I encountered and hopefully will act as a reference point for future ethnographers as they attempt to tease out new problems and possibilities in ethnographic research.

The Philosophical Underpinnings of Ethnography: Ontology and Epistemology

Distance does not guarantee objectivity, it merely guarantees distance

Scriven, "The Methodology of Evaluation"

Despite the differences alluded to above, ethnographic approaches claim to represent a uniquely humanistic, interpretive approach, as opposed to supposedly "scientific" and "positivistic" positions (Atkinson & Hammersley, 1994). Many ethnographic researchers, this one included, proffer a position of "engaged advocacy" that rejects the dominant positivist, "scientific" model of research for it fails to capture the true nature of social settings (Atkinson & Hammersley, 1994; Hammersley & Atkinson, 1995; Harding, 1986; Maguire, 1991). This perspective employs "semi-structured" forms of data collection such as interviews, observations, textual analysis, verbal description and explanation as opposed to quantitative measurement and statistical analysis. Thus, there is a recognition that:

> Human behavior is complex and fluid in character, not reducible to fixed patterns; and it is shaped by, and in turn produces, varied cultures. Adopting this conception of the social world, qualitative method often involves an emphasis on process rather than structure, a devotion to the study of local and small-scale social situations in preference to analysis at the societal or the psychological levels, a stress on the diversity and variability of social life, and a concern with capturing the myriad perspectives of participants in the social world. (Hammersley, 1989: 1)

The aim is to recognize the central importance of human action and meaning in the construction of the social world (Hollands, 1985). Ethnography then attempts to place specific encounters, events and understandings into a fuller, more meaningful context through the transformation of meaning into a written or visual form (Tedlock, 2000). To understand the social world, scholars attune methods of inquiry to its nature rather than conceptualizing it in terms of variables and the relationships between them.

Such a critical ethnographic approach recognizes that "participants" (and we should include the researcher under this label) are fundamentally attached to the worlds they inhabit. As a result, there is no effort to adhere to the positivistic canons of "science" that call for distance between the researcher and those being studied (objectivity). Rather, the researcher recognizes that he or she is playing an important part in the production and interpretation of data and thus acknowledges this role in the written account of the research (Tedlock, 2000). The critical ethnographic researcher then, gendered and multiculturally situated, approaches the world (either their own or that of others) with a set of ideas that specifies a set of questions. These questions are examined in various ways (Denzin & Lincoln, 1994a) which adhere to these ontological assumptions. Given this, there is recognition that social reality will not be the same for all people and a commitment to defining meaning through the eyes of those being studied. This has clear implications for the ways in which the researcher goes about gathering knowledge of the social world. Such an approach can be described as epistemological for it refers to the ways in which knowledge is gained through qualitative research.

Knowledge of the social world is gained through a fluid and flexible design that often emerges as the project unfolds. Further, there is a commitment to understanding human actions within natural environments (rather than in controlled or sanitized laboratory conditions), environments that the researcher may well be a part of or influence due to the subjective nature of inquiry. Given the commitment to understanding human beings in their natural environments, ethnographic research often takes place over long periods of time in an attempt to capture the meanings people attribute to their actions (although see Berg, 2001 for a discussion of macro and micro ethnographies). As a result of these underpinnings, the data collected are often complex, unwieldy and in the form of spoken words. This has implications for analysis, an issue that shall be addressed later in this chapter. These ontological (a stance on how we comprehend life or "reality") and epistemological (given our stance on understanding humans, how we actually gain knowledge) underpinnings clearly impact the methodological tools employed. Given the broadness of the ethnographic approach, it is often considered to encompass all qualitative research (Atkinson & Hammersley, 1994). However, it is clear that the critical ethnographic approach is rooted in the ontological and epistemological stances outlined above. Hammersley and Atkinson have thus described ethnography in the following way: "In its most characteristic form it involves the ethnographer participating, overtly or covertly, in people's daily lives for an extended period of time, watching what happens, listening to what I said, asking questions – in fact, collecting whatever data are available to throw light on the issues that are the focus of the research." (1995: 1)

Putting Ethnography into Practice: The Methodological "Field"

> Before leaving Harvard I went to see Kluckhohn. In spite of the confidence I had gained from some of my training at Harvard, this last session left me frustrated. When I asked Kluckhohn if he had any advice, he told the story of a graduate student who had asked Kroeber the same question. In response Kroeber was said to have taken the largest, fattest ethnography book off his shelf, and said, "Go forth and do likewise."
>
> Hammersley and Atkinson, *Ethnography: Principles in Practice*

While there has been a proliferation of publications in recent years in respect to countering the hegemonic positivist scientific approaches to the gaining of "knowledge" and carving out a progressive and politically charged qualitative inquiry (see e.g. Denzin & Lincoln, 1994b, 1998a; 1998b; 1998c; 2000; Gubrium & Holstein, 1997; Prus, 1996; Rosenau, 1992), there has been a paucity of literature that actually details the *process* of conducting such research. This is not to deny that there are a multitude of excellent "handbooks" or "guidelines" on how to conduct qualitative research that deal with different strategies of inquiry, the art of interpretation, competing paradigms in the field and the experiences of conducting fieldwork (see for example Berg, 2001; Burton, 2000; Creswell, 1994; Miles & Huberman, 1994; Denzin & Lincoln, 1994b; Shaffir & Stebbins, 1991; Silverman, 2000). However, there are few authors who have focused on the actual "nuts and bolts," the "nitty gritty," of conducting ethnographic research. Indeed, in many discussions of qualitative research there has been a reluctance to lay bare the procedures associated with the analysis of data (Bryman & Burgess, 1994). This is despite the recognition in qualitative analysis that research design, data collection and analysis are simultaneous and continuous processes (Bryman & Burgess, 1994).

Martyn Hammersley and Paul Atkinson (1983; 1995) wrote *Ethnography: Principles in Practice* for the very reason that there is little advice for researchers wishing to embark on ethnography. The work of these authors (Atkinson & Hammersley, 1994; Hammersley, 1989; 1992; Hammersley & Atkinson, 1983; 1995) has been crucial in forming the way in which ethnography has been conducted within academe and sports studies and, on a personal note, by this author. Nonetheless, despite what can only be described as an excellent (although far from appreciated at the time!) "training" in research methodology as a Masters student at the University of Alberta, I found myself to be extremely unprepared, overwhelmed and daunted by the actual process of conducting ethnographic research. No matter how sure the student or faculty member may be about themselves, or indeed their political or philosophical beliefs, the practice of ethnography can be humiliating, belittling, at times dull, boring and downright exhausting. This is despite, at first glance, the conduct of ethnography seeming "deceptively simple" (Hammersley and Atkinson, 1995: 23). This is not meant to put the reader off conducting ethnography, for at the conclusion (if this is ever reached) of such a piece of research the researcher may well not only have found out a great deal about the issue at hand and about themselves, but be able to develop critical consciousness through pedagogical and/or community means. Perhaps such "non-advice" stems from an awareness of the non-programmed and unexpected nature of ethnography and the diversification and disagreement within ethnography inasmuch as there is now a great variation in prescription and practice (Hammersley & Atkinson, 1995). Despite the diversity in perspective and practice and perhaps the lack of a clear and concise "how to do ethnography" text, the following paragraphs attempt to provide an indication of the processes, procedures and tools of ethnographic research. This is not an "ethnographic prescription"; rather a consideration of a number of key issues and tools that frame ethnographic practices.

In contrast to quantitative colleagues, qualitative researchers claim to know relatively little about what a given piece of observed behavior means until they have developed a description of the context in which the behavior takes place, and attempted to see that behavior from the position of its originator (Van Maanen, 1988). This does not mean that a researcher would necessarily enter a research setting without any indication of what they are observing. Both Shaffir (1991) and Fetterman (1991) provide valuable advice for ethnographers at the initial entry stage. Shaffir (1991) focuses on issues of self-presentation, particularly addressing how the researcher might act or present the "aim" of the research to participants. Fetterman (1991) suggests the researcher be honest, patient, sincere and non-judgmental in their initial dealings with those with whom they are interacting. While ethnographic research cannot be predetermined, the researcher should be warned against entering the field without preparation. Indeed, it is suggested that the research should start with some form of "foreshadowed problems" (Berg, 2001; Hammersley & Atkinson, 1995).

Depending on the phenomena being studied, foreshadowed problems could be developed from social theory, from a surprising fact, from political opposition to the status quo, from an opportunity to study a unique occasion, from detailed documentation that exists about a given setting, organization or major event, and perhaps most commonly, from analysis of a wide range of literature. Indeed, no matter the type of ethnographic study, theory is embedded within ethnography, even if in the form of a sensibility or sensitivity that exists just below the surface (Willis & Trondman, 2002). In the pre-fieldwork phase and in the early stages of data collection, the researcher should aim to turn the foreshadowed problems into a set of questions, even if they have little or nothing to do with the original problems (Hammersley & Atkinson, 1995), that shapes the way in which research problems are developed. Miles and Huberman (1984; 1994) term these foreshadowed problems a conceptual framework for investigation that outlines the main dimensions to be studied and the presumed relationship between them. While a set of problems or framework may be prepared beforehand, it is important to recognize that the process is inductive rather than deductive and requires flexibility on the part of the researcher. The structure of the research – what groups and settings are investigated and by what methods, in order to find out what, and so on – cannot always be specified at the start, but often must be worked out as the research proceeds (Adler & Adler, 1991; Hammersley, 1989). Given that the categories of behavior may change while the fieldworker is in the field as the unexpected occurs, it is necessary to be flexible. Silverman (2000) provides an analogy of a zoom lens to explain this point. He suggests that the researcher may well start out with a broad focus, but after time in the field, will "zoom in" on specific issues that have emerged over the research period. This is especially important in research settings that are vast and complex in nature. In such settings, a narrowing down of what can be observed and when is important to avoid a broad brush or superficial account. As Wolcott (1990: 62) has proposed, after initial immersion within the field the researcher may be best advised to "do less, more thoroughly."

No matter how meticulous the planning, there comes a point, however, when little more progress can be made without beginning data collection (Hammersley

& Atkinson, 1995). Unlike a positivist approach, an ethnographic design is fluid. While foreshadowed problems can be identified, and to some extent research questions and themes developed, difficulties predicted and solutions suggested, much of what is observed and questioned emerges out of the early stages of data collection itself. Explanations or concepts tend not to be determined a priori (Hollands, 1985); rather they emerge from the interlinked data collection, analysis and interpretation phases. As such, much of the actual research design emerges from successes, failures and access in the field. Rather than hiding these issues, it is important to acknowledge the ebbs and flows of the ethnographic inquiry in order to aid the reader in understanding the interpretations drawn from the data.

Once a research setting or "field" has been identified, perhaps the most important issue for the researcher is gaining access to the often closed world of organizations, sporting clubs, television networks, advertising agencies, spectators or whatever is the focal point of the research. The researcher also has to decide whether they want the people whom they are investigating to be aware of their presence. This decision is as much an ethical decision as a design issue. While the researcher can choose to collect data covertly, the implications could be quite problematic. For example, the researcher might decide to infiltrate a group of spectators who are known for violent and aggressive acts. The researcher may need to make a personal decision in respect to engaging in such actions as the situation could become quite dangerous if the spectators discovered that the researcher had been covertly collecting data about them (see Adler & Adler, 1985; Berg, 2001 for accounts of the dangers of observation). On the other hand, covert research may well yield natural and highly informative thick description about a particular setting and people's actions within that setting.

Of course, gaining access to some organizations or settings will be dependent on official permission being granted by certain personnel. These personnel, who can legitimately grant or withhold access, can be termed "gatekeepers" (Atkinson & Hammersley, 1994; Berg, 2001; Burgess, 1991; Denscombe, 1998). While these personnel may provide one's initial entrée into a research setting, it should be remembered that they may well wish to paint a favorable picture of the particular setting. In so doing, they may exercise some degree of surveillance by blocking off certain lines of inquiry, or by shepherding the fieldworker in one direction or the other (Berg, 2001; Hammersley & Atkinson, 1995). As such, no matter how reliant upon gatekeepers, it is important that the researcher attempt to maintain some degree of control over who to talk to, when and where.

Once access is gained into the research setting (Adler & Adler, 1991; Bryman, 1988; McLaren, 1991) the researcher needs to make decisions about where and when to observe, who to talk to and what to talk about, as well as about what and how to record (Hammersley & Atkinson, 1995). These early decisions in the field are critical for they will lay the conceptual and methodological foundations for the entire project and thus aid in achieving the objectives of the study (Berg, 2001). Hammersley and Atkinson (1995) propose that there are three major dimensions along which such internal sampling occurs: time, people and context. Temporal divisions should be taken into account in order to capture and represent the entire range of persons and events under study. Further, the ethnographer is, in principle, in play all day. That is, the researcher needs to balance time in order to capture the full range of events and people yet be aware that long, uninterrupted periods of fieldwork are not desirable. Again following Hammersley and Atkinson (1995), the ethnographic researcher is well advised to resist the temptation to see, hear and participate in everything that goes on. Rather, a more selective approach will normally result in better quality data as well as identifying crucial times for fieldwork.

Within contemporary ethnographic practice there are an array of tools available to the ethnographer. Depending upon the subject matter, the epistemological orientation of the researcher and the focus of the inquiry, the ethnographer may find themselves, for example, analyzing culture through film, textual or televisual analysis, becoming a participant in a social setting and engaging in interviewing or observations, utilizing introspective methodology as a tool of auto-ethnography, or analyzing audiotaped and videotaped recordings of conversations and naturally occurring behaviors (Adler & Adler, 1999). Some of these tools (such as textual analysis and interviewing) are dealt with in other chapters in this volume. Although somewhat eschewed by postmodern and post-experimental researchers (see Flaherty, 2002; Manning, 2002; Snow, 2002), and perhaps shaped by my personal orientation and that which has tended to dominate sports studies, fieldwork has been the cornerstone of ethnographic practice, at least in as far as it provides for the transformation of experience into the presented form.

As was outlined earlier, there has been very little published literature, especially within the field of sports studies, which has dealt with the conduct of fieldwork (Adler & Adler, 1994). Thomson (1979) suggested critical sport ethnographers engaged in fieldwork need to keep a daily log of events and a field diary recording their own personal impressions; carry out formal and informal interviews and systematic observations; and use informants, diaries, autobiographical accounts and related documents. Despite the seemingly dated nature of Thomson's review, his guidelines for fieldwork are as pertinent today as they were twenty years ago (see also Berg, 2001; Gallmeier, 1988). It is also important for the researcher to allow themselves time to reflect upon the observations during immersion in the research setting. That is, as a researcher it can be important to hold something back and create a space in which analytic work can be conducted (Hammersley & Atkinson, 1995). This process can allow for the accurate recording of field notes and aid in the development of categories and concepts while in the field. The research process then entails a continuous movement between emerging interpretations of reality and empirical observations.

Denzin (1989) proposes that capturing a research setting through thick description can identify the meanings that are observed in interactions and the meanings persons bring to their experiences. The researcher can also use other techniques to try and grasp the complexity of the social world such as the use of a dictaphone or a video camera. Of course, these tools can be quite obtrusive, may alter behavior and thus negate the capture of human interactions in a natural setting. In essence, the key in collecting good quality ethnographic fieldwork data is to "focus on *naturally occurring, ordinary events in natural settings,* so that we have a strong handle on what "real life" is like'" (Miles & Huberman, 1994: 10, emphasis added). This returns us to the import of field notes as a place in which to record off-the-cuff comments and conversation, explanations for decisions, and discussions between participants as well as items at meetings and so on.

While engaging in fieldwork, and again depending upon the degree of detachment the researcher has from the setting, the researcher may engage in what can be termed "ethnographic conversations" (Spradley, 1979). These conversations can occur at unexpected times and can be spontaneous, elicited by either the researcher or by a member of the group being studied. Within these ethnographic conversations, the researcher may not have a script (as might be expected in a formal interview) or ask each person the same "questions." Rather, conversations may be confirmation of something that has been observed or an informal chat with a person that may aid rapport with participants or a "subject" who wishes to share information may seek the researcher out. These conversations can allow for discussion to flow in a natural way and as such can be flexible and adjustable to the issues that emerge. Despite the seemingly relaxed method of ethnographic conversations, the researcher should attempt to maintain some control over them, ensuring that they have some relevance to the research agenda (Bryman, 1988; Spradley, 1979). In this regard, the researcher needs to consider who to ask, how to ask and how to analyze (Hammersley & Atkinson, 1995). Of course, this is a hard line to follow given that one of the aims of the ethnographic approach, especially in participatory research, is for those being researched to identify their experiences, meanings and understandings of everyday life. People often select themselves or nominate others for interviews in participant observation studies or are identified by the researcher (Hammersley & Atkinson, 1995). As with observations, rather than attempting to talk to the whole population, key actors, or gatekeepers, need to be identified. The context where people are talked to is also important, for people may behave or respond differently according to context (Hammersley & Atkinson, 1995). It is generally recognized that interviews should take place on the participants' own grounds (Henderson, 1991; Silverman, 2000; see also Amis, this volume). Specifically, it is suggested that they take place on the participants' own territory and that the context is organized by the respondent. Such locations may not be the most appropriate environments for intrusive data collection tools such as a dictaphone. Given the spontaneity of such situations, it could be inappropriate to ask the participant to wait while one sets up such a device.

Of course, all ethnographies are unique, so when to "leave the field" is an issue that can be hard to conceptualize. Generally speaking, and following Glaser and Strauss (1967), ethnographers should leave the field once the data being presented to them consistently replicates earlier findings, that is, once data saturation has been reached. While this may be the case in large-scale ethnographies of culture, "micro-ethnographies" (Berg, 2001; Wolcott, 1990) that are perhaps not as longitudinally dependent, may well end due to the conclusion of a season (e.g Gallmeier, 1988; 1991; Giulianotti; 1995; 1996) or an event (e.g MacNeill, 1996; Silk, 1999b; 2001). Even in these "shorter" research studies, time is spent in other people's social worlds and friendships, acquaintances and relationships can be established that the researcher may find are hard to disengage from, in both a physical and emotional sense (Berg, 2001; Stebbins, 1991; Taylor, 1991).

"On Writing Ethnography": Representation, Validity and Voice

> To generalise is to be an idiot. To particularise is the lone distinction of merit. General knowledges are those that idiots possess.
>
> William Blake, in Foot, "A Passionate Prophet of Liberation"

> What can a generalization be except an assertion that is context free? Yet it is virtually impossible to imagine any human behaviour that is not heavily mediated by the context in which it occurs.
>
> Guba and Lincoln, *Fourth Generation Evaluation*

While they have been somewhat artificially separated in this chapter for the purposes of discussion, it is important for the ethnographer to be aware that research design, data collection and analysis are simultaneous and continuous processes (Burgess, 1984). Imagine, for example, attempting to draw distinctive lines between these phases in the conduct of an introspective auto-ethnography. Depending on the type of ethnographic practice undertaken, upon leaving the field or completing data collection, the ethnographic researcher will be presented with often unwieldy and unstructured data, normally in the form of words from field notes, transcripts and documents. Two fundamental aspects of this data concern how to continue analysis of this data and how to ensure credibility and legitimacy in the (re)presentation of ethnographic data. Analysis will inevitably involve data reduction, data display and interpretation, or conclusion drawing (Huberman & Miles, 1998) in an effort to provide some coherence and structure to the data while retaining a hold of the original accounts and observations from which it is derived (Ritchie & Spencer, 1994). Unlike the "scientific" researchers, the ethnographer generally does not attempt to generalize their data beyond the specificities and peculiarities of the social setting under investigation. Rather, the written account should provide an in-depth, rich and informed account of the particularities of the site (although see Silverman, 2000 for an account of "generalizations" in qualitative research). This does not mean that qualitative researchers are not concerned with the process of analysis and "writing" up. Far from it, recent years have seen an explosion in the literature that attempts to deal with the dual crises of representation and legitimation (Denzin, 2002; Denzin & Lincoln, 1994a; 2000; Richardson, 1994; 2000a; 2000b) in qualitative analysis and in the final (written) account.

There are a number of ways in which ethnographic data can be analyzed. Most qualitative researchers use computers, but few use software packages designed specifically to aid qualitative analysis (Richards & Richards, 1998). There are a small number of software packages available, such as NUD-IST, HyperRESEARCH, Atlas, Ethnograph, that can aid in the management of data, the coding and retrieval of pieces of data, the indexing and exploration of data and the formation of theory (Richards & Richards, 1998). While perhaps appealing to the ethnographer, such packages have been criticized for they could kill off the intuitive art of qualitative analysis (Richards & Richards, 1998; Stroh, 2000). As opposed to using computer analysis, the ethnographer may choose to use a more hands-on approach that allows for the researcher to maintain more of a hold on the data. Such analytic approaches may be a long way from formalization or standardization and could involve the researcher listening to interviews, reading and re-reading field notes and perhaps coding the data as emergent themes are sought (see Huberman & Miles, 1998). Ryan and Bernard (2000), for example, suggest that the process is likely to involve sampling (selecting units or texts for analysis), finding themes (often inductively), the building of code books, the marking of texts, and some form of iterative process in which the analyst becomes more and more grounded in the data and develops increasingly richer concepts and models of how the phenomenon being studied really works. There is still a great deal of work to be done in respect to the analysis of qualitative data; indeed, it is perhaps something often neglected by the ethnographer who zealously collects data and then, quite legitimately, asks, "what now?"

One approach that has attempted to standardize qualitative analysis has been titled "framework" (Ritchie and Spencer, 1994). Ritchie and Spencer (1994) developed framework as an analytical process by which to analyze unstructured qualitative data. Framework involves a number of distinct yet highly interconnected stages. While this could be seen as a highly mechanical approach, it should be stated that it does not necessarily have to be conducted in a systematic and disciplined order. Rather, the approach relies on the creative and conceptual ability of the analyst to determine meaning, salience and connections (Ritchie & Spencer, 1994). The five stages of the approach are familiarization, identifying a thematic framework, indexing, charting, mapping and interpretation. Such an approach can aid in the link between analysis and data collection. That is, analysis will also generate the mechanics of where, when and with whom interviews and observations will take place.

No matter what type of analysis takes place, it is important that the ethnographer provides a clear account of the process and thus lays the process open to the reader. As Lincoln and Guba (1985) have expressed, the process should be constructed and mapped out for the reader, allowing him or her to follow the path and key decisions taken by the researcher from the conception of the research through to the findings and conclusions derived from the research. The researcher should not be afraid to critically reflect on what did, or did not, go well in respect to data collection and analysis. By making such accounts accessible, the research community can widen its pool of knowledge and extend its methodological base (Ritchie & Spencer, 1994). Such accounts, under the influence of a postmodernism that frees the ethnographer from scientific writing, promote a far more self-conscious text that has to struggle with a whole set of claims related to authorship, truth, validity and reliability and bring to the fore some of the complex political/ideological agendas hidden in our writing (Richardson, 2000c). There are a number of considerations to be taken into account in this respect – how credible, trustworthy or faithful the text is to the setting, the issue of reflexivity and that of a connection between the final text and the world written about (see e.g. Harrison et al., 2001). At the very least, the ethnographer needs to be fair, balanced and conscientious in taking into account multiple perspectives, interests and realities that will exist within any social setting.

There are a number of formal ways in which the ethnographer can rethink the positivist canons of validity and reliability. Specifically, the ethnographer can undertake a number of strategies that allow the account to be credible, trustworthy or legitimate. First, the ethnographer can engage in a strategy called "peer debriefing." This process involves "exposing oneself to a disinterested peer in a manner paralleling an analytical session and for the purpose of exploring aspects of inquiry that might otherwise remain implicit within the inquirer's mind" (Lincoln & Guba, 1985: 308). Such a process allows another suitably qualified person (perhaps a graduate student or faculty member) to explore the inquirer's biases, clarify interpretations, and "do their best to play devils advocate" (Lincoln & Guba, 1995). Second, the ethnographer can return transcripts, field notes and interpretations to those in the field to allow participants to check records and establish credibility (Hanson & Newburg, 1992; Lincoln & Guba, 1985). However, it is important here that the researcher maintains some critical distance and enters into a dialogue with participants if differences emerge. In this way, the process becomes less a "check" of interpretations and more a site through which new dialogue and data can be elicited. Third, the ethnographer needs to acknowledge their presence within the field of study. The basic issue here can be framed as one of "relative neutrality and reasonable freedom from unacknowledged researcher biases – at the minimum explicitness about the inevitable biases that exist" (Miles & Huberman, 1994: 278).

However, such criteria tend to be based on the domain assumption that there is a fixed point or object that can be triangulated. That is, through the deployment of different methods (such as interviews, observations, documents, member checking and so on), there is still an attempt to validate data (Richardson, 2000a). Building upon this critique, Laurel Richardson (2000a) proposes the need to look beyond the triangle – a rigid, fixed, two-dimensional object. Displacing triangulation is crystallization. For Richardson we should no longer triangulate, but crystallize, given the crystal,

> ... combines symmetry and substance with an infinite variety of shapes, substances, transmutations, multidimensionalities, and angles of approach. Crystals grow, change, alter, but are not amorphous. Crystals are prisms that reflect externalities and refract within themselves, creating different colors, patterns and arrays, casting off in different directions. What we see depends on our angle of repose... Crystallization, without losing structure, deconstructs the traditional idea of validity, and crystallization provides us with a deepened, complex, thoroughly partial, understanding of the topic. Paradoxically, we know more and doubt what we know. Ingeniously we know there is always more to know. (Richardson, 2000a: 934)

Crystallization opens ethnography to self-reflexivity, to the personal and biographical, to the complex political and ideological agendas that have been heretofore hidden in our work. This further displaces claims to truth and indeed the desires to speak "for" others (Richardson, 2000a). No longer can ethnography be carried out as if in some autonomous realm that is insulated from the wider society and from the particular biography of the researcher (Hammersley & Atkinson, 1995). Yet, is it enough to bracket details such as personal characteristics (ethnic origin, age, gender and sexuality) and then move on to a written account evacuated by the author? Clearly, the crisis of legitimation not only problematizes and provides qualitative counters to the traditional criteria used to evaluate qualitative research: a serious rethinking of such terms as validity, generalizability and reliability (Sparkes, 1995), it is coupled with a crisis of representation – how to write ethnographic accounts – and with a crisis of praxis (Denzin, 2002).

As has been highlighted in the introduction to this chapter, there has been a literary turn in ethnography. This has lead to a shift in ethnographic writing that has lead to several different ways of describing, inscribing, interpreting and (re)presenting (Denzin, 1994a). This shift emerged from recognition that ethnographic representations, especially in anthropology, have fundamentally been the products of asymmetrical power relations. This led to a development of new forms of representation which could include the multiple voices of those being represented and a rejection of the authoritative, realist and objectivist style of writing ethnography (James et al., 1997). The watershed of this thought was the publication of Clifford and Marcus's (1986) *Writing Culture: The Poetics and Politics of Ethnography*. The responses to this text caused a regermination of the ways in which ethnographies are represented, from questions of epistemology through to those of the political projects of ethnographers (James et al., 1997). The turn to writing "fiction" or literary analysis is an attempt to remove the false distinction between "science" and "rhetoric," thus reaffirming the essential dialectic between the aesthetic and humanist, on the one hand, and the logical and scientific, on the other (Atkinson & Hammersley, 1994). Sparkes (1992; 1995) and others, such as Denzin (1989; 1994; 2002), Atkinson (1992), Altheide and Johnson (1994), Clough (2000) and Richardson (1994; 2000a), have considered alternative ways of (re)presentation, such as ethnography as drama, fiction or poetry. However, Sparkes (1995) warns against researchers rushing out to produce alternative forms of representation with which they might not be familiar. This is not to reject such representations outright; rather it is an acknowledgment that such "textual radicalism" (Hammersley, 1993) is currently plagued by problems associated with their actual construction and with the integration of the research process into these representations (Sparkes, 1995).

Some regard the role of the ethnographer as being able to amplify the voices of subjects; others see the task as close to ideological critique in the deconstruction of accounts in an effort to understand how they were produced and the presuppositions on which they are based (Hammersley & Atkinson, 1995). What is clear is ethnographers "write culture" (Clifford & Marcus, 1986) as opposed to recording an objective reality that is "out there" (Denzin, 1989). However, this process of writing culture is still problematic to many ethnographers. As Krizek has proposed, "many of us do ethnography but write in the conservative voice of science... In short, we often render our research reports devoid of human emotion and self-reflection. As ethnographers we experience life but write science" (Krizek, 1998: 93). This style of writing is inconsistent with the philosophical underpinnings of ethnographic research. As Andrews Sparkes has eloquently surmised:

> The style of no style is the style of science. The stripped down, abstracted, detached form of language; the impersonal voice; and the statement of conclusions as propositions or formulae involves a realist or externalising technique that objectifies through depersonalisation. This technique allows the text to give the impression that its symbols are inert, neutral representations that exist quite independently of the interests and efforts of the researcher, who is presented as a neutral and disengaged analyst. (1995: 161)

Writing ethnography goes beyond description and neutral representation – ethnographic texts tend to be reconstructions of social life that require contextualization, reframing, interpretation and judgement of participants voices, actions and meanings. These reconstructions raise a number of issues that surround the author's place in the text, issues relating to voice, who speaks, who is excluded and how voices are interpreted. Again, as Sparkes elucidates: "Whose voices are included, how they are given weight, along with questions of priority and juxtaposition, are not just textual strategies but are political concerns that have moral consequences. How we as researchers chose to write about others has profound implications, not just for how readable the text is but also for how the people the text portrays are 'read' and understood" (1995: 159).

Denison and Markula (this volume) have described the narrative turn in sports studies research in which there has been a shift from a detatched, objective researcher who records and reports facts alone to a researcher who plays an integral part in the research process and whose voice is alive and well in the final form. Clearly, classic forms of representation have not disappeared, but are gradually becoming only one form of expression among a number of visible forms of social description (Sparkes, 1995). Yet, adopting a different genre does not in and of itself ensure a better product. Rather, just as with "traditional" forms, criteria for evaluating newer forms of representation are beginning to emerge. At present there are a number of questions that arise with the use of those forms of expression that counter the dominant forms within the sports studies literature: "What is a good story? Is just a good story enough? What must be added to story to make it scholarship? How do we derive concepts from stories and then use these concepts to understand people? What – precisely – would have to be added to transform story material from the journalistic or literary to the academic?" (Josselson, 1993 in Sparkes, 1995: 183). These questions are perhaps presently at the forefront of qualitative inquiry, and as scholars in sports studies become more familiar with these approaches, and perhaps engage with literary and creative forms of expression, then we will be in a better position to address these issues. At present, however, it is perhaps useful, as Denzin (2000; 2002) does, to think about these issues in relation to praxis. Denzin (2000) proposes qualitative inquiry that is attached to new and less foundational interpretive criteria. For Denzin (2000) these criteria exist alongside, and indeed are interrelated to, three interpretive practices: a civic, intimate and literary journalism; a call for critical, performance-based, ethnographies that simultaneously write and study performances (how people enact cultural meanings in their daily lives); and a variation on a Chicano/a and African American aesthetic and the relation between these practices and CRT. This type of co-participatory ethnography brings the audience into the text, creates shared emotional experiences, is political, moves people to action and reflection, moves towards the presentational (as opposed to representational) and builds collaborative, reciprocal, trusting, friendly relations with those studied (Denzin, 2000). Furthermore, such ethnographic work will speak to the logic and cultures of the community in question, creating and enacting emancipatory, utopian texts grounded in distinctive styles, rhythms, idioms and personal identities of local folk and vernacular culture. These texts are sites of resistance, places where meanings, politics and identities are negotiated – they transform and challenge all forms of cultural representation: black, white, Chicano/a, Asian American, Native American, straight, and gay (Denzin, 2000). In this sense, such texts are more than personal; they are political and take place in relation to the following commitments: that the world of human experience is studied from the point of view of the historically and culturally situated individual; that qualitative researchers persist in working outwards from their own biographies to the worlds of experience that surround them; that researchers continue to value and seek to produce works that speak clearly and powerfully about these worlds; and that the world is not just described, but changed – these texts will be performance-based and informed by civic, intimate and public journalism (Denzin, 2000).

If we seek a politics of liberation and moral and oppositional ethnographic works that "takes sides," ethnography has an exciting place within the future of a democratic sports studies. Making a difference can be achieved through ethnographic works that relate to these new criteria upon which our work is judged. Of course, these do not necessarily replace existing criteria, but exist, perhaps (un)comfortably, alongside them. Indeed, as Richardson (2000a) suggested, there are many criteria from which to judge ethnographic expression. Richardson (2000a) holds creative analytical practice to five such criteria: substantive contribution (grounded, if not deeply embedded, in a social science perspective); aesthetic merit; reflexivity; impact; and expression of a reality. Yet, such expressions may not be open to all – what of the graduate student or the assistant professor who is attempting to negotiate the halls of an academy that is dominated by science, if not by the corporate world (and these are of course far from mutually exclusive). Yet, and following Richardson (2000a: 938), to create a truly enriched, diversified, socially engaged and non-hegemonic community of sports studies scholars, there is a need to challenge the "medieval vision" of intellectual thought; otherwise we will continue to exclude and be complicitous with those who "discipline and punish postmodern ideas within social science."

In sum, the post-structural and postmodern influence upon ethnographic research within sports studies clearly impacts upon the authority of the researcher, the expression and presentation of data and the political potentialities of qualitative research. There remains a plethora of questions surrounding how voices are staged, who speaks, whose story is being told, who maintains control of the narrative, and by implication, the purpose to which the story is put (Sparkes, 1995). How we achieve a dispersed authority and write multiple voices within the field of sports studies will continue to be a place for lively debate and for the enactment of an emancipatory agenda. There will remain space in which the author of the academic text may have the final word, yet this space must exist alongside multiple voices which have an ability to talk back, have their own opinions and constitute their own (re)presentations. I am sure that some may render this problematic, for the researcher may still hold some (imperialist) power. Yet, in terms of praxis and engaging in a political project and perhaps intervention, transformation or emancipation in the social world, there may be times when it is important for the author to maintain an authoritative voice, take sides, and indeed make decisions about the impact of certain voices lest he/she offer a rampant polyphony, a mere tourist experience (Smith, 1993 in Sparkes, 1995). Indeed, in my own research, focussing on those who control resources and the official pedagogies that circulate in the media (television production personnel), it was important to allow (yes, give) voice, yet remain critical and evaluative of this voice.

Doing Ethnography: Critical Reflections on the 1998 Kuala Lumpur Commonwealth Games

Within this chapter I have attempted to lay out the philosophical underpinnings of the ethnographic approaches, highlight how the methodological tools are framed within these ontological and epistemological positions and discuss ways in which ethnographic data can be analyzed, legitimated, and (re)presented. In this final section, I offer a confessional tale, which provides some brief critical reflection on the ethnographic process, issues and problems that arose during an ethnographic study of the 1998 Kuala Lumpur Commonwealth Games (Kuala Lumpur 98). While ultimately personal, critical and revealing, this section will, I believe, allow the reader to assess some of the issues inherent in ethnographic research and hopefully aid in the conduct of ethnography within sports studies.

The Kuala Lumpur 98 Project

The Kuala Lumpur 98 project emerged from a series of interviews with production personnel at Television New Zealand (TVNZ) and the Executive Producer of the Kuala Lumpur Host broadcaster unit. These personnel became the gatekeepers (Burgess, 1991) and provided the opportunity to study both the Kuala Lumpur 98 Host broadcaster and the TVNZ rights holder. Prior to fieldwork, foreshadowed problems (Miles & Huberman, 1994) emerged from the nature of the setting and pre-fieldwork research. These problems were developed from a thorough review of the literature on televised sport production, globalization, cultural studies and critical political economy approaches to the study of the sport media. Investigation was initiated over two years prior to the actual event and extended after the event, with interviews, observations and analysis being conducted at TVNZ's studios in Auckland and Wellington. In addition to the ethnographic data collection there were many accounts of a written nature – the research setting has existed, at least in document form, since SUKOM, the organizing committee, first produced its bid for the Games in 1993. This documentation was analyzed using inductive content analysis that allowed the themes and patterns to emerge from the documents (Henderson, 1991). This data was important for it provided the context, revealed some of the taken-for-granted assumptions which actors (the production crew) brought with them to the research setting, gave an indication of the research site and enabled the creation of a number of foreshadowed problems and research questions. The following objectives for the fieldwork emerged: to comprehend the actions of broadcast crews and to determine which meanings about the Games circulated and which did not, which stories were told and about what, which arguments were given prominence, what cultural resources were made available and to whom and the technological conditions in which the Games were recreated by the media.

Observations and interviews were used in combination in the hope that they would be able to play off each other. Following Thomson (1979), field notes were overtly recorded during my immersion in the field. On return to my private hotel room at the conclusion of a period of observation I also kept a diary of the events observed. The field notes included accounts of brief, informal conversations I had conducted with employees, discussions between those involved in the reproduction of the Games, meetings between crew, Host and Client broadcasters which I attended, the key decisions that were made and the choices that were offered to the production crew, as well as descriptive accounts of the setting and methodological issues and concerns. Back at the hotel following the completion of a piece of fieldwork, I would transfer my field notes onto a laptop computer.

In addition, I used a video recorder while in the field to record the settings, the work routines of the crews and of some of the decisions being made. Initially I was concerned that this practice may not be appropriate for the setting, may influence the actions and decisions of the crew or may affect the relationships I had formed with the participants. Thus, for the first few days in the field, I made no recordings. However, at the end of the first week of observations, I noticed that a number of the crew were recording the setting and work routines for their own purposes. Indeed, some crew members had purchased new video cameras while in Malaysia for their own personal use and used them quite regularly in the International Broadcast Center (IBC). At this point, I blended in with the crew as I started to take video footage of the labor process involved in the recreation of the Games. I had also planned to use a Dictaphone, which I hoped would aid in recording interviews and informal discussions. However, due to time constraints, access and the nature of the work environment this was not possible. During the time in Kuala Lumpur I was an accredited crew member. This involved traveling to Kuala Lumpur with the crew, staying in the "team" hotel and eating, socializing and working with the crew.

Ethnographic Critiques, Reflections and Problematics

Gaining access to the organization was very much a first step. From initial immersion I had to try to gain rapport, become accepted and maintain a critical space (Berg, 2001; Bryman, 1988; Hammersley & Atkinson, 1995; Shaffir, 1991). Denzin (1989) proposed that during early stages of research there may be hostility to the researcher's presence, but in the latter stages the researcher often finds herself/himself being treated as one of the group. Indeed, despite the fact that prior to my arrival the crew members had been advised of my presence, there were a number of tense and stressful encounters in Kuala Lumpur. During the first few days of data collection, I felt quite removed from the TVNZ crew as they went about their familiarization routines. To elucidate, I offer an extract from my field notes written as I sat in the gymnastics venue on the third day I was in Kuala Lumpur:

> Despite the fact that I am in an extremely busy and exciting environment, sitting in world-class, brand new, purpose-built venues, it is not really me who is busy . . . at this stage I feel sort of out of touch and lonely I guess due to my not wanting to get into the nitty gritty until I have been properly introduced. I am not totally immersed in the broadcasting culture as yet which is what I had hoped for. At least I can take some comfort in knowing that I am not alone in this, as a number of the freelancers are just standing around and will not really do much until rehearsals start.

Acceptance, at least by the majority of the crew, was dependant upon the Executive Producer of the Games formally introducing the research objectives (and I was not even sure of them at this point, so how he explained them to the crew baffled me) at the first formal production meeting prior to the Games. Following this official introduction, crew members made an effort to introduce themselves to me and allowed opportunities to observe and ask questions. For example, one of the TVNZ news cameramen approached me after the meeting, asking, "so you learning heaps? I'm off out tomorrow, taking shots of the city. You should come out with me at some stage." Despite best intentions and broadcast accreditation, data collection was extremely reliant on access and gatekeepers. The Executive Producer for example was crucial in allowing me to enter closed meetings between the highest echelons of the host broadcaster and the rights holders.

Throughout the fieldwork, the generosity of the crew was remarkable. On one occasion a presenter who knew my intentions gave up her pass to the production area of the main stadia during the opening ceremony to allow me to collect the data required. Some crew members, with the best of intentions, would seek me out to "give me another page in the thesis" that detracted from the issues that I was looking to focus on. This was as problematic as it was helpful as various personnel attempted to "shape" the ethnographic experiences. In the interest of being patient and sincere (Fetterman, 1991) I had little choice but to go along on, at times, worthless journeys that added little to the research.

There were also differences between some of the crew, and at various times people with different opinions sought me out to see if I would be supportive of their particular positions and thus become some type of ally. Maintaining some type of control over the research and some neutrality among the crew became a very difficult pathway to follow. Further, some of the crew were keen to introduce themselves to me, perhaps out of wariness or curiosity. At one point for example, early in the research process, one of the directors approached me in an effort to explain his role, but perhaps equally to work out if I was a danger to him:

> "Hi, we haven't formally met, I haven't got a clue what a thesis is ... can you explain what you are doing and what you'll get out of observing me." I explained the aims of the research and he asked if anyone had actually explained to me how his show was going to work (at the actual on-air production desk). I replied no, so he asked me to sit with him and he explained to me the chroma key, the graphics, the way it would go live and his role. (field notes)

Throughout data collection I had access to the shuttle vans that transported crew back and forth between venues, hotels and the IBC. These buses were unreliable, often late and frequently "hijacked" by sports teams needing to get to a venue for competition. Thus getting around the vast research site was difficult. Early on in the research, it became clear that the site was too vast to attempt to "see everything" and that transport and geography were going to be two important factors that affected the data collection process. I therefore had to make a number of early decisions in respect to the pathway the research would take. I had to manage myself temporally and attempt to be in a position where I could collect the richest data. Initially, I had to pursue a number of avenues to determine when and where the most important data would be offered. The research started out with a wide perspective, yet the realities of the site meant the research had to follow the zoom lens metaphor alluded to above (Silverman, 2000). This approach offered more time to record the observations and interviews accurately and with greater quality than attempting to be "everywhere at once." With regard to achieving the objectives of the research, the IBC and the venue production trucks were major sites of data collection. However, I did not want to discard the possibility that there may be other avenues of analysis in other locations. Thus, in order to get a full picture early on in the research, I took advantage of the fact that the TVNZ crew with which I was accredited had been given the first day off once in Malaysia to recover from the flight. On this day, I explored the research setting:

> I decided to get a more complete picture and just to check that I was not ruling out any possible lines of inquiry too early. I moved on the shuttle to the National Sports Complex (Bukit Jalil) and took some general descriptions and shots of this complex and of the athletes' village. I then went to the aquatics and gymnastics complexes for some shots of the setting up of the cameras here. I took some description shots, until the security guards took my video camera away ... am now going to attempt to get to the MPC (Main Press Center) to further check out possible lines of inquiry... The MPC is a different ball game, with a whole new set of work routines, structures, language and practices ... this is just all too much. (field notes)

A major consideration in the ethnographic research arena is the continual management of access and acceptance. On the first day of broadcasting, I was invited by the Executive Producer to sit with him in the studio. Within a number of days, the crew had accepted that this was "my place." Thus, in the IBC, when TVNZ was on air I had a prime position from which to observe the productions:

> In the IBC, the spot I sit in has become my own now after a few days. At least during the on-air broadcasts. It is the seat next to [the Producer's] which is located directly behind the main production desk where the Director, vision mixer, technical Director, script counter & graphics people are, who sit directly in front of the screens. (field notes)

During the observations at the venues, however, I often had to change seats in the production truck. I believe this was due to not being totally immersed in the culture at the venues and the cramped conditions in the truck.

"Impression management" (Goffman, 1959; 1963) aids integration and rapport, acts as a symbol of membership and reduces differences between researcher and those being studied to make people feel at ease with the researcher's presence (Hammersley & Atkinson, 1995; Shaffir, 1991). Through dressing in the same way as the crew (TVNZ sent a "uniform" prior to the Games), my personal appearance matched the crew's. Further, I stayed in the same hotel and wore the same accreditation as the team and I quickly learnt the rules of dress and demeanor from social interactions with the crew. The climate was also a significant factor in relation to dress, allowing for little variation from a pair of sandals, shorts and a t-shirt for all involved, from Executive Producer down through the ranks.

Hammersley and Atkinson (1995) point out that the younger the researcher is, the more potential they have to adapt to the "incompetent" position of the outsider and establish good relationships with participants. As a result, and indeed given the temporal demands, many ethnographers are only able to conduct a small number of ethnographies within their lifetime. Luckily, a vast majority of the TVNZ crew were of a similar age to myself and had similar interests. On the second day, I was approached by one of the presenters who asked me to join him and a number of the crew in the bar that evening to watch a football (soccer) game. I had been approached as I was English and the presenter presumed I must be interested in football. As I was in the process of establishing relationships I accepted the offer. Immediately I established a common bond with some of the crew, who by the end of the evening had taken to mocking the team I follow, Bolton Wanderers. Rapport with the crew grew throughout the Games. Various members of the crew would often ask me what I had done during the day, or I would chat with them about an incident I had observed. This aided the relationships forged with many of the crew who, over time, became more amenable to my presence and questioning. Instead of constantly pumping participants on matters of research interest then, I spent time with them in social situations, establishing rapport with more "ordinary" topics of conversation. Such neutral "ethnographic conversations" (Spradley, 1979) were not totally divorced from the aims of social research; indeed they yielded new information on participants and formed new lines of inquiry (Hammersley & Atkinson, 1995).

Another indicator of being accepted by the crew was the nicknames I was given as the ethnography progressed. These revolved around my "student" status at the time. I became known as "Tax" (as in tax bludger) after being pressed by a few members of the TVNZ crew on my funding for the project. Later, I became known as "Rocko" (as in rocket scientist) after one of the presenters had talked to me about the nature of a Ph.D. As I was overtly recording some observations in the IBC one day, the presenter walked past and said "You and your notebooks, how many have you got Rocko?" The humor within the process of establishing relationships was highlighted by a discussion I had with a director and the Executive Producer. I was inquiring about the way in which the script was put together when the Director asked if the research would be published as a book. He continued:

Director: yep, I can't wait for the book, an undercover expose of our work...
Executive Producer: yeah right.
Director: ...but with more sex scenes inserted. I wonder who'll play me – Brad Pitt I presume.
Executive Producer: More like Jack Nicholson.

This banter and general interest in the research and me as researcher continued and grew as the project went on, climaxing on the final evening we were in Kuala Lumpur. On this evening, I was singled out by one of the commentary team who put a Host Broadcaster hat on my head and said, "Right, you are no longer a researcher, you are part of the broadcast team, so stop taking notes and concentrate on "relaxing" with the rest of us."

On reflection, I do not believe I would have achieved the rapport that I did with the majority of the TVNZ crew had I not been able to frame observations around their lifestyles. This involved long work hours and then down time, normally in the hotel bar. During this down time, alcohol was consumed and the crew openly talked about a number of issues key to the research. As the researcher, balancing rapport and acceptance with the influence of alcohol on memory and the construction of field notes became an issue that at times I struggled with. This was especially the case when the crew seemed able to survive on very little sleep, while I wanted to ensure that on retiring to the hotel room I could continue the process of recording, analysis and interpretation. As such, for over a month, I operated on less than four hours sleep a night, which had emotional, personal and health consequences and caused me to question my professionalism (see Asher & Fine, 1991). Indeed, frustrations at my professional capabilities at this point almost lead to my quitting the setting. Once in the field, I consistently wondered if I was following the right pathways, collecting any meaningful data or providing a worthy representation of my academic institution and myself. There was a real need for constant support and clarification, but nowhere (or no one) to turn to for validation of my actions. As Gurney (1991) has suggested, one is never really in a position of knowing exactly what the correct decisions are until after the fact, by which point it may be too late to salvage the data and/or the rapport.

In establishing such relationships, the researcher may well have to contend with "going native." This involves abandonment of the critical distance in favor of the joys of participation and bias from over-rapport (Hammersley & Atkinson, 1995). While I involved myself socially with the crew, I believe the nature of the research site prevented my "going native." First, the temporal and contextual nature of the setting did not allow for the researcher to be considered native. Second, the setting did not forward the joy of participation for the research site was complex, stressed and strained. Climatic, geographical and environmental stressors in Kuala Lumpur were far from conducive to enjoyment. Furthermore, while I was able to establish a rapport with the majority of the TVNZ crew, ethnic and cultural differences and a perceived power relation meant that this was more difficult to achieve with the Malaysian crew members. This was not just a personal issue, as many of the TVNZ crew found it difficult to gain acceptance in, and comprehension of, Malaysian cultures.

Gender was also a crucial factor in this respect. Of the sixty TVNZ crew, fourteen were female, the rest male. Female members of the crew often socialized together, a situation that did not allow me to develop as much of a relationship with them as I did with the male members of the crew. This was important out of the social setting as well, for the lack of an "established" relationship may have hindered the openness of the female crew to my research. It was probably the case that the world of which I was a part of was a western, patriarchal and logocentric man's world. My personal background allowed me to enter into this world, participate and, hopefully, interpret. Without a doubt, the research can be critiqued for providing an incomplete or half-meaningful account of the production crew due to my failure to fully engage women and "other" cultures. Clearly then, as Tedlock (2000) outlines, this ethnography could equally be seen as heroic to some, yet ludicrous to others – different ethnographers, in this case those from non-western cultures, those who share a history of colonialism or those who are female would have created quite different accounts of the same setting (see also Gurney, 1991). However, as Tedlock (2000) reminds us, just being born female does not result in feminist consciousness and just being born into an ethnic minority does not automatically result in "native" consciousness. In this regard, it is hoped being a western male did not work to close my consciousness; rather it is hoped the reader can find some comfort in the efforts (not all successful) to bridge the gulf between self and other by revealing both parties as vulnerable experiencing subjects working to co-produce knowledge (Abu-Lughod, 1993).

A further issued faced during the ethnography was in respect to physical danger. While the danger may not have been as real as it was perceived, there was a time when I felt in grave physical danger. This revolved around a political situation that unfolded during the fieldwork, the way in which the TVNZ crew wanted to report this and the censorship of the Malaysian Ministry of Information. Whether or not the actual threat existed, the perception was that the group of which I was a part may be excluded from the IBC, deported from Malaysia and even threatened physically by armed forces. Fortunately, this situation (and the consequences that would derive from such actions) did not materialize; however, those that highlight dangers in ethnography (see Adler & Adler, 1985; Berg, 2001 for example) can never prepare the researcher for the adrenaline, fear and emotion felt during the research process.

In gaining access to such a closed, chaotic and private environment, it was expected to some degree that I, as researcher, prove my worth through participation. Indeed, some of the tasks I was asked to undertake allowed for a greater understanding and explanation of some aspects of the televised sport labor process. Both I and the Executive Producer were mindful that I completed my own objectives, and as a result, at the beginning of the Games I was not asked to play much of a participatory membership role. Menial tasks such as sorting out athletic results as they came in to the studio or obtaining information for a crew member were conducted on a daily basis. However, as the Games progressed and the environment became a little more intense, the demands of the crew began to extend:

> The Producer has requested me for the morning shift. They have asked me to be a VTR operator this morning for 2/4 hours; this is due to a shortage of staff for the number of events coming in live today. The environment became frenzied and chaotic with people running all around me, taking tapes out of the machines I was using and putting new one in, telling me to start new log sheets, make sure I got accurate log times and in/out times, which at the time I didn't even know what that meant ... it meant I really learnt about what was considered important for editors, that is I was living out the question I had posed yesterday in terms of what would go into a highlights package or a montage. (field notes)

The tasks I undertook for the crew aided in my acceptance, justified my presence in the field and allowed for a greater comprehension of the labor process. Yet, at times, issues of reciprocity (Harrison et al., 2001) took away from time observing and as the tasks became more complex the environment became increasingly stressful. Further, there was pressure to say yes to more tasks as time in the field continued (see Adler & Adler, 1987, for a discussion of roles in ethnography). It became increasingly difficult to maintain a critical distance and space to achieve the research objectives. This was achieved through finding excuses to maintain distance, which to some degree altered both the sites observed and the people interviewed.

The research site was a frenzied chaotic environment, with participants working long hours in extreme weather conditions, unable to get around freely, and spread out over a vast geographical area. Consequently, many of the pre-arranged structured interviews were called off. In one instance the Executive Producer for one of the Host Broadcaster venues was called away to an emergency meeting, after I had traveled to meet him. A different occasion saw the Executive Producer of the TVNZ broadcasts fall asleep in the TVNZ minivan on the way back to the hotel, at a time we had arranged to talk! Such situations were a part of the research process, and had to be accepted as a part of the flexible ethnographic process, no matter how frustrating they were. It was my belief at the time that pressing for interviews at such inopportune moments may have hindered the building of relationships and the quality of data collected. However, this had an impact upon the actual research design. These formal and in-depth interviews were an important part of the design and in order to complete them I had to re-enter the field after I had disengaged from it. This meant cost and time implications that were not part of the original grant, a major concern for any graduate student.

It is important to offer a brief comment on the data collected. Not surprisingly, the data collected was mostly in the form of field notes and interview transcripts that reported other people's words and actions. This was supplemented by analysis of over 125 hours of broadcast footage and numerous official documents. I handled all the data and the framework process was followed. This process was time-consuming and exhausting; it did mean, though, that I was able to gain a strong handle on all the data. However, perhaps my biggest disappointments came in the ways in which I treated the data. The writing followed the normative social science criteria in which authority was claimed through a number of interrelated ways. Following Sparkes' (1995) critique of realist tales, the realist tales produced from this work often spoke with an impersonal voice (I disappeared, yet I was everywhere at the same time). I made conscious decisions to include voices that supported the point I was attempting to make, orchestrating voices to serve my theoretical needs as the absent, disembodied author. In essence through experiential authority, interpretive omnipotence, and interpretive credibility the written expression of the Kuala Lumpur project became a transparency to the realm of events, with few alternative points of view, a textual positivism (Sparkes, 1995).

Furthermore, these interpretations were, at various times throughout the analytical process, sent to gatekeepers at TVNZ, to personnel at the Kuala Lumpur 98 Host Broadcaster and to other participants. This process of "credibility" and "legitimation" was extremely informative, if not a little humbling. Despite my best efforts, there were interpretations I had made that, according to participants, had quite simply "missed the point." The process did prove to be exceptionally insightful and a dialogue took place in regard to some of the interpretations I had made. Yet, had I actually achieved anything? Does research such as this actually make a difference? Yes, I took sides, but did the work go beyond merely describing the social world, making recommendations for changing it? As much as was possible, the "results" challenged the TVNZ Producer to reconsider, at least theoretically, some of TVNZ's production practices:

> The more I read of this work of yours, the more I thought this claim of ours to be internationalist was actually hard to justify, especially at an event like a Commonwealth Games. I started thinking more about this. Are we nationalistic or are we internationalist? The same with us coming out with the *preferred thinking* of the Host country. A lot of that is unintentional, or certainly not deliberate; it is not something that is written down in a manual as being policy... When you go out with the intention of showing the event, it is all you've got time for. You haven't got the airtime to put in stories about the slums next to the main stadium, nor have you got the resources and the manpower. You've got the resources for the event and it is just all go for that. Again, it is the way it is worked out. If we all stopped and thought about it we might end up changing our ways perhaps, or if someone came in and said "right, you've got to this time with the Olympics in Sydney, do some stuff about the down and outs in Kings Cross." It would then take away from the actual event, which is why we are there. It falls into a news and current affairs area to come up with that sort of activity. I'm not sure now if that is right or wrong Michael, I honestly don't. You started me thinking, as I read through it I got a bit precious about the whole internationalist debate and got a bit defensive... It is an interesting debate, how populist should we be? (TVNZ Producer – emphasis added)

I am of course not sufficiently naïve, or narcissistic, to suggest that this work has, in Denzin's (2000) terms, transformed the official pedagogies that circulate in the media, or indeed enhanced moral discernment and promoted a critical consciousness among media professionals. Further, I of course worry about those voices not included within the parameters of this study, those of the diverse peoples of Malaysia who I acted on behalf of (without permission and with my agenda), yet never spoke to and to whom I never gave anything back. Ethnographies such as this fall down in many ways and can be critiqued against the new and emergent criteria which ethnographic research is being judged. Yet, in another way, in a pedagogical sense, the utility of such ethnographic work is in providing visions of "what it means to live in a world that has been radically altered by global capitalism, transnational corporations, and new electronic technologies ... expanding the public nature of pedagogy to include how knowledge, values, identities and social practices are produced and disseminated across a wide range of cultural sites and social locations" (Giroux, 2001: 9). Thus, in the classroom as in the community, we as sports studies educators can draw upon our various ethnographic works to articulate knowledge to effects and learning to social change, using our pedagogy as a form of socially engaged citizenship to create the conditions that encourage and enable public participation and engagement with a vastly changing set of historical circumstances (Giroux, 2001). It is this vision, of multiple and competing forms of ethnographic research in sports studies, co-existing (even if not comfortably) side by side, expressed in various forms relevant to engagement of the community in question, that can potentially be the most progressive and emancipatory for a contextual sports studies. This is a field characterized by diversity, not by a meta-narrative that asserts that one form of ethnography (or ethnographic expression) is necessarily better suited to the key issues of our time, and a field that has displaced, as opposed to discarded, only traditional (or medieval as Richardson, 2000a would say) forms of ethnographic research. However, ethnographic inquiries that contribute to a contextual sports studies must, at the least, be judged in respect to the collective and individual reflection and critical action they produce. This includes conversations that cross the boundaries of race, class, gender and nation and how each instance of qualitative inquiry promotes the development of human agency, resistance and critical consciousness (hooks, 1990: 111, in Denzin, 2000).

References

Abu-Lughod, L. (1993). *Writing Women's Worlds: Bedouin Stories.* Berkeley: University of California Press.

Adler, P. & Adler, P. (1985). *Wheeling and Dealing.* New York: Columbia University Press.

—— (1987). *Membership Roles in Field Research.* London: Sage.

—— (1991). Stability & Flexibility: Maintaining Relations Within Organized and Unorganized Groups. In W. Shaffir & R. Stebbins (eds). *Experiencing Fieldwork: An Inside View of Qualitative Research.* London: Sage

—— (1994). Observational Techniques. In N. Denzin & Y. Lincoln (eds). *Handbook of Qualitative Research.* London: Sage.

—— (1999). The Ethnographers' Ball – Revisited. *Journal of Contemporary Ethnography*, 28, 5, 442–50.
Altheide, D. & Johnson, J. (1994). Criteria for Assessing Interpretive Validity in Qualitative Research. In N. Denzin & Y. Lincoln (eds). *Handbook of Qualitative Research*. London: Sage.
Anderson, L. (1999). The Open Road to Ethnography's Future. *Journal of Contemporary Ethnography*, 28, 5, 451–9.
Archetti, E. & Romero, A. (1994). Death and Violence in Argentinean Football. In R. Guilianotti, N. Bonney & M. Hepworth (eds). *Football, Violence and Social Identity*. London: Routledge.
Armstrong, G. (1993). Like that Desmond Morris? In D. Hobbs & T. May (eds). *Interpreting the Field*. Oxford: Oxford University Press.
Armstrong, G. & Guilianotti, R. (eds) (1997). *Entering the Field: New Perspectives on World Football*. Oxford: Berg.
Armstrong, G. & Harris, R. (1991). Football Hooligans: Theory and Evidence. *Sociological Review*, 39, 427–58.
Asher, R.& Fine, G. (1991. Fragile Ties: Shaping Research Relationships with Women Married to Alcoholics. In W. Shaffir and R. Stebbins (eds). *Experiencing Field Work: Qualitative Research in the Social Sciences*. London: Sage.
Atkinson, M. (2000). Brother, Can You Spare a Seat? Developing Recipes of Knowledge in the Ticket Scalping Subculture. *Sociology of Sport Journal*, 17, 151–70.
Atkinson, P. (1992). *Understanding Ethnographic Texts*. London: Sage.
Atkinson, P., Coffey, A. & Delamont, S. (1999). Ethnography: Post, Past and Present. *Journal of Contemporary Ethnography*, 28, 5, 460–71.
Atkinson, P. & Hammersley, M. (1994). Ethnography & Participant Observation. In N. Denzin & Y. Lincoln (eds). *Handbook of Qualitative Research*. London: Sage.
Auge, M. (1997). *Non-Places: Introduction to an Anthropology of Supermodernity*. London: Verso.
Barker, C. (2000). *Cultural Studies: Theory and Practice*. London: Sage.
Beal, B. (1995). Disqualifying the Official: Exploring Social Resistance through the Subculture of Skateboarding. *Sociology of Sport Journal*, 12, 252–67.
Becker, H., Geer, B., Hughes, E. & Strauss, A. (1961). *Boys in White: Student Culture in Medical School*. Chicago: University of Chicago Press.
Berg, B. (2001). *Qualitative Research Methods for the Social Sciences* (4th edition). Boston: Allen & Bacon.
Bethanis, P. (2000). The Shadowboxer. *Sociology of Sport Journal*, 17, 1, 81–2.
Bruce, T. (2000). Never Let the Bastards See You Cry. *Sociology of Sport Journal*, 17, 1, 69–74.
Bryman, A. (1988). *Quality and Quantity in Social Research*. London: Routledge.
Bryman, A. & Burgess, R. (eds) (1994). *Analysing Qualitative Data*. London: Routledge.
Burgess, R. (1984). *In the Field: An Introduction to Qualitative Research*. London: Allen & Unwin.
—— (1991). Sponsors, Gatekeepers, Members and Friends: Access in Educational Settings. In W. Shaffir & R. Stebbins (eds). *Experiencing Fieldwork: An Inside View of Qualitative Research*. London: Sage
Burton, D. (ed.) (2000). *Research Training for Social Scientists: A Handbook for Graduate Students*. London: Sage.

Carlisle-Duncan, M. (2000). Reflex: Body as Memory. *Sociology of Sport Journal*, 17, 1, 60–8.
Clifford, J. (1986). Introduction: Partial Truths. In J. Clifford & G. Marcus (eds). *Writing Culture: The Poetics and Politics of Ethnography*. Berkeley: University of California Press.
Clifford, J. & Marcus, G. (eds) (1986). *Writing Culture: The Poetics and Politics of Ethnography*. Berkeley: University of California Press.
Clough, P. (2001). On the Relationship of the Criticism of Ethnographic Writing and the Cultural Studies of Science. *Cultural Studies ↔ Critical Methodologies*, 1, 2, 240–70.
Creswell, J. (1994). *Research Design: Qualitative and Quantitative Approaches*. London: Sage.
Crossett, T. & Beal, B. (1997). The Use of "Subculture" and "Subworld" in Ethnographic Works on Sport: A Discussion of Definitional Distinctions. *Sociology of Sport Journal*, 14, 1, 73–85.
Dal Lago, A. & De Biasi, R. (1994). The Social Identity of Football Fans in Italy. In R. Giulianotti, N. Bonney & M. Hepworth (eds). *Football, Violence and Social Identity*. London: Routledge.
Denison, J. & Rinehart, R. (2000). Introduction: Imagining Sociological Narratives. *Sociology of Sport Journal*, 17, 1–5.
Denscombe, M. (1998). *The Good Research Guide*. Buckingham, UK: Open University Press.
Denzin, N. (1989). *The Research Act: A Theoretical Introduction to Sociological Methods* (3rd edition). Englewood Cliffs, NJ: Prentice Hall.
—— (1994). The Art and Politics of Interpretation. In N. Denzin & Y. Lincoln (eds). *Handbook of Qualitative Research*. London: Sage.
—— (1997). *Interpretive Ethnography*. London: Sage.
—— (2000). The Practices and Politics of Interpretation. In N. Denzin & Y. Lincoln (eds). *Handbook of Qualitative Research*. London: Sage.
—— (2002). Confronting Ethnography's Crisis of Representation. *Journal of Contemporary Ethnography*, 31, 4, 482–90.
—— (2004). The War on Culture, The War on Truth. *Cultural Studies ↔ Critical Methodologies*, 4, 2, 137–42.
Denzin, N. & Lincoln, Y. (1994a). Introduction: Entering the Field of Qualitative Research. In N. Denzin & Y. Lincoln (eds). *Handbook of Qualitative Research*. London: Sage.
—— (1994b). (eds). *Handbook of Qualitative Research*. London: Sage.
—— (1998a). (eds). *The Landscape of Qualitative Research: Theories and Issues*. London: Sage.
—— (1998b). (eds). *Strategies of Qualitative Inquiry*. London: Sage.
—— (1998c). (eds). *Collecting and Interpreting Qualitative Materials* London: Sage.
—— (2000). *Handbook of Qualitative Research* (2nd edition). London:Sage.
Donnelly, P. (1985). Sport Subcultures. *Exercise and Sport Science Reviews*, 13, 539–78.
Duncan, M.C. (1998). Stories We Tell Ourselves about Ourselves. *Sociology of Sport Journal*, 15, 95–108.
Dunning, E., Murphy, P. & Waddington, I. (1991). Anthropological Versus Sociological Approaches to the Study of Soccer Hooliganism: Some Critical Notes. *Sociological Review*, 39, 3, 459–78.

Fetterman, D. (1991). A Walk Through the Wilderness: Learning to Find Your Way. In W. Shaffir & R. Stebbins (eds). *Experiencing Fieldwork: An Inside View of Qualitative Research*. London: Sage

Fine, G.A. (1979). Small Groups and Culture Creation: The Idioculture of Little League Baseball and Teams. *American Sociological Review*, 44, 733–44.

—— (1987). *With the Boys: Little League Baseball and Preadolescent Culture*. Chicago: University of Chicago Press.

Fine, M. (1992). Passions, Politics and Power: Feminist Research Possibilities. In M. Fine (ed.). *Disruptive Voices: The Possibilities of Feminist Research*. Ann Arbor: The University of Michigan Press.

Flaherty, M. (2002). The "Crisis" in Representation: Reflections and Assessments. *Journal of Contemporary Ethnography*, 31, 4, 508–16.

Foot, P. (1996). A Passionate Prophet of Liberation: A Review of Blake by Peter Ackroyd (Sinclair-Stevenson, 1995) and *Witness against the Beast – William Blake and the Moral Law* by E.P. Thompson (Cambridge University Press, 1993). *International Socialism*, quarterly Journal of the Socialist Workers' Party (Britain), Issue 71 (available at: http://pubs.socialistreviewindex.org.uk/isj71/blake.htm).

Gallmeier, C. (1988). Methodological Issues in Qualitative Sport Research: Participant Observations Among Hockey Players. *Sociological Spectrum*, 8, 213–35.

—— (1991). Toward An Emergent Ethnography of Sport. *Arena Review*, 13, 1–8.

Geertz, C. (1973). *The Interpretation of Cultures: Selected Essays*. New York: Basic Books.

Giroux, H. (2001). Cultural Studies as Performative Politics. *Cultural Studies <–> Critical Methodologies*, 1, 1, 5–23.

Giulianotti, R. (1995). Football and the Politics of Carnival: An Ethnographic Study of Scottish Fans in Sweden. *International Review for the Sociology of Sport*, 30, 191–224.

—— (1996). Back to the Future: An Ethnography of Ireland's Football Fans at the 1995 World Cup Finals in the USA. *International review for the Sociology of Sport*, 31, 323–48.

Glaser, B. & Strauss, A. (1967). *The Discovery of Grounded Theory*. Chicago: Aldine.

Goffman, E. (1959). *The Presentation of Self in Everyday Life*. New York: Anchor.

—— (1963). *Behavior in Public Places*. New York: Free Press.

Gold, R. (1958). Roles in Sociological Field Observations. *Social Forces*, 36, 217–23.

Gruneau, R. (1989). Making Spectacle: A Case Study in Televised Sport Production. In L. Wenner (ed.). *Media, Sports, and Society*. London: Sage.

Guba, E. & Lincoln, Y. (1981). *Fourth Generation Evaluation*. London: Sage.

—— (1994). Competing Paradigms in Qualitative Research. In N. Denzin & Y. Lincoln (eds). *Handbook of Qualitative Research*. London: Sage.

Gubrium, J. & Holstein, J. (1997). *The New Language of Qualitative Method*. Oxford: Oxford University Press.

Gurney, J. (1991). Female Researchers in Male-Dominated Settings: Implications for Short-Term Versus Long-Term Research. In W. Shaffir & R. Stebbins (eds). *Experiencing Fieldwork: An Inside View of Qualitative Research*. London: Sage.

Hallett, T. & Fine, G.A. (2000). Ethnography 1900. *Journal of Contemporary Ethnography*, 29, 5, 593–617.

Hammersley, M. (1989). *The Dilemma of Qualitative Methods: Herbert Blumer and the Chicago Tradition*. London: Routledge.

—— (1992). *What's Wrong with Ethnography? Methodological Explorations*. London: Routledge.

—— (1993). The Rhetorical Turn in Ethnography. *Social Science Information*, 32, 23–37.

Hammersley, M. & Atkinson, P. (1983). *Ethnography: Principles in Practice.* London: Routledge.

—— (1995). *Ethnography: Principles in Practice* (2nd edition). London: Routledge.

Hanson, T. & Newburg, D. (1992). Naturalistic Inquiry as a Paradigm for Doing Applied Performance Enhancement Research. *Contemporary Thought on Human Performance Enhancement*, 1, 71–105.

Harding, S. (1986). *The Science Question in Feminism.* Buckingham, UK: Open University Press.

Harris, J. (1987). Moving Toward Sociocultural Sports Studies. *Sociology of Sport Journal*, 4: 133–6.

Harrison, J., MacGibbon, L. & Morton, M. (2001). Regimes of Trustworthiness in Qualitative Research: The Rigors of Reciprocity. *Qualitative Inquiry*, 7, 3, 323–45.

Henderson, K. (1991). *Dimensions of Choice: A Qualitative Approach to Recreation, Parks and Leisure Research.* State College, PA: Venture Publishing Inc.

Hollands, R. (1985). *Working for the Best Ethnography*. Birmingham: Centre for Contemporary Cultural Studies.

hooks, b. (1990). *Yearning: Race, gender and cultural politics.* Boston: South End.

Huberman, A. & Miles, M. (1998). Data Management and Analysis Techniques. In N. Denzin & Y. Lincoln (eds). *Collecting and Interpreting Qualitative Materials.* London: Sage.

Ingham, A. & Donnelly, P. (1997). A Sociology of North American Sport: Disunity in Unity, 1965–1996. *Sociology of Sport Journal*, 14, 4, 362–418.

James, A., Hockey, J. & Dawson, A. (eds) (1997). *After Writing Culture : Epistemology and Praxis in Contemporary Anthropology.* London: Routledge.

Klein, A. (1986). Pumping Irony: Crisis and Contradiction in Bodybuilding. *Sociology of Sport Journal*, 3, 112–33.

—— (2000). Anti-Semitism and Anti-Somatism: Seeking the Elusive Sporting Jew. *Sociology of Sport Journal*, 14, 3, 213–28.

Krizek, R. (1998). Lessons: What the Hell Are We Teaching the Next Generation Anyway? In A. Banks & S. Banks (eds). *Fiction and Social Research.* London: Altamira Press.

Lewis, J. (1997). What Counts in Cultural Studies. *Media, Culture & Society*, 19: 83–97.

Lincoln, Y. & Guba, E. (1985). *Naturalistic Inquiry.* London: Sage.

Lofland, J. & Lofland, L. (1995). *Analyzing Social Settings* (3rd edition). Belmont, CA: Wadsworth.

Loland, N. (2000). The Art of Concealment in a Culture of Display: Aerobicizing Women's and Men's Experience and Use of Their Own Bodies. *Sociology of Sport Journal*, 17, 2, 111–29.

Lowes, M. (1997). Sports Page: A Case Study in the Manufacture of Sports News for the Daily Press. *Sociology of Sport Journal*, 14, 2, 143–59.

MacNeill, M. (1996). Networks: Producing Olympic Ice Hockey for a National Television Audience. *Sociology of Sport Journal*, 13, 103–24.

Maguire, J. (1991). Human Sciences, Sport Sciences, and the Need to Study people "In the Round." *Quest*, 43, 190–206.

Malinowski, B. (1967). *A Diary in the Strict Sense of the Term.* New York: Harcourt Brace.

Manning, P. (2002). The Sky is not Falling. *Journal of Contemporary Ethnography*, 31, 4, 490–8.

Marsh, P. (1978). *Aggro: The Illusion of Violence*. London: Dent.

McLaren, P. (1991). Field Relations and the Discourse of the Other: Collaboration in Our Own Ruin. In W. Shaffir & R. Stebbins (eds). *Experiencing Fieldwork: An Inside View of Qualitative Research* London: Sage

McRobbie, A. (1994). *Postmodernism and Popular Culture*. London: Routledge.

—— (1996). All the World's a Stage, Screen, or Magazine: When Culture is the Logic of Late Capitalism. *Media, Culture, and Society*, 18, 335–42.

Miles, M. & Huberman, A. (1984). *Qualitative Data Analysis*. London: Sage

—— (1994). *Qualitative Data Analysis: An Expanded Sourcebook* (2nd edition). London: Sage.

Miller, E. (2000). Dis. *Sociology of Sport Journal*, 17, 1, 75–80.

Paraschack, V. (1997). Variations in Race Relations: Sporting Events and Native Peoples in Canada. *Sociology of Sport Journal*, 14, 1, 1–21.

Patton, M. (1990). *Qualitative Evaluation and Research Methods* (2nd edition). London: Sage.

Prus, R. (1996). *Symbolic Interaction and Ethnographic Research: Intersubjectivity and the Study of Human Lived Experience*. New York: SUNY Press.

Richards, T. & Richards, L. (1998). Using Computers in Qualitative Research. In N. Denzin & Y. Lincoln (eds). *Collecting and Interpreting Qualitative Materials*. London: Sage.

Richardson L. (`1994). Writing: A Method of Inquiry. In N. Denzin & Y. Lincoln (eds). *Handbook of Qualitative Research*. London: Sage.

—— (1998). Writing: A Method of Inquiry. In N. Denzin & Y. Lincoln (eds). *Collecting and Interpreting Qualitative Materials*. London: Sage

—— (2000a). Writing: A Method of Inquiry. In N. Denzin & Y. Lincoln. *Handbook of Qualitative Research* (2nd edition). London: Sage.

—— (2000b). New Writing Practices in Qualitative Research. *Sociology of Sport Journal*, 17, 1, 5–20.

—— (2000c) Evaluating Ethnography. *Qualitative Inquiry*, 6, 2, 253–5.

Ritchie, J. & Spencer, L. (1994). Qualitative Data Analysis for Applied Policy Research. In A. Bryman & R. Burgess (eds). *Analysing Qualitative Data*. London: Routledge.

Rosenau, P. (1992). *Post-Modernism and the Social Sciences: Insights, Inroads, Intrusions*. Princeton, NJ: Princeton University Press.

Rowe, D. (2000). *Amore Impropre*, or "Fever Pitch" sans Reflexivity. *Sociology of Sport Journal*, 17, 1, 95–7.

Ryan, G. & Bernard, H. (2000). Data Management and Analysis Methods. In N. Denzin & Y. Lincoln (eds). *Handbook of Qualitative Research* (2nd edition). London: Sage

Sanders, C. (1999). Prospects for a Post-Postmodern Ethnography. *Journal of Contemporary Ethnography*, 28, 6, 669–75.

Sands, R. (2000). *Sport Ethnography*. Champaign, IL: Human Kinetics.

Scriven, M. (1967). The Methodology of Evaluation. In R. Tyler, R. Gagne & M. Scriven (eds). *Perspectives on Curriculum Evaluation*. AERA Series on Education, No. 1. Chicago: Rand-McNally.

Shaffir, W. (1991). Managing a Convincing Self-Presentation: Some Personal Reflections on Entering the Field. In W. Shaffir & R. Stebbins (eds). *Experiencing Fieldwork: An Inside View of Qualitative Research*. London: Sage

Shaffir, W. & Stebbins, R. (eds) (1991). *Experiencing Fieldwork: An Inside View of Qualitative Research.* London: Sage

Silk, M. (1999a). Reconstructing Meanings: The Media Reproduction of Kuala Lumpur 98. Unpublished Ph.D. thesis, University of Otago, New Zealand.

—— (1999b). Local/Global Flows and Altered Production practices: Narrative Constructions at the 1995 Canada Cup of Soccer. *International Review for the Sociology of Sport*, 34, 113–23.

—— (2001). Together We're One? The Place of the Nation in Media representations of Kuala Lumpur 98. *Sociology of Sport Journal*, 18, 277–301.

—— (2002). "Bangsa Malaysia": Global Sport, the City and the Mediated Refurbishment of Local Identities. *Media, Culture and Society*, 24, 6, 771–90.

Silk, M. & Amis, J. (2000). Institutional Pressures and the Production of Televised Sport. *Journal of Sport Management*, 14, 267–92.

Silk, M. Slack, T. & Amis, J. (2000). An Institutional Approach to Televised Sport Production. *Culture, Sport and Society*, 3, 1, 1–21.

Silverman, D. (2000). *Doing Qualitative Research: A Practical Handbook.* London: Sage

Snow, D. (2002). On the Presumed Crisis in Ethnographic Representation: Observations from a Sociological and Interactionist Standpoint. *Journal of Contemporary Ethnography*, 31, 4, 498–507.

Sparkes, A. (1992). Writing and the Textual Construction of Realities: Some Challenges for Alternative Paradigms in Physical Education. In A. Sparkes (ed.). *Research in Physical Education and Sport: Exploring Alternative Visions.* London: Falmer Press.

—— (1995). Writing People: Reflections on the Dual Crises of Representation and Legitimation in Qualitative Inquiry. *Quest*, 45, 188–95.

Spradley, J.P. (1979). *The Ethnographic Interview.* New York: Holt, Rinehart & Winston.

Stacey, J. (1999). Ethnography Confronts the Global Village. *Journal of Contemporary Ethnography*, 28, 6, 687–97.

Stebbins, R. (1991). Do We Ever Leave the Field? Notes on Secondary Fieldwork Involvements. In W. Shaffir & R. Stebbins (eds). *Experiencing Fieldwork: An Inside View of Qualitative Research.* London: Sage

Stoddart, B. (1994). Sport, Television, Interpretation and Practice Reconsidered: Televised Sport and Analytical Orthodoxies. *Journal of Sport and Social Issues*, 18, 76–88.

Stoller, P. (1999). Back to the Ethnographic Future. *Journal of Contemporary Ethnography*, 28, 6, 698–704.

Stroh, M. (2000). Qualitative Interviewing. In D. Burton (ed.). *Research Training for Social Sciences: A Handbook for Postgraduate Students.* London: Sage.

Sugden, J. & Tomlinson, A. (eds) (1994). *Hosts and Champions: Soccer Cultures, National Identities and the USA World Cup.* Aldershot: Avebury/Ashgate.

—— (1995). Hustling in Havana: Ethnographic Notes on Everyday Life and Mutual Exploitation between Locals and Tourists in a Socialist Economy under Siege. In G. McFee, W. Murphy and G. Whannel (eds). *Leisure Cultures: Values, Genders, Lifestyles* (LSA Publication 54). Brighton: Leisure Studies Association.

—— (1998). *FIFA and the Contest for World Football: Who Rules the Peoples' Game?* Cambridge: Polity Press.

—— (1999). Digging the Dirt and Staying Clean: Retrieving the Investigative Tradition for a Critical Sociology of Sport. *International Review for the Sociology of Sport*, 34, 4, 385–97.

Sykes, H., Chapman, J. & Swedberg, A. (2001). *Wearing The Secret Out: A Dramatic Performance of Life History Research about Homoeroticism and Homophobia in Physical Education.* Ethnographic video and paper presented to North American Society for the Sociology of Sport. San Antonio, Texas. Oct–Nov.

Taylor, S. (1991). Leaving the Field: Research, Relationships and Responsibilities. In W. Shaffir & R. Stebbins (eds). *Experiencing Fieldwork: An Inside View of Qualitative Research.* London: Sage

Tedlock, B. (2000). Ethnography and Ethnographic Representation. In N. Denzin & Y. Lincoln (2000). *Handbook of Qualitative Research* (2nd edition). London: Sage.

Thomson, R. (1979). Participant Observation in the Sociological Analysis of Sport. *International Review of the Sociology of Sport*, 12, 99–109.

Tsang, T. (2000). Let Me Tell You a Story: A Narrative Exploration of Identity in High-Performance Sport. *Sociology of Sport Journal*, 17, 1, 44–59.

Turner, G. (1996). *British Cultural Studies: An Introduction* (2nd edition). Boston: Unwin Hyman.

Van Maanen, J. (1988). *Tales of the Field: On Writing Ethnography.* Chicago: University of Chicago Press.

Vidich, A. & Stanford, M. (1994). Qualitative Methods: Their History in Sociology and Anthropology. In N. Denzin & Y. Lincoln (eds). *Handbook of Qualitative Research.* London: Sage

Wheaton, B. (2000). "Just Do It": Consumption, Commitment and Identity in the Windsurfing Subculture. *Sociology of Sport Journal*, 17, 254–74.

Whyte, W. (1943). *Street Corner Society.* Chicago: University of Chicago Press.

Willis, P. & Trondman, M. (2002). Manifesto for Ethnography. *Cultural Studies ↔ Critical Methodologies*, 2, 3, 394–402.

Wolcott, H. (1990). *Writing up Qualitative Research.* London: Sage.

Wood, M. (2000). Disappearing. *Sociology of Sport Journal*, 17, 1, 100–02.

Young, K. (1988). Performance, Control and Public Image of Behavior in a Deviant Subculture: The Case of Rugby. *Deviant Bahavior*, 9, 275–93.

5

Interviewing for Case Study Research

John Amis

I like data. I like the process of exploration, of discovery, of uncovering some of what is happening in the world around us, and trying to understand why it is happening. Furthermore, I believe that the underlying basis of any such understanding depends on gaining an appreciation of how individuals construct their social world, and interact with it. In this sense, I side with Altheide and Johnson (1994) and their supposition that the social world cannot be taken as a literal world but should instead be viewed as one that is individually constructed and interpreted. In other words, we make sense of the world around us based on our individual values and experiences, and thus we all interpret events in our lives, even shared events, differently. It is this interpretation that constitutes the basis and source of social reality (Burrell & Morgan, 1979), and thus frames our understanding of the social world within which we exist.

Researching within an interpretivist paradigm might perhaps predispose analysis of the social world to taking a qualitative form. Indeed C. Wright Mills (1959) has highlighted the danger of reducing our study of the social world to statistical aggregations, arguing that such a course of action brings with it an inherent danger that the accompanying results may fail to fit "reality." The debate as to whether qualitative and quantitative approaches represent different epistemological stances or are merely different tools for data collection that can be used interchangeably has been ongoing throughout the social sciences (see, for example, Bryman, 1988). Within the interpretive paradigm, qualitative approaches have been dominant and have generally drawn on interviewing as a major method of data collection. That said, quantitative methods can, of course, be very useful and I have used them in my own work. Care is needed, however, to ensure that data are appropriately contextualized and interpreted, something that is often lacking in quantitative research. Bauer, Gaskell and Allum's (2000: 8) mantra of "no quantification without qualification, no statistical analysis without interpretation" exemplifies this point. Interviews that are used to collect quantitative data will likely be much more structured than those that are qualitatively oriented, an issue to which I return below. While both have utility, given the focus of this book, my concentration in this chapter will be on using interviews to collect qualitative data.

Understanding various interpretations of social life requires a position of relativism: the realization that realities are multiple and exist in people's minds (Sparkes, 1992). The most logical way to access these realities is to talk to people. Within most social science disciplines, interview-based research has predominantly featured "individualistic" interviewing (Madriz, 2000) in which a single interviewer explores pertinent issues with a single participant. However, there have recently been increased emphases on "focus group" interviews in which one or two interviewers – sometimes termed facilitators or moderators – engage with multiple participants. While typically associated with market and political-opinion research, focus group research has become particularly prominent with those participating in feminist (e.g., Madriz, 2000) and/or participatory action research (e.g., Frisby et al., 2005; Kemmis & McTaggart, 2000).

In either individualistic or focus group interviews, the interviewer attempts to gain insight into the inconsistencies, contradictions and paradoxes that are a quintessential part of our daily lives. Interviews offer a depth of information that permits the detailed exploration of particular issues in a way not possible with other forms of data collection. For this reason, interviews have been described as critical to understanding what has happened, how it has happened, and why (Pettigrew, 1990; Pettus, 2001). I share this perspective, and for this reason interviews have featured heavily in my own work. Primarily, I have used interview data to form the backbone of studies that have been used to explore phenomena such as sport sponsorship decision-making (Amis et al., 1997; Amis et al., 1999; Shaw & Amis, 2001), the causes of organizationally-based conflict (Amis et al., 1995), the strategic management of a transnational brand (Amis, 2003) and the institutionalized pressures on televised sport production (Silk & Amis, 2000). It should be noted that interviews should not be carried out to the exclusion of other forms of data collection. Participant observation and ethnographic methods can also be very important forms of data collection when building case studies; the use of documents, popular press, electronic media and other forms of data are also important. However, the chapter that follows has been written with the intention of exploring the use of interviews as a major source of qualitative data in the construction of case studies.

To this end, the chapter is organized in the following way. In the next two sections different types of interview are explored, along with the epistemologies most usually associated with them. The ethics of interviewing are then considered followed by a discussion of how an interview guide might be constructed. Some key issues of research design, notably the selection of different research sites and gaining the requisite access to appropriate individuals, are then considered. Some techniques for conducting interviews are then presented, along with sections dealing with data interpretation and analysis and writing up. The chapter is concluded with some summary remarks. Although for the sake of clarity each of these sections is discussed separately, it is important that they are viewed as being tightly interwoven. For instance, the type of interview that is carried out will play an important part in the way in which the data are interpreted, analyzed and written up. Thus, although the "what, when, where and why" of interviewing are covered in the earlier sections followed by issues concerned more with the actual "how" of carrying out the interview, analyzing the data and writing up, the interview process can be thought of as a constant interplay back and forth among each of the topics discussed.

Individualistic Interviews

The most common form of interview in social science research is the one-to-one version in which a single interviewer asks an individual a range of questions related to a particular set of issues. Although it is preferable for these to be conducted face-to-face in order to ease the building of rapport and collection of non-verbal data, there also might be times when one-to-one interviews have to be conducted by telephone or electronic mail (see, for example, Shaw & Amis, 2001) or even electronic instant messaging; of course the virtual absence of non-verbal cues and the more structured interaction can be drawbacks to these formats. For ease of discussion, the comments that I make will refer specifically to face-to-face interviewing unless otherwise stated. However, the basic principles discussed are largely transferable to other media and formats.

As Patton suggested, "interviewing begins with the assumption that the perspective of others is meaningful, knowable, and able to be made explicit" (1990: 278). This "perspective" can be uncovered in a variety of ways depending in large part on the style of the interview adopted. The approach taken will depend on two things: the nature of the problem being addressed and the epistemology of the researcher.

The researcher's ontological and epistemological positions will inevitably shape the ways in which the research is designed and the data are collected and presented. In other words, it is misleading to believe that the research question will in and of itself lead to the method of data collection. However, it is also the case that no method of data collection is inherently linked to any single ontological or epistemological position. Bauer et al. (2000) suggested that the research process could be split into four separate and independent dimensions: design principles, data elicitation, data analysis and knowledge interests. In other words, design and method are not inextricably linked. For example, as Bauer et al. (2000) went on to point out, critical research depends on contextualizing and challenging accepted or unconsidered norms and values. This can often be better achieved through the production of quantifiable and easily understood statistics as opposed to a supposedly more in-depth qualitative approach that critical theorists usually favor. However, positivist and post-positivist researchers will tend to hold more of an external-realist ontology (Burrell & Morgan, 1979) and will likely favor a closed interview style that will in turn result in a more deductive approach to knowledge generation. Conversely, those who favor more interpretive or critical approaches will tend more towards a more open-ended approach to interviewing. I now briefly consider four interviewing formats.

Closed Interviewing

Closed or structured interviewing involves the interviewer following a pre-determined protocol in exactly the same way for each interview. The tone, pace and direction of the interview is controlled by the interviewer, with all respondents receiving the same set of questions in the same order. In this way, the interviewer attempts to sanitize the process by reducing the impact of the interviewer on the interview process as much as possible. Questions are tightly tied to the preconceived ideas of the researcher and have only a single interpretation, resulting in the data effectively being pre-coded (Berg, 2001). The most suitable items for questions in this type of interview are those that are direct, precise and require minimum interpretation by the interviewer. Because of this, care must be taken that the choices forced on the individual do not result in a distortion of the data collected (Patton, 1990). The limited set of response categories for each question results in the findings lending themselves to quantitative analysis, although such interviews can also provide useful qualitative data. Market research interviews, typically conducted in shopping malls, at sporting events or over the telephone, are good examples of research that utilizes this type of design.

Standardized Open-ended Interviewing

This approach to interviewing is similar to the one outlined above in that the questions delivered to each informant are exactly the same, again arising from predetermined themes. However, the nature of the response to each question is left open to the individual being interviewed. As such, the data collected may be subjected to qualitative or quantitative analyses. This approach is useful if the time available to carry out each interview is limited. It allows the interviewer to focus on specific, pre-determined issues while providing the participant with the flexibility to provide the most appropriate response without being constrained by narrow response categories. It is normal to also include some open-ended questions, usually at the end of the interview, to elicit additional explanatory information (Patton, 1990). An example of this arises in some of the work that has been carried out on Canadian National Sport Organizations (NSOs) (e.g., Amis et al., 2002, 2004a; Kikulis et al., 1995a; 1995b; Slack & Hinings, 1994). A major data source for some of this work comprised a series of interviews in which members of the NSOs were asked questions relating to the complexity, formalization and centralization of their organizations. While these questions were delivered in a consistent manner, the interview participants had some degree of flexibility in the responses that they could provide. Some questions were quite precise, such as those designed to uncover the number of committees, gender distinction among coaches, and existence of particular volunteer and professional roles. Others were less prescriptive and asked participants to explain, for example, how formalized procedures were for the selection and evaluation of coaches, and how these areas had changed over recent years. These formal questions were supplemented with more open-ended questions designed to allow interview participants to provide opinions regarding the various changes that were unfurling in their organizations and the sport system in general. From these data, various conclusions were drawn regarding the nature of change in these NSOs.

General Interview Guide

The general interview guide comprises a number of questions that center on predetermined themes. Unlike the two types of interview described above, the interviewer is ascribed much greater flexibility with respect to how the interview is carried out. The order of questions can vary, additional exploratory questions can be inserted, and the pace of the interview can be adjusted depending on the responses provided by the participant.[1] The utility of this type of interview is that there is a structure that ensures that certain themes will be covered and helps to keep the individual focused on particular issues, but there is also the flexibility to develop questions as new themes emerge in the course of the interview. The open-ended questions also allow the participant to provide the most appropriate responses to particular questions, reflecting the diverse ways in which different individuals view the social world. Importantly, this type of interview allows the interviewer to adapt the language of the questions to that most suitable for the participant, something to which I return later.

This approach has been probably the most popular method of interviewing within those qualitative studies that have appeared in the sports studies literature. For instance, the interviews that were carried out by Sally Shaw and myself for a study that investigated the sponsorship of women's sport were framed by a number of questions that centered on particular themes: the reason for entering into a particular agreement, the objectives of the decision-maker, and how the sponsorship fitted into the organization's overall marketing strategy. However, questions were adapted depending on the responses gained in previous interviews and whether the interview was with a sponsor or a sport organization member; furthermore, additional questions were inserted as the interview progressed to follow-up on particular issues, such as how decisions were made or why some sports were targeted over others (Shaw & Amis, 2001).

Informal Conversational Interview

The informal conversational, or unstructured, interview represents an attempt to understand complex behavior without the imposition of any prior categorization or framework that may limit responses (Fontana & Frey, 1994). The intent is to access the perspective of the person being interviewed rather than tainting responses with any preconceived ideas. Clearly, this approach most accentuates the subjective epistemology that underpins much interview-based research. It is the most flexible of the four techniques described here and allows the interviewer most freedom to set the direction of the interview depending on the responses of the participant. The informal conversational interview usually requires the greatest amount of time to complete, as the interview is likely to range in a variety of directions. Often termed ethnographic interviewing (Spradley, 1979), this approach is frequently combined with other data collection methods such as participant observation. This method of interviewing is explored more fully by Silk in the previous chapter. Indeed, the data collection that Silk carried out at the 1998 Commonwealth Games in Kuala Lumpur made considerable use of this type of interviewing (see Silk, 2002; Silk & Amis, 2000).

Focus Group Interviews

> I'd rather talk this way, with a group of women . . . When I am alone with an interviewer, I feel intimidated, scared. And if they call me over the telephone, I never answer their questions. How can I know what they really want or who they are?
>
> María Fernández, a 25-year-old Dominican woman, cited in Madriz "Focus Groups in Feminist Research"

There is some discussion in the literature as to when a one-to-one interview is likely to be more effective than a focus group. Clearly, the nature of the topic, research objectives, types of respondent and skills and personal preferences of the interviewer will all be important in making the decision (Gaskell, 2000). The purpose of focus groups is to "learn through discussion about conscious, semiconscious and unconscious psychological and sociocultural characteristics and processes" (Berg, 2001: 111). Focus groups can be very rewarding in that they allow access to a larger number of individuals in a shorter period of time than do one-to-one interviews. For this reason, focus groups have tended to be more popular in commercial settings, notably market and political research, while academics have predominantly preferred the greater depth that it is perceived can be obtained from one-to-one interviews (see Fontana & Frey, 2000; Gaskell, 2000). However, the dominance of individualistic interviewing may also be a function of the traditional dominance of positivist and post-positivist research paradigms across the social sciences and the perceived greater "reliability" and "validity" of data emanating from such interviews (Madriz, 2000).

As alternative forms of inquiry have gained prominence, such as participatory action research, so focus groups have gained in prominence as a method of data collection in various academic disciplines. As the quote at the opening of this section indicates, many participants feel more comfortable in a group setting with their peers. This can be particularly true when researching with women of color who typically experience a "triple subjugation" based on class, race and gender oppression, a position exacerbated with women who are "undocumented" (Madriz, 2000). Thus, focus groups can act to overcome the intimidation of an individualistic interview, and can instead serve to "expose and validate women's everyday experiences of subjugation and their individual and collective survival and resistance strategies" (Madriz, 2000: 836). In order to further raise confidence levels among participants, it is usually advisable to ensure homogeneity in areas such as class, race and gender across the focus group. It is similarly advisable to utilize an interviewer who shares common characteristics with the focus group (e.g., in terms of race, class, gender) (Madriz, 2000). Clearly, the more sensitive the nature of the research, the more important this issue can become.

Wendy Frisby and her colleagues have found a similar utility for the use of focus groups, of various sizes and composition, in their participatory action research investigating restrictive policies and practices hindering access to community-based recreation programs for women on low income in British Columbia. There have been a number of research pieces that have stemmed from the ongoing work of Frisby and her colleagues to which interested readers are referred (e.g., Frisby et al., 1997; Frisby & Fenton, 1998; Frisby & Hoeber, 2002; Frisby & Millar, 2002). A useful consideration of the epistemological and methodological issues that were encountered by the group, and strategies that were used to address various issues – several of which are typical when using focus groups in participatory action research – is provided in Frisby et al. (2005).

Focus groups can also play a useful role in overcoming the hierarchical power relationship that has traditionally been a feature of one-to-one interviewing. In overtly highlighting the negotiated account that emerges from the interview, the interviewer can develop a closer relationship with interview participants. Thus, while there is little doubt that the interviewer still shapes the research process, the dynamic, explorative type of discussion that typically weaves through stories, memories, explanations and disagreements, can ensure that the dominant voices that emerge are those of the participants (Harrison et al., 2001).

Focus groups allow members to challenge each other, develop positions of consensus, and build on each other's ideas. Thus, they can be stimulating and dynamic environments in which to collect data. As Rubin and Rubin (1995) suggested, the goal is to let people spark off each other such that new perspectives and understandings may emerge. It is not the purpose of focus groups to develop a consensus of opinion but to allow people to consider and present their own views in the context of others (Patton, 1990). The outcome is a "multivocal" account that is more dynamic than those typically associated with individualistic interviewing (Madriz, 2000).

Facilitating focus groups does require a skillful interviewer. The interviewer must prevent the interview from becoming dominated by one or two strong personalities and must encourage recalcitrant participants to engage with the discussion. It is important that the interviewer emphasize that it is acceptable, even desirable, for participants to disagree with each other. In this way, the potential for "groupthink" to overcome the usefulness of a potentially enlightening data collection method can be lessened (Fontana & Frey, 2000; Madriz, 2000).

To help keep things manageable, Kreuger (1994) suggested that for complex issues, the number of participants should be kept to about seven. While the degree of structure that the interviewer wishes to impose upon the discussion will vary according to the epistemological basis of and objectives for the research, it is important that the interviewer retains a focus on the overall intent of the interview. Consequently, at the start of the interview, in addition to establishing a rapport, it is sometimes a good idea to establish some informal ground rules that indicate how the focus group will be conducted. Berg (2001) noted that issues of confidentiality are much more difficult to control with focus groups as opposed to individualistic interviews and thus suggested gaining a very explicit signed confirmation from all participants that the information discussed will remain confidential. This is particularly important when dealing with sensitive or proprietary information.

Power, Integrity and the Ethics of Interview Research

Irrespective of the format chosen, the inherent human interaction involved with interviewing necessitates that the rights of those participating in the research are protected. The moral and ethical responsibilities of the interviewer are straightforward to relay, but often more problematic to follow. It is to these that I now turn. It may seem odd to be discussing ethics so early in the chapter. However, it is vital that ethical considerations are taken into account at the very outset of the research project. When designing any research involving data collection from people, researchers are morally, and often legally, required to ensure that those involved with the research will come to no harm. This is not always as simple as it may seem for, as Punch (1994: 85) has suggested, "fieldwork is a *demanding* craft that involves both coping with multiple negotiations and continually dealing with ethical dilemmas" (emphasis in the original).

The focus on the protection of human participants involved in research projects largely stems from the atrocities committed during World War II by researchers in German concentration camps. This led to the Nuremburg Code, adopted by the United Nations General Assembly in 1946, which stated that voluntary consent must be given by those involved in research projects (Seidman, 1998). Despite this, there have been multiple cases of individuals being harmed or even killed in the name of research.

For example, Milgram's (1963) (in)famous electric shock study in which individuals were deceived into believing that they were causing severe pain to others and Lofland and Lejeune's (1960) study in which students posed as alcoholics to gain entry into Alcoholics Anonymous meetings both highlighted the psychological harm to which unwitting individuals can be exposed through disguise and deception. Although interviewing is often considered to be non-problematic from an ethical standpoint, there are multiple examples of research in which participants have been placed in vulnerable positions. Humphrey's (1970, 1972) study of homosexual behavior in which he observed actions in a public toilet, took car license plate numbers, followed the individuals home and then interviewed them under the guise of another study illustrated the way in which research participants have been deliberately deceived. More recently, Hobbs (1989) justified a willingness to engage in certain questionable research activities by holding that he was adhering to the ethics of the East End of London criminal subculture that he was studying. Adler (1985) faced similar ethical dilemmas in her ethnographic study of drug dealers in California in which she made extensive use of interview data. Since much of this work was carried out, and particularly following Milgram's (1963) laboratory work and other medical research carried out on "captive" populations, there has been continued debate as to how research participants can be better protected. One concrete outcome of this has been the establishment of an Institutional Review Board for the Protection of Human Subjects (IRB), or similar body, in most organizations that carry out research on people. While it is incumbent upon researchers to follow the guidelines administered by the IRB at their institution, Kent (2000a) provided a useful summation of how to proceed in his "rules" for ethical research.

The first of Kent's (2000a) rules is *veracity* whereby researchers are obliged to tell the truth, avoid misleading or deceiving potential participants, and report results truthfully. Linked to this is the notion of autonomy, whereby individuals have the right to self-determination and should thus be able to make an informed choice as to whether to be interviewed or not. There is some debate in the literature as to the extent to which this rule is actually followed. For example, Punch acknowledged that while it is not acceptable to lie about intentions of the research or the actions that will be carried out, "some dissimilation is intrinsic to social life and, therefore, also to fieldwork" (1994: 91). Punch held that in order to get "accurate" data it might be necessary to not be totally open about the nature of the proposed research. By contrast, others have argued that anything other than total honesty is unacceptable. Much feminist research, for example, has held that any form of deception is unacceptable. Some feminist researchers have also opposed the viewing of (female) participants as objects and have perceived participants as being subjugated to abuse through the one-way power relationships that are the feature of much interviewing (Fontana & Frey, 1994). The acknowledgement of an inherent power relationship in interviewing is important. Research can empower if participants are given knowledge that then enables them to control and perhaps change some aspect of their own lives. However, research is also capable of disempowerment if the information that is provided is misused (Crow, 2000). Indeed, this is viewed by some as not just an ethical but also an epistemological and methodological issue. It has been pointed out that the intimacy required for the acquisition of meaningful data will not become manifest without an open and honest research relationship (Oakley, 1981). This is particularly seen as important by participatory action researchers in which any attempt to "dupe" participants would be to undermine the processes that the interviewer wants to examine (Punch, 1994).

Of course, consideration of the participants' roles in the research process raises the important issues of reciprocity and equity. In the type of action research projects outlined earlier, there may be clear benefits accruing to the participants, but in most interview-based research, such direct benefits may not be so apparent. In some cases, resentment can arise if participants perceive that the researcher is gaining money and/or prestige from writing about "their" lives. In fact, the very nature of the interviewing process makes the process almost inevitably inherently inequitable. However, fairness is something that interviewers can strive for: taking a real interest in the lives and actions of the research participants, being fair and honest, and acting with integrity are all ways in which we can try to ensure that any benefits that accrue are not entirely one way (Seidman, 1998).

The second rule that Kent (2000a) suggested that ethical researchers should follow concerns the *privacy* of the individual. It is important for the researcher to appreciate that just because the individual consents to take part in a particular study, s/he does not automatically grant unlimited access to all parts of her/his life. The individual is perfectly entitled not to discuss any issue that s/he feels unwilling to do so, and should not be pressured to do so by the interviewer.

The notion of *fidelity*, Kent's (2000a) third rule, concerns the integrity of the researcher and involves ensuring that any explicit or implicit promises made by the interviewer to individuals, society, funding bodies, or any other actor in the research are kept. These might include promising to provide reports on the research to various interested parties, allowing individuals to review interview transcripts, ensuring that reported facts are correct and not compromising the professional standards of the discipline. This rule should be regarded as virtually inviolate.

Finally, the issue of *confidentiality* is one of the most important rules that interviewers need to respect. If an individual agrees to take part in a study, s/he should not be able to be identified in any outcome of the study in any way unless s/he gives express permission to be so. This protection extends to the individual's organization, family, friends and colleagues. It is sometimes difficult to maintain confidentiality if a participant is a well-known person or member of a prominent organization. There are also times when the identification of the individual or the organization might add depth or clarity to the findings. In either of these cases, it is worth asking for permission from the participants to release the identity of them or their organization. For example, in a study that explored the sponsorship of the Canadian Freestyle Skiing team by Owens-Corning, we felt that by identifying the organizations involved, readers would gain additional insight into the nature of the sponsorship being discussed by being allowed to appreciate more fully the symbiotic relationship that was seen as integral to the success of the sponsorship (Amis et al., 1997). However, if permission is not forthcoming it is incumbent upon the research team to protect the identity of those interviewed at all costs. This may involve using pseudonyms (e.g., Amis et al., 1995; 1997) or even simply not using some interviews. If pseudonyms are used in the text, they should be carefully selected so that they protect the identity and dignity of the participant, but do not distort the data (Seidman, 1998). Thus, characteristics such as gender, role and geographical location should not be changed unless doing so is paramount for the protection of the participant.

Confidentiality also extends to protecting participants during the research process. One frequently used method of uncovering suitable participants is to ask those who have been previously interviewed for suggestions of who else to interview, a process known as "snowball sampling." It is necessary to ensure that the participant making the recommendation does not mind having his/her name "dropped" to encourage the participation of others. Further, the name of the participant should not be used beyond the immediate recommendations made. A second issue that requires consideration is the use of identities in transcripts. If anybody beyond the immediate researcher may have access to the transcripts, such as in a common workspace, care must be taken to ensure anonymity of participants even at this stage of the research process.

Before carrying out interviews of any type the interviewer should normally get the participant to sign an informed consent form. This confirms that the individual understands exactly what they are being asked to do, and provides authorization for information to be collected in a manner that is neither coercive nor deceitful, thus protecting her/his autonomy. Kent (2000b) outlined five elements that need to be met to protect this right.

1. Potential participants must be provided with sufficient information so that they can discern the potential benefits and risks of participating in the study.
2. The researcher must ensure that the individual understands the information given. The language and style that is used must be appropriate for the individual, and the information provided must be clear and comprehensive.
3. Agreement to participate must be granted voluntarily, with no explicit or implicit pressure applied. In a number of universities, researchers collect data from students in return for course credits. It is certainly questionable as to whether such participants are free from at least an implicit pressure to participate and thus whether their participation is truly voluntary.
4. The competence of potential participants to provide consent must be established. This can be problematic if a researcher wishes to interview members of vulnerable groups, such as children or the mentally ill. It is normal in these circumstances to secure proxy permission from somebody in a legally responsible position, such as a parent, but this of course assumes that the parent can state what the participant would do if s/he was competent.
5. Consent must be physically obtained from participants. Kent (2000b) suggested that verbal consent is sometimes sufficient for non-invasive data collection such as interviewing; I suggest that the interviewer gain written consent whenever possible.

A good way of deciding the appropriate way to proceed is to consult with the interviewer's IRB or equivalent. In fact, it has become compulsory in virtually all research institutions, particularly those that receive any form of public funding, to consult with the IRB prior to conducting any interview research. Although an exemption will often be granted from having to go through a lengthy formal review process, an application to the IRB must usually still be made.[2]

Several writers have suggested that at times it is necessary to hide the true nature of the research in order to gain meaningful data (e.g., Punch, 1994). This can range from simply omitting some details of the research in which one is engaging to hiding the fact that there is any research going on at all. Adler's (1985) drug dealing study and MacIntyre's (1999) work on organized soccer violence in England both highlight the way in which data can be collected from very unstructured interviews in the form of informal conversations supplemented by direct observation of participants activities. While not intended as an academic study, MacIntrye's work is recommended as an excellent illustration of the major issues involved in covert research, including gaining access to the research site, fitting in, data collection, exiting the scene and dealing with issues of personal safety. Clearly there can be difficult ethical issues to consider when dealing with covert interviewing. Some researchers have justified their covert approach on the basis that it investigates illegal or unsocial activities. However, it is important that the ethics involved in interviewing any individual, no matter what activities s/he has been engaged in, be carefully considered prior to initiating any research project. In deciding how to proceed, the interviewer should "draw upon his or her values and experiences and the cultural context when considering what action to take" (Kent, 2000a: 62). If any such deception is to be carried out, the justification for it must be clearly laid out both in the proposal for and final reporting of the research. In particular, it must be pointed out to the appropriate IRB. Participants should also be debriefed at the end of the research if this is practical.

While interviewing does not carry the same threat of harm as some other data collection methods, interviewers can place their respondents in a vulnerable position and do have an obligation to follow the ethical procedures laid down by their institutions. Punch provides a good note on which to finish this section: "I echo Hughes's and Becker's summons to "simply go out and do it." But I would add that before you go you should stop and reflect on the political and ethical dimensions of what you are about to experience. Just do it by all means, but think a bit first" (1994: 95).

"Follow-ups and Probes": Developing an Interview Guide

Although the precise nature of the interview guide will depend on the interview type, there are certain principles that are worth adhering to in all cases. These are briefly reviewed here. First, it is important that the interviewer have a sound, up-to-date knowledge of the relevant literature that underpins the study. This helps to ensure that the research problem being addressed is relevant and timely, and also that appropriate conceptual themes are used to inform the questions to be used in the interview. It is a good idea at this stage to start with a broad outline of the relevant theoretical categories that the researcher wishes to address. As specific knowledge of the context in which the interviews will take place is gathered, such as details about individuals, organizations, events and/or the socio-economic and political contexts, more specific questions can be developed as necessary. Depending on the type of interview planned, additional questions can be inserted following pilot testing of the guide or they can be inserted as appropriate during the course of the interview. The less structured the interview, the more general the interview instrument, and the less rigidly it should be followed. In more unstructured interviews the interviewer tends to rely more on her/his theoretical and contextual knowledge to explore issues raised by the individual (Gaskell, 2000). Rubin and Rubin (1995) also noted that the nature of the interview will likely influence the level of detail provided in the interview guide. In "cultural interviews" aimed at understanding how participants view and interpret the social world, there will likely be a small number of "main" questions intended to cover major events or examples with "the bulk of the work ... done with follow-ups and probes" (Rubin & Rubin, 1995: 178). Thus, the intent is to provide general themes rather than precise questions. However, in "topical interviews" based on particular events, more specific questions are provided based on previous research: "the researcher guides the discussion to keep on target and obtain answers to [key] questions. The purpose is to avoid omitting a crucial step in a process or a critical event in a decision, lest the resulting narrative be misleading" (Rubin & Rubin, 1995: 197).

There are a number of points to consider with respect to the wording of the questions to be used. These are crucial because, as Patton (1990) has pointed out, perhaps the most important element governing a response is the way in which a question is asked. The first point to contemplate is the language that will be used. The interviewer needs to learn the language used by the individuals to be interviewed. This includes technical language, colloquialisms and slang terms that form common parlance in the environment under investigation. The interviewer may also be required to understand different definitions of commonly used words. For example, Henderson (1991) reported that a group of farm women that she was studying felt that they had no leisure time, but that when questions were reworded to use "free time" or "fun activity," responses were forthcoming: while they certainly engaged in meaningful and enjoyable activities, they did not perceive these to be "leisure," nor did they feel that they had designated "leisure time." Issues of language can be particularly important when interviewing individuals of different ages and those from different educational or cultural backgrounds: if meaningful responses are to be obtained, it is important that questions are asked at the "same level" of the participants (Berg, 2001). Henderson (1991) suggested that these problems can be somewhat alleviated by spending time with the individuals to be interviewed. Furthermore, Rubin and Rubin (1995) recommend engaging in extensive background research and even preliminary interviewing if there is a lack of published information in order to lessen the likelihood of being presented with a normative or idealized account of particular events, and to allow for more effective follow-up questioning around key issues. Learning about participants beforehand also adds to the interviewer's credibility.

The style of the question is also important. Interview questions should be neutral and singular, thus allowing the individual to answer in her/his own terms without having any suggestion as to how to respond provided by the interviewer.

Further, questions should only focus on a single issue. Multiple questions can result in confusion and may also cause the interviewer to lose control of the interview if the participant responds with a long monologue. When possible, it is also advisable to avoid affective wording of questions that is likely to promote an emotional response (Berg, 2001; Rubin & Rubin, 1995). The more emotional an individual gets about a particular issue, the more likely it is that the answer will be an extreme representation of how s/he feels about a particular subject and may obscure reference to other issues. Finally, care may need to be taken when asking "why" questions (Patton, 1990). Asking why something occurred presupposes that a cause and effect relationship is clearly apparent and known to the participant. In reality, there may be a number of factors that impinge upon a particular action, so it may be advisable to word questions more precisely to explore one or more of these perceived contingent factors more fully.

The final point that I briefly consider here is the sequence in which questions should be asked. It is a good idea to start the interview with relatively straightforward, non-controversial questions. This helps to get both the interviewer and the participant accustomed to their roles, and helps to build rapport. I usually start with contextual questions that locate the individual in the organization, event or phenomenon that I am studying. Patton (1990) cautioned against asking too many demographic questions because of the danger of the participant becoming bored. He suggested that any demographic data be gathered towards the end of the interview. It is also preferable to ask questions referring to current events first. This establishes a reference point against which past and/or future events can be compared. Be aware, however, that responses to questions about past and future events are not as likely to be as reliable as those referring to current ones (Dutton et al., 2001).

Sampling and Access

As I have previously stressed, interviewing involves a constant interplay back and forth among the different steps involved in design, implementation and analysis. This is particularly apparent with issues of sampling and access: there is little point in designing a worthwhile study only to be unable to gain access to the necessary informants, nor is their any point in carrying out meaningless interviews just because one is able to gain access to a particular research site. Instead, the two steps go hand in hand, although I consider the two separately for ease of discussion.

Sampling

The issue of sampling proceeds at two levels. First there is a decision to make as to what case to focus on – be it an organization, group, or particular issue. It is important here to define what is to be included and excluded in the case (Stake, 2000). Second, there is a need to identify participants able to provide appropriate levels of insight to the phenomena being studied. I briefly discuss each of these in turn.

In terms of selecting appropriate cases, there is a need to decide whether to look for cases that fit particular theoretical questions that the researcher wants to explore, or whether to focus on a particular case and to use whatever theoretical approaches would be most appropriate. This is somewhat determined by the ontological position of the researcher. A realist would take the view that cases are empirically discoverable and just need to be found, a nominalist view would be that cases are theoretically and socially constructed by researchers for the purposes of carrying out a particular investigation (Burton, 2000). Irrespective of whether the view is taken that cases emerge or are constructed, there are a number of issues that need to be addressed.

First, the researcher should decide whether to compare different cases or concentrate on a single case. Both of course have merit. A single case allows a greater depth of analysis into a particular phenomenon, as in Pettigrew's (1985, 1987) examination of change at ICI or Sack and Nadim's (2002) investigation of Starter Corporation. By contrast, a comparison of cases allows the emergence of particular characteristics that may provide insight into reasons for the differences among the cases, as in Pettigrew and Whipp's (1993) work on British industry and some of the work that I have been involved with on organizational conflict (Amis et al., 1995), corporate sponsorship strategies (Amis et al., 1997; 1999; Shaw & Amis, 2001) and organizational change (Amis et al., 2004b). Within single or multiple cases, it can also be useful to adopt an embedded approach in which data are collected and analyzed at various levels, such as societal, government, organization, subunit and/or individual (Yin, 1994). This can provide conceptual insights that might otherwise remain hidden. What is important in either single or multi-case designs is how particular research sites are selected.

It is highly unlikely that cases will be selected by means of the probability sampling that researchers engaged in quantitative studies tend to favor; normally cases will be selected on the basis of particular characteristics that they possess. It is also possible to focus on certain critical incidents that may allow particular dynamics to unfurl as O'Brien and Slack (1999) did with their investigation into the professionalization of the sport of rugby union. In short then, sites in which interviews are going to be conducted will likely be selected on the basis of particular theoretical and/or empirical criteria. It is important that the rationale for the selection of such cases is clearly laid out in the reporting of the research.

It is a similar scenario when deciding whom to interview. Rather than simply selecting who to interview at random, individuals should be chosen on the basis of particular insights that they can provide on the events being studied, be they television personnel as in the work by Silk (2002) or those involved in the strategic management of the Guinness brand (Amis, 2003). This is termed purposive sampling (Berg, 2001). It is important that categories are devised and parameters established to ensure that those being interviewed can indeed provide a meaningful contribution (Stroh, 2000a), and so that different perspectives on a particular incident can be gained. Interviews should be carried out with different individuals until new issues stop emerging (Henderson, 1991). It may be beneficial to carry out repeat interviews with certain individuals who are particularly pertinent to the phenomena being studied. In fact Seidman's (1998) phenomenological interviewing protocol calls for a series of three interviews with the same informant spaced about 3–7 days apart. While it may not be always possible to secure the time required to engage in such a process, the utility of being able to explore different aspects of the participant's views and understanding following an opportunity for mutual reflection is clearly appealing.

Depending on whether the research design is cross-sectional or longitudinal, interviews may be spaced over a comparatively short period of time or spread over a longer period. While cross-sectional designs can be useful, longitudinal designs are almost imperative for studies that are intended to explore dynamic phenomena such as organizational change processes (Pettigrew, 1998). Again, the reason for adopting a particular design and selecting certain individuals must be made clear in the output from the research.

Access

While the selection of research cases and participants is important, gaining access to useful informants is a major determinant of success. Problems with gaining access to conduct research are a recurring theme in social science research (Bryman, 1988). Overcoming such problems requires patience, persistence, research and often a little luck. Carrying out interviews in a particular setting requires the researcher to identify a gatekeeper and potential sponsor, roles often played by the same individual. A gatekeeper is a person who controls access to a research environment. It is through her/him that participants can be identified and accessed. A sponsor is somebody within a research site who is willing to support the research and use her/his influence to persuade individuals to agree to being interviewed. It is important that these individuals are identified and that relationships with them are actively cultivated. In addition, the role of serendipity should not be downplayed: it is important that researchers take advantage of lucky encounters with influential individuals who may be able to help the research process.

An example of gaining access to a particular research site, and particularly the role of serendipity, persistence and then the cultivating of a good relationship with a gatekeeper and sponsor, is provided by a recent research project. I wanted to investigate the strategic management of a transnational brand, and particularly the various ways in which sport is used in different locations. From previous work, I had got to know the Commercial Director of the English Rugby Union, who suggested that I contact the account manager of one of the team's sponsors, Guinness. I contacted this individual and explained my ideas; he in turn suggested that I contact a senior Guinness Director. When he heard the names of the individuals who had recommended that I contact him, the Director agreed to meet with me. It took several telephone and e-mail messages before we were able to fix a date for the interview, but once we met, he was very forthcoming. I quickly established a rapport based on several common interests, including sport and some of my other research projects. I subsequently carried out a follow-up interview with him, and he also recommended other people for me to interview in an example of the snowball sampling process referred to earlier. One of these individuals informed me that he would not normally have agreed to an interview, but given the fact that the Director was supportive of my research, he agreed to do it. This highlights the important role that the Director played as both a gatekeeper and a sponsor. The rapport that we developed was clearly important. I made sure that I followed through on my promise to send him copies of interview transcripts, field notes and research findings of the research prior to submission for publication. In return, he allowed me to identify Guinness in my research, something that clearly added value to my research by permitting me to use much more detail and imagery than I would have been able to do if I had been required to protect the identity of the firm (e.g., Amis, 2003). He also agreed to provide me with access to a number of documents that I might otherwise not have gained. As Henderson (1991) has pointed out, establishing reciprocity, generosity and responsibility are crucial to the ongoing development of a research relationship.

Gaining access is an issue that has to be continually dealt with as new lines of inquiry develop and new potential participants emerge. Of course, gatekeepers will not always be directors as in the case cited above. It is often good practice to establish a rapport with secretarial staff and personal assistants: these are people who often have the power to schedule meetings, forward telephone calls and relay messages. As such, they can play a determining role in the success or failure of interview-based research.

Interviewing Protocols: Rapport, Empathy and Neutrality

In the section above, I noted the importance of building a rapport with gatekeepers and sponsors. It is of course also important that a rapport is similarly developed with the individuals to be interviewed. Inevitably, participants will draw an immediate impression of the interviewer, whether the first contact be by telephone, by e-mail or face-to-face. As such, it is important that the interviewer project an air of professionalism at all times, and act in a manner appropriate to the task in hand. It is the task of the interviewer to provide a setting in which the individual will respond accurately and honestly (Patton, 1990). Denscombe (1998) has suggested that the level of education, class, sex, age and ethnicity can all effect the amount of information a participant is prepared to divulge, and the level of honesty s/he will use. Of course, there are some things that the interviewer can do nothing about, but Denscombe recommends that care be taken to present oneself in a neutral way that will not negatively impact the individual. It is also worth considering who in the interview team should carry out the interviews particularly if questions are going to touch on sensitive issues. Interviewers should question how age, education, gender, race, or class might affect the willingness of particular individuals to divulge information and, if possible, adjust accordingly (see Madriz, 2000). As Henderson (1991) pointed out, the interviewer is the research instrument and thus must take responsibility for a bad interview. As such, anything that s/he can do to improve the likelihood of gaining an open and honest interview should be carefully considered. In this respect, social skills can be more important in data gathering than skills of a more technical nature (Sparkes, 1995).

While it is important to establish a rapport, the degree of intimacy that is established between the interviewer and the participant should be carefully considered. Denscombe (1998) for example cautioned against the interviewer getting too close to the participant, suggesting that the interviewer should remain neutral throughout. Henderson (1991) similarly advised against becoming too intimate with the participant, suggesting that interviewers should be "value neutral." However, as I noted above, other researchers have suggested that developing a closer relationship between interviewer and participant can provide greater insight than would otherwise be the case. This, it has been suggested, also helps to overcome the traditional paternalism associated with interviewing that does not allow emotions or other sensitivities to intrude and can in turn enhance the experience for both interviewer and participant (Fontana & Frey, 1994). I recommend that the interviewer decide on a position that fits with her/his epistemology and personality and proceed on that basis, though if an approach can be adopted that is more likely to positively resonate with the participant, that can clearly be beneficial.

It is important to remember that the interview is an interaction that must be actively managed by the interviewer. Thus, the participant must be kept on track, particularly if s/he has a tendency to provide long-winded responses. It is not rude to gently interrupt the participant to get her/him back to the relevant topic provided that it is done with sensitivity and respect. In my experience, most individuals who are long-winded recognize their proclivity for verbosity, are quite used to being interrupted, and do not draw any offence.

When and Where to Interview

It is necessary for an interviewer to be flexible in order to fit in as much as possible with the schedule of the participant. Henderson (1991) suggested allowing two hours for an in-depth qualitative interview; my experience would certainly support that, although the schedule of the participant may preclude an interview of that length. Consequently, a time for the interview must be established such that the individual will be willing and able to devote her/his attention to the interviewer's questions. It is also worth considering the types of questions being asked, and consequently whether it would be better for the interview to be conducted in work time or free time, in the participant's office, the interviewer's office or a neutral venue. In order to minimize the inconvenience for the participant, it is usually a good idea to offer to go to a location of their choosing, though it must be one in which the interview can be carried out in private, ideally in a location free from distractions. It is also worth considering whether the particular time of the year will affect the interviews. I foolishly tried to arrange interviews with a leading sponsor of the English Football Association Premier League and league personnel just prior to the start of a new season. Although both groups were positive about my research, the time frame that I proposed was impossible for them and the research never got started. Quite understandably, they were more concerned about the new season than they were about my research! Thus, it is worth investigating any external pressures that may be on the potential participants when trying to schedule particular interviews.

Avoiding Dangerous Situations

Whenever one is carrying out interviews in field situations, personal safety should be a major concern. Thankfully, most of the time interviews are completed in a pleasant environment with no problems. However, there are cases when interviewers have not been so fortunate. Inevitably, female interviewers can be particularly vulnerable (Fontana & Frey, 1994). Howell (1990) discussed a number of crimes that may be encountered in the field, including theft, rape and assault. Some individuals have ended up in dangerous situations because of the nature of the research that they are carrying out. For example, Adler's (1985) study on drug dealers in California and MacIntyre's (1999) work on soccer violence placed these researchers in highly dangerous situations. However, even for more mundane topics, it is sound advice for any interviewer to ensure that they know the place where the interview is going to be carried out, carry a mobile telephone, have a knowledge of where help can be obtained quickly, and have told other people where they are going and why. Situations in which interviews are conducted late at night or in deserted buildings should be avoided if at all possible.

Carrying Out the Interview

There are a number of different ways to carry out an interview. The first factor to consider is the nature of the interview itself. Once access has been gained, a face-to-face interview is usually quite straightforward to arrange and relatively painless for the interviewer to control. A telephone interview is also normally quite simple to carry out, although clearly the benefit of face-to-face interaction is lost. If a telephone interview is carried out, it will likely be more effective if it is with an individual with whom the interviewer has previously met and developed a rapport. This will increase the likelihood of more accurate and honest responses to the questions being asked. It is certainly not advisable to do an interview "cold," but to at least establish contact by telephone, e-mail or letter first (Berg, 2001). Because of the increased emotional distance from the participant, electronic interviews are usually a method of last resort. They can be effective, but are most appropriate for follow-up questions designed to elucidate additional insights or interpretations.

When the necessary informed consent has been gained, the interview can be started. It is a good idea to have practiced the interview first, and to know the question schedule as well as possible. However, no matter how well I know the topics to be covered, I always keep a hard copy of the questions to hand, both to record when particular questions have been covered, and to note any additional field notes beyond the verbal answers provided. It also allows the insertion of additional questions for inclusion later in the interview.

Once started, there are a number of points that will help the flow of the interview. First, the interviewer should try to avoid interrupting the participant unless, as noted above, the interview is going badly off-track. The less an interviewer talks outside of asking questions, the more likely it is that the individual's responses will be untainted by the opinions of the interviewer. As Fontana and Frey (1994) suggested, the role of the interviewer is to try to be encouraging, but non-evaluative of any responses provided. The rapport that is established with the participant should not undermine the neutrality of the interview. The individual needs to feel that s/he can respond in any way to a question without that response engendering favor or disfavor, shock, embarrassment, or disdain with the interviewer; the interviewer should simply try to convey empathy and understanding. Denscombe (1998) similarly advised that an interviewer be sensitive to the individual and able to empathize, but also be willing to explore any inconsistencies and continually try to assess if the participant is being accurate, exaggerating, or trying to please the interviewer. Denscombe recommended maintaining eye contact throughout and looking for non-verbal cues to assess the veracity of what is being said. At the end of the interview the individual should be invited to add any further relevant points before the tape recorder is turned off and the interview scene exited.

Recording and Transcribing

Irrespective of the type of interview, the ways in which data are to be recorded should be established prior to the start of the interview. It is standard procedure to record the interview on audio tape, thus leaving the interviewer free to manage the interview and take field notes without having to worry about trying to make copious notes. If possible, a focus group should be video recorded to ease identification of participants. In both cases, permission must be obtained from the participant(s). It is important that the respondent be shown how to stop the recording, or at least have the opportunity to get the interviewer to stop recording, at any time. There may be some things that the participant is willing to discuss, but only "off the record." This is perfectly normal and should be respected. Of course, the direct use of such data is not permitted, although they might be useful in a general sense to provide more insight into a particular incident. It is also recommended that the interviewer check the sound quality at the start of the interview. A short sound test with the individual to ensure that the equipment is working properly and that the environment is conducive to good quality sound recording can save a great deal of time and frustration when it comes to transcribing the interview. It is also good practice to have spare batteries and cassettes readily available.

Even if the interview is recorded, field notes remain an important source of data and should be as detailed as possible. It is helpful to record as much about the context of the interview as possible. This may include the physical setting and any non-verbal cues transmitted by the participant. It is important that as soon as the interview is concluded, the field notes are written up as fully as possible. The longer the time between the interview and the writing up of field notes, the greater the likelihood that important details will be lost. When the field notes have been completed, it is possible to then modify the interview instrument. Ideally this should be done after the interview has been transcribed, but it is most important that the structure of the instrument be considered after each interview and before the next one. In this way, the interviewer can ensure that the most appropriate questions are asked in each interview (Dutton et al., 2001).

It is worth adding a note on interview transcribing. The transcription should include, as much as possible, both verbal and non-verbal cues (Seidman, 1998). Non-verbal data can be added from the field notes that have been recorded, and help to provide a more in-depth understanding of the context in which the interview was carried out. Such data can also help uncover any hidden meanings and/or provide certain emphases: laughter, silences, or carefully considered responses to a question can all be illuminating. Patton (1990) suggested that a researcher should anticipate spending four hours transcribing for every hour of interview tape. An advantage to transcribing the interviews oneself is that it increases the familiarity of the researcher with the data and can aid interpretation. However, it can be onerous and time-consuming, particularly with a large number of interviews, and thus getting professional transcription should be considered. The interviewer must then go through the tape and the transcript to ensure that the wording and meanings are clear. If the interviewer has to transcribe the interview her/himself it is worth considering buying voice recognition software to re-record the interview directly into a word processing file. Although voice recognition systems do require training, they can provide a valuable shortcut for interviewers who are not proficient typists, something to which I can readily attest! There are a number of voice recognition systems available several of which are quite user-friendly and reasonably inexpensive. It can also be trained to recognize different voices and thus might be a worthwhile investment for a research unit or group of graduate students.

Credibility, Legitimacy and Initial Interpretations

It may seem strange to include a section on interpretation before discussing coding and analysis, but it is important to realize that data interpretation begins as soon as data collection starts. As soon as we enter the field, we are absorbing and interpreting data. As we listen to responses to interview questions and record field notes, we are inevitably making judgments about what to record and what to disregard. We also, consciously and subconsciously, immediately start making connections between different constructs and concepts. As Sparkes (1992) has pointed out, we are not "empty vessels," thus everything we see or hear is analyzed against the frame of reference we bring to the field, a frame that is both epistemologically and conceptually based. Consequently, the way in which we collect data is, in some ways, less important than the methods of interpretation (Sparkes, 1992). Given, then, that as soon as we start collecting data we are also interpreting them, there are a number of issues that will arise and need to be considered before formal coding and analysis are started.

Participant Checking

Participant checking involves returning the transcript, once it has been reviewed by the interviewer, and any relevant field notes to the participant and asking her/him to check that the content is an accurate reflection of what was said. While it will be impossible for the individual to accurately remember all that transpired, this should still help ensure that what was said forms an accurate reflection of her/his thoughts and feelings at the time, important for the credibility and veracity of the study. In addition to checking the accuracy of what was *said*, it is also important that the accuracy of the researcher's *interpretation* of what was said is checked. It is therefore good practice to provide the participant with the interviewer's interpretation, often in the form of a final report. The interpretations of the interviewer may still be appropriate even if a participant disagrees with them (Seidman, 1998). However, if there is some disagreement, the interviewer or research team must decide whether to modify the analysis or thank the participant for her/his additional insights and proceed as originally planned. The purpose of these steps is to be able to present sufficient evidence to the reader that the researcher's interpretation of the data is both sound and credible (Lincoln & Guba, 1985; Sparkes, 1992).

Triangulation

When interpreting the data collected, it is also worth noting that participants are unlikely to be self-critical and may in fact exaggerate their roles in particular situations; it is also possible that the respondent may provide a socially desirable answer rather than an accurate one (Denscombe, 1998; Fontana & Frey, 1994); further, there may be some hidden agenda that the participant is working to of which the interviewer has no knowledge, but that mitigates against the individual providing honest answers (Altheide & Johnson, 1994). It should be appreciated that human recall of events is not perfect, and that even with the best of intentions, individuals may not be able to recall particular events as accurately as they would like, a point acknowledged by Dutton et al. (2001) in their study of change in a hospital in which their prime mode of data collection was to get participants to reconstruct past events. As Denscombe (1998) has pointed out, we forget most of what we see, engage in selective attention and perception, and have an accentuated disposition to remember some things rather than others, depending on our personal experiences, emotional state, and so on. No matter what the cause, the point being made is that interview data collected from one source should be compared with data from other sources, a process known as *triangulation*. These other sources can include other interviews and/or other types of data. Rubin and Rubin (1995) noted that interviewing involves "weaving together" often contrasting accounts to provide a coherent narrative. This emphasizes the subjective nature of qualitative research and the role that the researcher plays in constructing *a* view of reality, an issue to which I return in the next section.

The idea of data triangulation is not new. As Fontana and Frey (1994) have pointed out, Booth (1902–3) combined unstructured interviews with survey research and participant observation in order to gain insights into the lives and habits of London's working classes. Indeed, observation can be a very useful method of data collection ranging from a very passive form of direct observation to full participation in various activities by the researcher. Archer (2001) for example spent a period of time simply observing what was happening in a sports store in which he had previously conducted a number of interviews; Silk, by contrast, actually took part in the television production of the Canada Cup of Soccer (Silk, Slack & Amis, 2000). Both methods are effective ways of supplementing the data collected through interviews.

A further additional source of data is written documentation, either from official or non-official sources. Berger and Luckman (1967) suggested that representations of the world around us are constituted in communication processes. As a result, official organization documents, minutes of meetings, memoranda, letters and popular press articles can all provide useful data to supplement those gathered during interviews. There are of course other sources of data that can also be useful, including electronic mail, websites, audio and video productions, and physical artifacts. While it is not possible to engage in a detailed discussion of each of these here, the various sources of data should, of course, converge upon some common themes (Yin, 1994).

Credibility and Legitimacy

In addition to triangulating different sources of data and methods of data collection, as noted above, consideration should also be given to triangulating with different theoretical perspectives and different researcher interpretations. This last point is particularly important when it comes to reassuring the reader and other researchers that the work is both credible and legitimate. There has been considerable debate as to how qualitative researchers who reject the quantitatively-based notions of validity and reliability can nevertheless establish that their findings have credibility and legitimacy. This has led to a so-called "crisis of legitimation" (see Denzin & Lincoln, 2000). If we reject the notions of validity and reliability, how, and should, we claim that what we are studying has any relevance beyond the immediate context of the research site? While there is not the room to do justice to this debate here, there are two steps worth pointing out that will enhance the credibility of interview-based research. The first involves conducting an audit trail that will allow another researcher unconnected with the project to follow the research process, from conception, through data collection, to analyses and conclusions (Lincoln & Guba, 1985; Yin, 1994). In this way it is possible for claims that are made to be thoroughly checked against the data collected. Second, it is a good idea to engage in what Lincoln and Guba (1985: 308) call "peer debriefing." This involves providing a colleague with no direct involvement with the research with an open and detailed explanation of the cognitive and data collection processes in which the researcher has engaged. This "disinterested peer" tries to uncover the interpreter's biases and clarify interpretations, and generally plays the role of "devil's advocate." An example of both of these can be seen in the Silk and Amis (2000) paper referred to earlier.

It is also necessary at this juncture to consider issues of reflexivity. Accounts favored by scientific writers and epitomized in the social sciences by Van Maanen's (1988) "realist tales" result in the interviewer being absent from the text, with the data presented as incontrovertible truth that would have been similarly found by any other researcher following the same methods. Others have argued that this is a misrepresentation and that in fact the researcher, far from being a neutral conveyor of information, is inextricably a part of the data that s/he collects. Along with this has gone the debate as to how we go about representing those whom we study in our research, a so-called "crisis of representation" (Denzin & Lincoln, 2000). How do we decide whom to interview? On what basis do we prioritize our various participants' contributions? How do we decide what information to include and what to leave out? Consequently, as Geertz (1988) commented, getting "their" lives into "our" work has moved from being a technical challenge to a moral, political and epistemological one. Sparkes suggested that, "the knower and process of knowing cannot be separated from what is known, and facts cannot be separated from values" (1992: 27). Thus, any methods that are used to collect data, including statistical ones, cannot be free from interpretation. As a consequence, issues such as class, race and gender, and the role that researchers play by inevitably prioritizing some voices and ignoring others become central debates. Again, it is impossible in the space allotted to do justice to this debate. However, it is important that the interviewer understands the ways in which s/he will affect the data that are collected. The ways in which this is accounted for in any analysis will largely depend on the ontological and epistemological position that is held. I suggest that, at a very minimum, all interviewers should include in their account their own position with respect to the research. This may include personal beliefs, interests, experience, expertise, age, gender and ethnicity; anything, in fact, which the researcher feels may affect the interpretation of the data. This allows the reader to adopt a critical stance to the research that would otherwise be impossible (Altheide & Johnson, 1994).

Coding and Analysis

"Data interpretation and analysis involve making sense out of what people have said, looking for patterns, putting together what is said in one place with what is said in another place, and integrating what different people have said" (Patton,

1990: 347). As I noted above, interpretation begins from the moment data collection begins. Thus it is a good idea to start formal coding as soon as possible, ideally after the first one or two interviews. This allows the interviewer to get an early appreciation of the data, to start identifying themes, and if necessary, to modify the interview instrument. The purpose of coding and analysis is to make sense of the mass of data that rapidly accumulates (Patton, 1990). Coding helps to provide a structure and coherence to what will generally be an unwieldy, unstructured, amorphous mass without losing the feel for the original data. Of course, the first requirement is to come up with an appropriate data storage and management system that allows easy retrieval of both electronic and "hard copy" data. An alphabetic filing system with a regularly updated index is the simplest way to store interview transcripts, although, as mentioned earlier, care must be taken to protect the identity of participants if the data are likely to be viewed by other people.

Burgess (1984) suggested that research issues are either preconceived or emerge from the data. Stroh (2000a) differentiated a little more finely, suggesting that themes may originate in predetermined research questions, in the research instrument, from concepts or categories used by other researchers, from the data, or from the socio-cultural context. No matter from where these themes originate, they are categorized by a system of codes that are used to associate particular chunks of the interview text with corresponding themes. There are a number of ways of doing this.

Miles and Huberman (1994) suggested that code definitions must be precise so that they can, if necessary, be easily recognized by other researchers. Codes should also be as close as possible to the name of the theme with which they are associated. For instance, in a study into organizational conflict, it became apparent that the two major antecedents for conflict occurring were the interdependent and differentiated nature of conflicting sub-units (see Amis et al., 1995). Thus, codes used included "DIFF" and "INT" to identify chunks of text in the interview transcripts that suggested that the differentiated or interdependent nature of an organization had contributed to conflict taking place. These codes should be recorded in the left margin of the text. I feel that it is best if the interviewer codes the data as different reviewers are likely to have varying interpretations of the data. However, it is a good idea to get a second researcher to independently review the data. This will provide additional insight into conceptual linkages and interconnectedness of the codes that may have been missed by the interviewer, and also provides an additional check against preconceived biases that may have unduly influenced the analyses. Differences of opinion should be resolved through discussion and, if necessary, the introduction of a third coder.

Initial coding is likely to be descriptive with codes applied to identify particular chunks of data. As the researcher gets to know the data better, coding can become more interpretive to identify what each chunk of data represents. Gradually, more inferential and explanatory pattern codes can be used to identify particular themes, patterns, and linkages (Miles & Huberman, 1994). These can be recorded in the right margin. These conceptual linkages will often form when the researcher is doing something other than directly analyzing the data: it is a good idea that they are written down as soon as possible before the fallibility of one's memory turns a potentially valuable insight into a frustrating lost connection. Lincoln and Guba (1985) suggested that as well as adding new codes, researchers should always be willing to re-interrogate the data to explore new themes, linkages and relationships. Ideally, this process should continue until no new themes emerge and categories are "saturated." Often, however, as field work continues, new themes keep emerging; thus it is time and resource constraints that frequently dictate when the research process is terminated. As a consequence we tend to reach a position in which, as Van Maanen sagely noted, "we know that our analysis is not finished, only over" (1988: 120).

Depending on the approach taken, initial codes may be drawn from a conceptual framework constructed from a review of previous research. Alternatively, a more inductive approach may be favored, such as the grounded theory method advocated by Glaser and Strauss (1967). Here, the researcher tries to avoid imposing any preconceived notions of what s/he might find, and waits to see what themes emerge from the data. The analysis is continued ideally until no more themes emerge. This grounded approach is not as unstructured as it may at first appear. Strauss (1987), for example, suggested that, as a starting point, the researcher could code for various conditions, strategies and tactics, interactions among different actors, and consequences of particular actions. From here, more specific codes will likely start to emerge.

It is also possible to develop a mid-range general set of codes that sits between the inductive and *a priori* schemes described above. Denis, Lamothe and Langley are proponents of this approach, suggesting that a "partly deductive (theory inspired) and partly inductive (data inspired) ... approach can be very fruitful because it allows one to gain creative insight from the data without necessarily denying or reinventing concepts that have been useful previously" (2001: 812). Lofland (1971) and Bogdan and Biklen (1992) have both suggested mid-range coding schemes. While the nature of the initial themes will clearly depend on the specific context in which the research is being conducted, I suggest the following as a possible starting point if dealing with some form of organizational analysis:

1. Setting – locating the organization in its socio-political economic context; this should help identify key environmental pressures (institutional, resource, cultural, political, etc)
2. Organizational activities – the main activities in which the organization engages
3. Values/beliefs/culture – shared understandings, perspectives (likely to be multiple)
4. External linkages – identifying relationships that exist between the organization and key environmental actors
5. Internal linkages – key relationships within the organization

6. Individual actions – more specific activities of individuals tied to a particular theme

It is possible to explore these points from both what is expected in certain situations and what actually occurs, although care must be taken not to simply slip into a continual process of description rather than analysis. As more familiarity with the data is gained, codes can be adapted, added, discarded and even split up if necessary. In fact, this process of revising codes is important to the ongoing development of the analysis (Miles & Huberman, 1994).

The complexity and sheer volume of qualitative data make the use of software packages such as NUD*IST, HyperRESEARCH, Ethnograph and ATLAS/ti appealing. Indeed they can be useful in the storage, coding and retrieval of data. However, while there are claims that they can help with theory construction, software packages cannot actually do the analysis – this still has to come from the researcher. Indeed, some commentators have suggested that such software can distance the researcher from the data (e.g., Stroh, 2000b). There has also been debate as to whether the formal logic of the software is appropriate for qualitative analysis (Gaskell, 2000). Consequently, while interviewers may wish to experiment with these packages, simple word processing software will probably be sufficient for most researchers. However, for those who wish to explore this further, Weitzman (2000) provides an account as to what data analysis software can and cannot do, and how to go about selecting among different packages while Stroh (2000c) provides an insightful "hands-on" lesson in using the NUD*IST version 4 package.

Writing Up: "A Process of Discovery"

Many researchers see writing up as the final part of the research process. Given my previous comments it should be no surprise when I say that writing up should begin as soon as possible. I try to get students to write an introduction *before* they have collected any data. In this way, ideas are being formulated and revised from an early stage. Even if utilizing a grounded approach, it is incumbent upon the researcher to develop an understanding of what other research has been carried out in the area and how the current project may extend understanding in a particular area. Irrespective of the epistemology and methodology adopted, writing an introduction early on, that will almost certainly be subsequently revised as understanding develops, helps the researcher to begin to articulate her/his ideas in a coherent manner. Burgess suggested "the final report relies upon the researcher blending together personal experiences with theories and data in order to make some contribution to our understanding of the social world" (1984: 183). In this sense, writing is more a process of negotiated discovery by interviewer and participant(s) than simply a singularly produced narrative produced by the researcher. Thus, the earlier one starts to write, the more one is likely to discover. As Richardson (2000) has suggested, writing should be a dynamic, creative process in which the writer does not wait until s/he is sure of what s/he wants to say before starting to write.

While I advocate an early start to the writing process, there are some points worth considering before one starts to write. The first is the style of writing. Qualitative writing is generally considered more engaging if written in an active rather than a passive voice (Richardson, 2000). It is therefore a good idea to write in the first person and try to draw the reader into the text. That said, it is important to know the audience for whom one is writing: some journals and disciplines favor particular styles so it is worth finding out about particular conventions in advance.

The crises of representation and legitimation discussed earlier will also affect the way in which the writing is approached. In large part, this will be determined by the epistemological position of the researcher. However, the need to consider the way in which realities of lived experiences are shown, and whose voices are privileged over others in the research and why should not be underplayed. Van Maanen (1988) detailed a number of alternative writing genres. A realist approach will likely see the author vanishing from the text as s/he attempts to provide a sanitized account of the individual's experiences. Data in the text will be used to support the prevailing viewpoint with no alternative explanations allowed to creep in. However, Van Maanen also provided other styles in which the role of the researcher is made explicit in the text. "Confessional tales" make explicit the researcher's journey of discovery through the research process in what Van Maanen described as an autobiographical account. "Impressionist tales" are written more in the fragmented form of a novel with attempts to establish truth considered meaningless because the reader is not present in the field; instead, the author exhibits a concern for coherence, interest and fidelity. Van Maanen (1988), Sparkes (1995) and Richardson (2000) have noted various other styles of writing that consider the need to account for the multiple realities that constitute the social world and also take account of the reflexive nature of qualitative research. However, the choice of writing should not be arbitrary but should instead be a product of the nature of the research experience and the epistemological position of the researcher (see Sparkes, 1995).

The question as to how to use the data in the text also needs to be considered. Denscombe (1998) suggested that while textual extracts can provide a voice, they are inevitably biased and should therefore only be used as illustrations or supporting evidence rather than as unequivocal proof of a particular position. That said, the use of extracts from the interview is absolutely vital in qualitative research. As well as providing evidence for particular claims, quotations provide color, add interest and enhance the legitimacy and credibility of the account. Jackson (2000) provided a number of points to ponder when considering how to use quotations:

- How should quotes be attributed – how much detail of the informant should be provided?

- To what extent should the data be cleaned – should minor syntax mistakes be corrected, or silences excluded?
- Should the interviewer's questions be used – were questions inferential or neutral?
- Should longer or shorter extracts be used – several short quotes or fewer longer ones?
- Can the extracts be rearranged – can quotes be spliced together or their order changed?

As Jackson (2000) noted, there are no right answers, but the position taken needs to be ethically and professionally defensible, and justified in the text. No matter what approach we take, we should not feel that we have to, or are able to, write anything other than a partial account. "Our subjects always know more than they can tell us, usually even more than they allow us to see; likewise, we often know more than we can articulate" (Altheide & Johnson, 1994: 491). If we accept this, we will sleep more easily than if we strive for some unattainable perfection.

Research Exemplars

Throughout the text I have referred to various pieces of research that should be useful in helping readers gain a more comprehensive understanding of the use of interviews in sports studies case study research. In particular, I have provided examples from the sports studies literature that highlight the various issues discussed. The exemplars below should further illuminate the processes involved in the design and implementation of interview-based case study research. When my own work is drawn upon here and throughout the chapter it is because of my intimate knowledge of it rather than any belief as to its particular insightfulness.

Sack and Nadim (2002) used interview data as the basis for a detailed case study on Starter Corporation. Writing from a realist perspective, Sack and Nadim (2002) chronicle the history of the firm from its founding in 1971, through its initial public offering in 1993 and development into a leader in the apparel industry, through its decline and ultimate bankruptcy in 1999. The real utility of Sack and Nadim's (2002) paper is in highlighting the value of using interview data to construct a single-case study that can provide rich insight into the details of the life history of an organization. A criticism is the lack of detail provided as to how the interview data were collected and analyzed. A single-case study, this time of an English rugby union club, is similarly a feature of O'Brien and Slack's (1999) work. Using data collected from twenty semi-structured interviews, the paper provides detailed insight into some of the dynamics of change involved in the professionalization of English rugby.

Several of the case studies that have featured in my own work have, in contrast to Sack and Nadim 2002 and O'Brien and Slack 1999, been used comparatively. Amis et al. (1997), for example, provided two cases that were used to contrast the sponsorship activities of one firm that used sponsorship as a pillar of its marketing activity and another that regarded it as a luxury to be enjoyed only in times of munificence. Shaw and Amis (2001) explored the differences between two firms that had very different philosophies underpinning their sponsorship of two women's international sport teams. Finally, Amis et al. (1995) used four case studies to examine some of the antecedents of conflict in voluntary sport organizations. A criticism of all of these pieces, in common with much of the interview research that is carried out under the banner of sport management, is their lack of accounting for the inevitable reflexivity of the interview process. This issue is considered in much more detail in my examination of the utilization of image and reputation as key strategic resources by Guinness (see Amis, 2003). Finally, reflexivity along with several other issues associated with focus group interviews are discussed in the body of work emanating from Frisby and her colleagues, cited earlier. In particular, from a methodological standpoint, readers are referred to Frisby et al. (2005).

Conclusion

This chapter has touched on a number of different topics that will, I hope, provide at least a rudimentary framework from which to plan and complete interview-based research. The reason for trying to be reasonably comprehensive rather than, say, just focusing on the interview guide or data interpretation, is that I believe that all of the topics covered here, as I have said several times, are inextricably intertwined. It makes no sense to me to try to design an interview guide without considering the ethical issues involved in carrying out the research, or to ask how the data might be interpreted without examining how the research will be written up. All of these things should be considered at the very start of the design process, and revisited throughout. A number of these steps are perhaps worth highlighting.

First, decide on the type of interviews that will be carried out, ranging from highly structured with closed questions to very unstructured with a small number of general issues to explore. The design should arise naturally out of the research problem and the ontological and epistemological positions of the researcher. Second, be aware of the ethical responsibility that interviewing carries with it; the protection of the research participants should be of paramount importance throughout the design and execution of the study. Third, carefully construct the interview guide, thinking about the language, style and sequencing of the questions or themes to be covered. Fourth, decide on whether the interviews will focus on a single issue, event or organization, or multiple cases. Deciding on where the research will take place will likely be a combination of the satisfaction of theoretical criteria and pragmatic opportunity. Fifth, carefully plan the interview: try to consider everything from the practicalities of carrying out the interview, to the entering and exiting of the field, to building rapport, to personal safety. Sixth, start interpreting the data as soon as they are collected. Make field notes that do not just describe what happened, but also start to make conceptual linkages. Note the importance of data triangulation and reflexivity. Seventh, start coding and analyzing the data as soon as possible; be prepared to revise the codes over time. Finally, consider the writing style that will be used, and start writing as early as possible.

When I sat down to start writing this chapter, I had three main intentions. The first was to provide some insight into the techniques of using interviewing as a method of data collection in case study research. The second was to explore some of the theoretical and epistemological debates that impact the interviewing process. The third was to get across my enthusiasm for interviewing. If I have done nothing else, I hope that I have conveyed my enthusiasm. The process of engaging with individuals and finding out about their interpretation of events in the social world is always stimulating: it may not be straightforward at times, but it is never boring and usually immensely gratifying.

Acknowledgments

My thanks to C. Roger Rees, two anonymous reviewers and the book editors for their astute comments on earlier drafts of this chapter.

Notes

1. There are a variety of terms used in the literature to refer to the individual being interviewed. These include interviewee, respondent, subject, informant and co-researcher. In using "participant" I follow the lead of Seidman (1998: 8) who reasoned that the term "seems to capture both the sense of active involvement that occurs in an in-depth interview and the sense of equity that we try to build in our interviewing relationships." See Seidman (1998) for an exploration of the use of different terminologies, and the possible drawbacks associated with them.
2. While researchers are of course advised to consult the regulations in place at their own institutions, the IRB requirements in place at The University of Memphis can be seen at www.people.memphis.edu/~irb/.

References

Adler, P.A. (1985). *Wheeling and Dealing: An Ethnography of an Upper-Level Drug Dealing and Smuggling Community.* New York: Columbia University Press.

Altheide D.L. & Johnson, J.M. (1994). Validity in Qualitative Research. In N.K. Denzin & Y.S. Lincoln (eds). *Handbook of Qualitative Research.* London: Sage.

Amis, J. (2003). "Good Things Come to Those Who Wait": The Strategic Management of Image and Reputation at Guinness. *European Sport Management Quarterly*, 3, 189–214.

Amis, J., Pant, N., & Slack, T. (1997). Achieving a Sustainable Competitive Advantage: A Resource-Based View of Sport Sponsorship. *Journal of Sport Management*, 11, 80–96.

Amis, J., Slack, T. & Berrett, T. (1995). The Structural Antecedents of Conflict in Voluntary Sport Organizations. *Leisure Studies*, 14, 1–16.

—— (1999). Sport Sponsorship as Distinctive Competence. *European Journal of Marketing*, 33, 250–73.

Amis, J., Slack, T. & Hinings, C.R. (2002). Values and Organizational Change. *Journal of Applied Behavioral Sciences*, 38, 356–85.

—— (2004a). Pace, Sequence and Linearity in Radical Strategic Change. *Academy of Management Journal*, 47, 15–39.

—— (2004b). The Role of Interests, Power and Capacity in Strategic Change. *Journal of Sport Management*, 18, 158–98.

Archer, C. (2001). Examining Sustainable Competitive Advantage in a Specialist Sport Retail Outlet: A Resource-Based Perspective. Unpublished Master's thesis, De Montfort University, UK.

Bauer, M.W., Gaskell, G., & Allum, N.C. (2000). Quality, Quantity and Knowledge Interests: Avoiding Confusions. In M. Bauer & G. Gaskell (eds). *Qualitative Researching with Text, Image and Sound: A Practical Handbook*. London: Sage.

Berg, B. (2001). *Qualitative Research Methods for the Social Sciences* (4th edition). Boston: Allen & Bacon.

Berger, P. & Luckman, T. (1967). *The Social Construction of Reality*. London: Allen Lane.

Bogdan, R. & Biklen, S.K. (1992). *Qualitative Research for Education: An Introduction to Theory and Methods* (2nd edition). Boston: Allyn & Bacon.

Booth, C. (1902–3). *Life and Labour of the People of London*. London: Macmillan.

Bryman, A. (1988). *Quantity and Quality in Social Research*. London: Routledge.

Burgess, R. (1984). *In the Field: An Introduction to Field Research*. London: Allen & Unwin.

Burrell, G. & Morgan, G. (1979). *Sociological Paradigms and Organizational Analysis*. London: Heinemann.

Burton, D. (2000). The Use of Case Studies in Social Science Research. In D. Burton (ed.). *Research Training for Social Sciences: A Handbook for Postgraduate Students*. London: Sage.

Crow, I. (2000). The Power of Research. In D. Burton (ed.). *Research Training for Social Sciences: A Handbook for Postgraduate Students*. London: Sage.

Denis, J.-L., Lamothe, L., & Langley, A. (2001). The Dynamics of Collective Leadership and Strategic Change in Pluralistic Organizations. *Academy of Management Journal*, 44, 809–37.

Denscombe, M. (1998). *The Good Research Guide for Small-Scale Social Research Projects*. Buckingham: Open University Press.

Denzin, N.K. & Lincoln, Y.S. (1994). Introduction: Entering the Field of Qualitative Research. In N.K. Denzin & Y.S. Lincoln (eds). *Handbook of Qualitative Research*. London: Sage.

—— (2000). Introduction: The Discipline and Practice of Qualitative Research. In N.K. Denzin & Y.S. Lincoln (eds). *Handbook of Qualitative Research* (2nd edition), pp. 1–28. London: Sage.

Dutton, J.E., Ashford, S.J., O'Neill, R.M., & Lawrence, K.A. 2001). Moves that Matter: Issue Selling and Organizational Change. *Academy of Management Journal*, 44: 716–36.

Fontana, A. & Frey, J.H. (1994). Interviewing: The art of science. In N.K Denzin & Y.S. Lincoln (eds). *Handbook of Qualitative Research*. London: Sage.
—— (2000). The Interview: From Structured Questions to Negotiated Text. In N.K. Denzin & Y.S. Lincoln (eds). *Handbook of Qualitative Research* (2nd edition). London: Sage.
Frisby, W., Crawford, S., & Dorer, T. (1997). Reflections on Participatory Action Research: The Case of Low-Income Women Accessing Local Physical Activity Services. *Journal of Sport Management*, 11, 8–28.
Frisby, W., & Fenton, J. (1998). *Leisure Access: Enhancing Recreation Opportunities for Those Living in Poverty*. Vancouver, BC: British Columbia Health Research Foundation.
Frisby, W. & Hoeber, L. (2002). Factors Affecting the Uptake of Community Recreation as Health Promotion for Women on Low Incomes. *Canadian Journal of Public Health*, 93, 2, 129–33.
Frisby, W. & Millar, S. (2002). The Actualities of Doing Community Development to Promote the Inclusion of Low-Income Populations in Local Sport and Recreation. *European Sport Management Quarterly*, 3, 209–33.
Frisby, W., Reid, C.J., Millar, S. & Hoeber, L. (2005, forthcoming). Putting "Participatory" into Participatory Forms of Action Research. *Journal of Sport Management*.
Gaskell, G. (2000). Individual and Group Interviewing. In M. Bauer & G. Gaskell (eds). *Qualitative Researching with Text, Image and Sound: A Practical Handbook*. London: Sage.
Geertz, C. (1988). *Works and Lives: The Anthropologist as Author*. Stanford, CA: Stanford University Press.
Glaser, B. & Strauss, A. (1967). *The Discovery of Grounded Theory: Strategies for Qualitative Research*. Chicago: Aldine.
Harrison, J., MacGibbon, L. & Morton, M. (2001). Regimes of Trustworthiness in Qualitative Research: The Rigors of Reciprocity. *Qualitative Inquiry*, 7, 3, 323–45.
Henderson, K. (1991). *Dimensions of Choice: A Qualitative Approach to Recreation, Parks and Leisure Research*. State College, PA: Venture Publishing Inc.
Hobbs, D. (1989). *Doing the Business*. Buckingham, UK: Open University Press.
Howell, N. (1990). *Surviving Fieldwork: A Report of the Advisory Panel on Health and Safety in Fieldwork*. Washington, DC: American Anthropological Association.
Humphreys, L. (1970). *Tearoom Trade: Impersonal Sex in Public Places*. Chicago: Aldine.
—— (1972). *Out of the Closet*. Englewood Cliffs, NJ: Prentice Hall.
Jackson, P. (2000). Writing up Qualitative Data. In D. Burton (ed.). *Research Training for Social Sciences: A Handbook for Postgraduate Students*. London: Sage
Kemmis, S. & McTaggart, R. (2000). Participatory Action Research. In N.K. Denzin & Y.S. Lincoln (eds). *Handbook of Qualitative Research* (2nd edition). London: Sage.
Kent, G. (2000a). Ethical Principles. In D. Burton (ed.). *Research Training for Social Sciences: A Handbook for Postgraduate Students*. London: Sage
—— (2000b). Informed Consent. In D. Burton (ed.). *Research Training for Social Sciences: A Handbook for Postgraduate Students*. London: Sage.
Kikulis, L.M., Slack, T. & Hinings, C.R. (1995a). Sector-Specific Patterns of Organizational Design Change. *Journal of Management Studies*, 32, 67–100.
—— (1995b). Does Decision Making Make a Difference? Patterns of Change within Canadian National Sport Organizations. *Journal of Sport Management*, 9, 273–99.
Kreuger, R.A. (1994). *Focus groups: A Practical Guide for Applied Research* (2nd edition). London: Sage.

Lincoln, Y.S & Guba, E.G. (1985). *Naturalistic Inquiry*. London: Sage.
Lofland, J. (1971). *Analyzing Social Settings: A Guide to Qualitative Observation and Analysis*. Belmont, CA: Wadsworth.
Lofland, J.F. & Lejeune, R.A. (1960). Initial Interaction of Newcomers in Alcoholics Anonymous. *Social Problems*, 8, 102–11.
MacIntyre, D. (1999). *MacIntyre Undercover*. London: BBC Worldwide Limited.
Madriz, E. (2000). Focus Groups in Feminist Research. In N.K. Denzin & Y.S. Lincoln (eds). *Handbook of Qualitative Research* (2nd edition). London: Sage.
Miles, M. & Huberman, M. (1994). *Qualitative Data Analysis: An Expanded Sourcebook* (2nd edition). London: Sage.
Milgram, S. (1963). Behavioral Study of Obedience. *Journal of Abnormal and Social Psychology*, 67, 371–78.
Mills, C.W. (1959). *The Sociological Imagination*. Oxford: Oxford University Press.
Oakley, A. (1981). Interviewing Women: A Contradiction in Terms. In H. Roberts (ed.). *Doing Feminist Research*. London: Routledge.
O'Brien, D. & Slack, T. (1999). Deinstitutionalising the Amateur Ethic: An Empirical Examination of Change in a Rugby Union Football Club. *Sport Management Review*, 2, 24–42.
Patton, M. (1990). *Qualitative Evaluation and Research Methods*. London: Sage.
Pettigrew, A. (1985). *The Awakening Giant*. Oxford: Blackwell.
—— (1987). Context and Action in the Transformation of the Firm. *Journal of Management Studies*, 24: 649–70.
—— (1990). Longitudinal Field Research on Change: Theory and Practice. *Organization Science*, 1, 267–92.
—— (1998). Success and Failure in Corporate Transformation Initiatives. In R.D. Galliers & W.R.J. Baets (eds.), *Information Technology and Organisational Transformation*. London: John Wiley and Sons Ltd.
Pettigrew, A. & Whipp, R. (1993). *Managing Change for Competitive Success*. Oxford: Blackwell.
Pettus, M.L. (2001). The Resource-Based View as a Developmental Growth Process: Evidence from the Deregulated Trucking Industry. *Academy of Management Journal*, 44, 878–96.
Punch, M. (1994). Politics and Ethics in Qualitative Research. In N.K. Denzin & Y.S. Lincoln (eds). *Handbook of Qualitative Research*. London: Sage.
Richardson, L. (2000). Writing: A Method of Inquiry. In N.K. Denzin & Y.S. Lincoln (eds). *Handbook of Qualitative Research* (2nd edition). London: Sage.
Rubin, H.J. & Rubin, I.S. (1995). *Qualitative Interviewing: The Art of Hearing Data*. London: Sage.
Sack, A.L. & Nadim, A. (2002). Strategic Choices in a Turbulent Environment: A Case Study of Starter Corporation. *Journal of Sport Management*, 16, 36–53.
Seidman, I. (1998). *Interviewing as Qualitative Research: A Guide for Researchers in Education and the Social Sciences* (2nd edition). New York: Teachers College Press.
Shaw, S. & Amis, J. (2001). Image and investment: Sponsorship and Women's Sport. *Journal of Sport Management*, 15, 219–46.
Silk, M. (2002). Bangsa Malaysia: Global Sport, the City and the Refurbishment of Local Identities. *Media, Culture and Society*, 24, 771–90.
Silk, M & Amis, J. (2000). Institutional Pressures and the Production of Televised Sport. *Journal of Sport Management*, 14, 267–92.

Silk, M., Slack, T., & Amis, J. (2000). An Institutional Approach to Televised Sport Production. *Culture, Sport, Society*, 3, 1, 1–21.

Slack, T., & Hinings, C.R. (1994). Institutional Pressures and Isomorphic Change: An Empirical Test. *Organization Studies*, 15, 803–27.

Sparkes, A. (1992). Writing and the Textual Construction of Realities: Some Challenges for Alternative Paradigms in Physical Education. In A. Sparkes (ed.). *Research in Physical Education and Sport: Exploring Alternative Visions.* London: Falmer Press.

—— (1995). Writing People: Reflections on the Dual Crises of Representation and Legitimation in Qualitative Inquiry. *Quest*, 45, 188–95.

Spradley, J.P. (1979). *The Ethnographic Interview.* New York: Holt, Rinehart & Winston.

Stake, R.E. (2000). Case studies. In N.K. Denzin & Y.S. Lincoln (eds). *Handbook of Qualitative Research* (2nd edition). London: Sage.

Strauss, A.L. (1987). *Qualitative Analysis for Social Scientists.* Cambridge: Cambridge University Press.

Stroh, M. (2000a). Qualitative Interviewing. In D. Burton (ed.). *Research Training for Social Sciences: A Handbook for Postgraduate Students.* London: Sage.

—— (2000b). Computers and Qualitative Analysis: To Use or Not to Use? In D. Burton (ed.). *Research Training for Social Sciences: A Handbook for Postgraduate Students.* London: Sage.

—— (2000c). Using NUD*IST Version 4: A Hands-on Lesson. In D. Burton (ed.). *Research Training for Social Sciences: A Handbook for Postgraduate Students.* London: Sage.

Van Maanen, J. (1988). *Tales of the Field: On Writing Ethnography.* Chicago: University of Chicago Press.

Weitzman, E.A. (2000). Software and Qualitative Research. In N. Denzin & Y. Lincoln (eds). *Handbook of Qualitative Research* (2nd edition). London: Sage

Yin, R.K. (1994). *Case Study Research: Design and Methods* (2nd edition). London: Sage.

6

Qualitative Methods in Sport-Media Studies

Darcy Plymire

Media research has a long history. Critics since the mid nineteenth century have worried about the effects of mass media on political discourse and individual behavior. Pundits at the dawn of the mass media age feared news and entertainment media might appeal to the lowest common denominator of human desire, peddling scandal and spectacle to a gullible and uncritical mass audience. Those fears have not diminished with time. Indeed every innovation in communications technology, from the printing press and the telegraph to the Internet and the cell phone, seems to spawn a new discourse on the decline and fall of civilization. Paradoxically those same technologies simultaneously provoke a parallel discourse on the wonders of technology.

Peters points out communications and media studies were not among the "social sciences" conceptualized by nineteenth-century thinkers, and though communications and media studies leaned heavily on the assumptions of nineteenth-century social science, they were "example[s] of a newer, nascent way of organizing inquiry" (1994: 374). Specifically, communications and media studies are not disciplinary fields; they are topical areas of study that can be approached from a variety of theoretical and methodological perspectives. Peters identifies three main traditions in communications research, each of which has its origins in the intellectual and social ferment of the 1930s: (1) the empirical "effects" tradition of Paul Lazersfeld, (2) the "humanistic" tradition of John Dewey and (3) the "critical" tradition pioneered by the Frankfurt School and more recently carried on by practitioners of critical cultural studies (e.g., Hall, 1977; 1980; 1985). The effects tradition and the critical tradition have been most influential in media research. As the name implies, the effects tradition strives to measure the effects of media consumption on audiences. Research from this perspective has produced some interesting findings. However, it is limited by the assumption that media directly cause particular behaviors and attitudes. For example, it is the lingering influence of the effects tradition that leads many people, including some media researchers, to suspect that playing video games with violent themes and content causes users to become inured to violence and, potentially, more apt to act violently.

More recently scholars working in the critical tradition have questioned whether media can have such strong effects, arguing instead that audiences are thoughtful and active consumers of media products who may resist or question messages rather than swallowing them whole. Work in the critical tradition is more often qualitative, as it seeks to understand the multiple levels of media production and consumption and to sort out the relationships between media producers, texts and consumers.

As sport became enmeshed with the media, throught the course of the twentieth century, interest in the relationships between sport and media grew. However, sport-media studies developed at a relatively late date. Wenner (1998) claims the publication of his first book, *Media, Sports, and Society*, in 1989, launched interest in sport-media studies. A review of the contents of the three most prominent journals in the sociology of sport, *Sociology of Sport Journal*, *Journal of Sport and Social Issues* and the *International Review for Sociology of Sport*, supports Wenner's claim. Prior to 1989 few sport-media pieces appeared in any of those publications. In contrast, over half of the studies appearing in those journals during the last five years of the twentieth century were sport-media studies of one variety or another. The timing of this boom in interest has had important consequences on the character of sport-media studies: the qualitative critical tradition has dominated the field of sport-media studies.

Sport sociology has deep roots in critical social thought, emerging as it did from the intellectual, cultural and social milieu of the late 1960s. Early sociological studies of sport included Scott's *The Athletic Revolution* (1971) and Edwards' *The Revolt of the Black Athlete* (1969). More significantly, by the late 1970s and early 1980s, critical Marxist (e.g., Brohm, 1978; Ingham, 1976) and feminist (e.g., Birrell, 1984; Theberge, 1981) analyses pushed sport sociology toward a radical reconsideration of sport and culture. Those radical streams combined with the interdisciplinary field of critical cultural studies to produce a flood of sport media analysis in the late 1980s and 1990s.

Choosing the Qualitative Approach

Graeme Turner (1990) argues that cultural studies is based on the principle that culture is constructed in language and through textual representations, and therefore, the way to understand culture is to study texts and contexts. Based on those principles the core business of cultural studies has become analysis of texts and contexts. Many sports studies scholars have concluded that the theories and methods of cultural studies make it ideal for sport-media analysis.

The rubric of critical cultural studies encompasses a variety of theoretical and methodological perspectives. Critical cultural studies shares with sociology the perspective that humans make sense of the world though symbolic interactions. The sociological perspective says that everything meaningful in human life is a product of human social interactions. Our social institutions – religion, education, government, sports and so forth – and our ideas – philosophies, ideologies, values – all are constructed or created through human social endeavor. However, cultural studies views cultural construction from a different perspective than sociology. In short, cultural studies tends to look at culture as a symbolic structure and thus focuses its attentions on the construction and interpretation of various cultural texts. In *The Long Revolution* Raymond Williams defined culture as, "a description of a particular way of life, which expresses certain meanings and values" (1975: 57). Williams termed the sense of the way of life of an era its "structure of feeling" (Turner, 1990: 57). In Tony Bennett's (1981) terms, a structure of feeling is a way of thinking and feeling shared by the people of a particular time and place. Adopting Williams's definition of culture, the job of the cultural critic becomes, "the clarification of meanings and values implicit and explicit in a particular way of life, a particular culture" (Williams, 1975: 57). One method of accomplishing that objective is critical textual "reading" of media products such as popular books, magazines, newspapers, and films (Nelson et al., 1992; Turner, 1990). Critical cultural studies views such documents as repositories of value and meaning that can help scholars to understand cultural belief systems and relationships of power among different cultural and social groups. Based on that assumption, critical cultural studies foregrounds inequalities of social power along multiple axes of race, class, gender, sexuality, and so on (Birrell & McDonald, 2000).

Theory and Method

Four categories of theories, interpreted through the lens of critical cultural studies, have influenced sport-media studies: (1) Marxist-based hegemony theory; (2) semiotics and structuralism; (3) post-structuralism; and (4) feminism.

Hegemony

Marx famously stated, "the ideas of the ruling class are in every epoch the ruling ideas," and the ruling class of a society is the "ruling *material* force of society" (emphasis in original), as it controls "the means of material production ... [and of] mental production" (Marx & Engels, 1981: 64). The ostensible purpose of the mass media is to entertain and inform, but as representatives of the ruling class, the media also reflect the "consciousness" of the ruling class who "rule ... as thinkers, as producers of ideas, and regulate the production and distribution of the ideas of their age" (Marx & Engels, 1981: 64). From a "vulgar" Marxist perspective, the so-called mass media in western democracies constitute the material means of mental production. Wealthy capitalists control the media, and the media construct and disseminate ideological messages that help maintain the status quo. This of course is an oversimplification, but one that illuminates why the more flexible hegemony theory of Antonio Gramsci has proved more useful to sport-media analysis than the deterministic readings predicted by vulgar Marxism.

Gramsci (1971) said the dominance of the ruling class was never complete: those with power must always negotiate with other groups and factions to maintain their hegemony. Writing in fascist Italy before World War II, Gramsci theorized fascists negotiated their power through a specific alliance with the middle class and with landowners, each of which perceived a stake in protecting capitalism against the incursions of working-class communists and/or socialists, who formed a politically and socially subordinated and resistant opposition. Sport-media scholars have appropriated and rearticulated Gramscian hegemony theory. Rather than conceptualizing hegemony as an alliance between clearly defined and mutually exclusive social classes and/or political groups, practitioners of sport and media studies have articulated hegemony theory to an analysis of social power relations around multiple axes of race, class, gender, sexuality and so forth (Birrell & McDonald, 2000). In short, hegemonic ideas, according to sport and media studies, may be produced by mass media and may reflect the interests of whites, men, the middle class and heterosexuals, but no grand alliance/conspiracy exists among white, heterosexual, middle and upper-class men to oppress women, people of color, the poor and/or homosexuals. Instead, the media tend to reproduce power because they rely on "common sense" ideology to attract and satisfy a broad audience. To paraphrase Stuart Hall (1980), the dominant ideas in any society are those which best reflect commonly held assumptions. In western democracies, those commonly held assumptions tend to reproduce inequalities along the aforementioned axes.

Semiotics

Semiotics is the study of signs and how signs work (Fiske, 1990: 40). A sign has two parts, the signifier, or physical form of the sign, and the signified, the mental concept to which the signifier refers. According to Swiss linguist Ferdinand de Saussure, who pioneered the science of semiotics, the meanings of signs are arbitrary and conventional. Furthermore, the meanings of signs are determined through their relationships to other signs within a given text. The meanings of texts are constructed by differentiating one sign from another and by placing signs in different contexts. For semiotics, the proper object of study is the text, because the text is the site where meaning is constructed. However, texts can never be studied out of context. The signs in a text are organized according to culturally specific codes or systems of signification. Furthermore, the producers of texts encode meaning under specific social and cultural conditions while readers decode texts under somewhat different conditions.

Semiotic theory adds two important dimensions to media studies that were missing in hegemony theory. First, whereas hegemony theory privileges the power of textual producers, who represent the dominant social class, semiotics focuses more attention on the activity of reading. Second, although semiotics originates in linguistics, it offers a theoretical premise from which to study a wide range of cultural practices as signifying practices. Despite these characteristics, semiotics is limited by the assumption that the meaning of a text is *determined* by its organization of signs. In the structural linguistics of semiotics, "Codes are, in fact, the systems into which signs are organized. These systems are governed by rules, which are consented to by *all* members of the community using that code" (Fiske, 1990: 64, emphasis added). Though any single sign may denote more than one thing, once a sign is encoded into a particular text, the structure of the text disallows some meanings. Thus the potential readings of the text are limited and the power of the reader is reduced.

Post-structuralism

Jacques Derrida unsettled the assumption that the structure of a text determined its meaning. Saussure thought the structure of a language determined all possible utterances. Derrida countered that the idea that language is a determining system relies on the assumption that signifiers/words refer to concrete and specific underlying concepts. That is, even though a single signifier may have more than one possible meaning, a reader may judge the intended meaning of the word/signifier from its usage. In essence, Derrida argued that signifiers/words do not refer to concrete mental concepts but to other signifiers. In other words, every signified is also a signifier, as language produces meaning through strings of metaphors that have no beginning or end. For example, a semiotician or a structuralist might say the meaning of the word "man" is fixed by its relationship to words like "woman" and "animal" – that is a man is by definition not a woman and not an animal. Derrida counters, the meaning of "man" cannot be determined by its relation to "woman" or to "animal" because the meanings of woman and animal are not fixed. Indeed, the multiple meanings of the three terms are constantly in play, thus any text about masculinity or femininity, for example, creates *aporias*, moments when the possible meanings of a text undermine the perception that the text has a literal or intended meaning.

Feminism

Feminism has no unitary theoretical position nor does it have a prescribed method of inquiry. Rather, feminism has been influential in sport-media studies because it suggests an object for analysis – gender – and offers a position from which to critique the social construction of gender within sport texts. Specifically, feminist researchers ask how sport-media texts produce and/or reproduce ideologies that affirm presumed sexual differences and inequalities of social power. The same logic can be and has been applied to the analysis of other social inequalities. Marxist/hegemony theory, semiotics and post-structuralist theories all have afforded feminists opportunities to interpret media texts and contexts.

Variants, Procedures and Challenges

Based on the accumulated influences of hegemony theory, semiotics, post-structuralism and feminism, sport-media scholars have pursued three avenues of research: (1) studies of textual production, such as the participant observation studies of media undertaken by Fishman (1980), Gitlin (1980; 1985), the Glasgow Media Group (1976; 1980; 1982) and Tuchman (1978); (2) studies of media texts such as Fiske's (1991) analyses of television programs and innumerable studies of advertising; and (3) studies of audience response to media content, such as Morley's (1980) examination of television audiences and Radway's (1991) reading of the romance novel.

In the field of sociology of sport, about 70 per cent of all studies of media and sport examine media products while 20 per cent are production studies and less than 10 per cent are audience studies. Textual analysis dominates the field for theoretical and practical reasons. Ethnographic production studies require access to sites of media production, and substantial commitments of time and material resources on the part of the researchers. Furthermore, the results of ethnographic studies do not generalize easily, as all production sites do not operate in the same fashion. Audience reception studies present the same problems of access, resource allocation, and generalizability as production studies, but they add another layer of methodological difficulty. Audiences for media texts are widely dispersed. Bringing people together to act as an audience for the sake of study creates an artificial situation that may lead audiences to respond differently than they would under ordinary conditions. Research subjects tend to give researchers the responses they think the researchers want, and/or subjects may be, "shy about expressing their thoughts and opinions in such a contrived situation" (Jhally & Lewis, 1992: 10).

Production Studies

Relatively few researchers have studied sport-media production. However, the completed studies offer insights into how sports reporters manufacture news (Lowes, 1997) and how gender and other identity categories influence news production (Pedersen et al., 2003; Whisenant et al., 2004), why newspaper work routines contribute to the marginalization of women's sports (Theberge & Cronk, 1986), how Olympic ice hockey coverage produces nationalism (MacNeill, 1996), and how the globalization of politics, economics and culture affects television production (Silk, 1999; 2001; Silk & Amis, 2000). These insights are essential because textual analysis and reception studies both are premised on the assumption that media producers tend to reproduce and/or represent the ideologies and interests of society's dominant classes. Production studies are reminders that fluid work processes and other environmental factors both participate in *and* mitigate against ideological reproduction.

A recent and fascinating trend in production studies is to examine how sport and media organizations mobilize in response to crisis. Wenner (2004) used a textual analysis of news stories to understand how corporate stakeholders framed the "crisis" of Janet Jackson's infamous "wardrobe malfunction" during halftime of the 2004 Super Bowl. Domingo (2003) explained how Chicago Cubs management mobilized within twenty-four hours to respond when a broken bat revealed team superstar, Sammy Sosa, was using a corked bat. These studies clearly illustrate how media and corporate elites mobilize language and symbols to consolidate their social and cultural hegemony.

Reception Studies

Marxist and post-structuralist forms of cultural studies assume the meaning of a text is formed through a complex interaction between producers, consumers and texts. Audiences are not passive receivers of culture but active interpreters. Though producers have a somewhat greater power to make and disseminate meanings, audiences have the power to resist hegemonic ideology and to create readings that give them pleasure (Fiske, 1991). To date, sports studies scholars have analyzed audiences in three ways. First, they have utilized quantitative, survey methods (e.g., Gantz & Wenner, 1995; Gantz et al., 1995a; Gantz et al., 1995b). Second, they have studied fans at live sporting events using ethnographic and other qualitative methods (White & Wilson, 1998). Third, they have conducted qualitative studies of sport-media consumers. The last is the smallest category, but such studies have utilized creative methods to address important issues. Duncan and Brummett analyzed the ways women resist the hegemonic ideology of televised football. Wilson and Sparks (1996) studied the different ways white and black teenagers interpret Nike advertising. Mitrano (1999) was a virtual observer of Hartford Whaler fans using the Internet to discuss the demise of their favorite ice hockey team. Bruce (1998) investigated how women's basketball fans challenged stereotypic depictions and descriptions of female players. And Plymire and Forman examined how sports fans use Internet newsgroups to negotiate the meanings of sex, gender and sexuality in women's sport (2000; 2001; Forman & Plymire, in press). Despite the relative paucity of audience reception studies, these works play an important role as they, like production studies, provide a context from which textual analysis can proceed.

Textual Analyses

The overwhelming majority of sport-media studies completed over the past decade have been textual analyses. Over that period, many researchers have made notable contributions; only a few can be mentioned here. Significantly, 63 per cent of the textual studies over the past decade have looked at the relationship between media representations and the perpetuation of patriarchal and sexist gender norms. Consistently, these studies have found that sports media tend to reproduce sexist ideologies of sexual difference that reify sport as a male preserve. Some examples: photographs of Olympic athletes emphasize sexual difference and reified patriarchal norms (Duncan, 1990). Print media and television cover male and female athletes differently (Kane & Parks, 1992) Images in *Sports Illustrated for Kids* depict more boys engaged in vigorous activity than girls (Duncan & Sayaovong, 1990). Magazine articles about women tennis players reinforce the image of sport as a male preserve (Hilliard, 1984). The Australian sport media legitimate masculine hegemony (McKay & Rowe, 1987). Advertisements in women's magazines portray women as sedentary consumers, despite the growth in women's sport and fitness participation (Duquin, 1989). And televised sport constructs a master narrative of masculinity (Messner et al., 2000).

Epistemology

Epistemology is the philosophy or theory of the basis or grounds of knowledge. Epistemologies for qualitative research differ significantly from traditional quantitative epistemologies in several ways. Qualitative research typically adopts an inductive approach to reasoning that contrasts to the deductive approach of quantitative social science. Quantitative deductive social science reasoning proceeds from the general or theoretical to the particular. A deductive scientist begins with a theory, derives testable hypotheses from that theory, and collects data to test the hypothesis. Social scientists call this form of reasoning "top down," as it works downward from theory to data.

In contrast, qualitative inductive reasoning proceeds from particular facts to general principles. Inductive researchers begin with broad research questions rather than with a specific theory and/or testable hypotheses. They collect data and build mid-range theories from the ground up. These grounded theories emerge from the data and are constantly subject to change and revision as new data is collected.

A deductive, positivist study begins with a general principle or theory that purports to explain all or part of social life. For example, the overarching theory of the effects tradition is that media have direct effects on social behavior, attitudes and values. Based on that theory, quantitative researchers derive axioms – propositions that are assumed without proof for the purpose of study. From those axioms the researchers suggest hypotheses – provisional theories that can be tested through experimentation. The researchers devise studies that will test the hypotheses, collect data, and finally, using statistical methods report to what extent the data support their hypotheses. If they find statistically significant relationships between the variables in their studies, then they can make strong, general theoretical statements. The validity of those generalizations is assured (in theory, at least) by the rigor of the empirical method. Positivist empiricists design their experiments to eliminate or neutralize the influences of extraneous variables so that they can make positive statements about reality. Positivism is the assumption that reality can be known precisely and exactly. Empirical research, which is the systematic and controlled collection of data, is fundamental to positivism. Positivist researchers assume they can know the answer to their research questions, if they strictly control their data identification and collection.

Qualitative research begins with a different understanding of "reality." Positivists assume there exists a single, objective reality that can be measured directly using proper instruments. Qualitative researchers are more skeptical. They assume reality is subjective and/or socially constructed. In other words, they presume the ways that human beings experience reality are the products of human social interaction. Moreover, though the material world exists, qualitative researchers assume the meanings of that world do not exist prior to human interpretation. Accordingly, though qualitative researchers also employ empirical methods of data collection, they do not assume, as positivists do, that their data provide an unambiguous or transparent perspective on an objective reality. That does not mean that qualitative researchers need not be careful with research design and/or methods. It does mean that qualitative researchers approach their data with a level of skepticism positivists need not. Reflecting the skepticism of the perspective, qualitative researchers use inductive reasoning, a different sort of logic than do positivist researchers.

Inductive researchers build general statements or theories on the basis of systematic observations. Thus, the generalizations derived from inductive research are more varied and specific because each particular research setting is liable to produce different findings. As a result of the particularity of grounded inductive research, its findings do not have as much external validity as deductive studies. That is, the results of one inductive study may not be generalized to a wide range of different situations. However, the results of qualitative research offer a more complex, and arguably, therefore, more accurate picture of social interactions, which can be complex and ambiguous. Therefore, well-designed qualitative studies can have very strong internal validity. That is they can claim to describe the research setting quite accurately, perhaps more so than deductive studies which sacrifice accuracy at the level of the individual case in order to make broad generalizations. Deductive, quantitative research privileges studies that utilize large, random samples of specific research populations. This sort of study allows the researcher to make broad generalizations. However, the same type of study requires the researcher to narrow his or her focus, so as not to allow extraneous variables to interfere with the controlled collection of data. As a result of this narrow focus, the complexity of social interactions is obscured. In contrast, the inductive approach allows qualitative sport-media researchers to embrace the complexity of interactions between producers, consumers and texts. Thus, qualitative researchers are more sensitive to emerging themes that may challenge received knowledge and existing theories. The goal of inductive research is not an objective or general theory but a thick description of the particular that may offer a starting point for future research.

Designing and Implementing Research

Typically, qualitative sport-media research begins with a general question about the relationship between the production and consumption of media content. For example, Lowes (1997) began his study of the sports department of a daily newspaper wondering why such publications devote most of their space to commercial spectator sports while virtually ignoring non-commercial participant-oriented sports. Similarly, Theberge and Cronk (1986) wondered why daily newspapers covered men's sports to the virtual exclusion of women's. Those general questions drove the organization of Lowes' and Theberge and Cronk's research. To address their general questions, they adapted strategies of studying journalistic work routines that had been utilized successfully in classic media studies (e.g., Tuchman, 1978). Their research questions were refined to address the impact of organizational structure on media content and/or the reproduction of hegemonic social values, such as the primacy of commercial and patriarchal values in mediated sport. Studies of sport-media production conducted more recently have shifted focus from the immediate influence of time-pressures work routines on individual workers to the influence of globalization on the "labor processes involved in the production of [an] event" (Silk, 1999: 113). Thus a goal of contemporary research is to identify and connect local practices to specific global economic, social and political forces (Andrews, 2003; Silk & Andrews, 2001).

The goals of textual analysis also reflect an interest in connecting specific practices to broader social and cultural forces. McDonald and Birrell (1999) recommend "reading" sporting events and celebrities as texts as a method of interrogating relationships of social power. By reading sport as a text, they argue, critics can "connect seemingly discreet incidents and events that are generated within the world of sport to the larger social world" (McDonald and Birrell 1999: 283). This is possible because "social life is composed of complex, often contradictory meanings and signifying systems accessible through ... innumerable cultural artifacts or texts." Furthermore, the meaning of a text is "ideologically coded and affected by political struggles related to age, race, and class divisions" (McDonald and Birrell 1999: 291). In other words, texts and their meaning are constituted in specific social and cultural practices and contexts, and those meanings may, to a great extent, be read from the text – if we know the context in which the text was constructed.

These broad assumptions have led a multitude of researchers to ask variations on the question, "Given current social and cultural conditions, what is the meaning of this/these sport-media texts?" Some specific examples give an idea of the range of possibilities suggested by this seemingly simple question. White and Gillett asked how advertisements in *Flex* magazine "promote and legitimate a dominance-based masculinity" (1994: 19) which helps men to cope with a perceived loss of social dominance and self-control. Messner, Dunbar and Hunt (2000) asked what do the most popular televised sports among boys tell young men about the meaning of masculinity in late capitalist, consumer culture. Plymire (1999) asked how and why did track and field journalists argue that record-setting Chinese women runners were guilty of using performance-enhancing drugs? Daddario asked how NBC's 1992 coverage of the summer Olympics used a "female narrative form" (1997: 104) derived from television melodrama to appeal to a desirable market segment of young female viewers.

Fewer studies of sport-media audiences have been completed, but identifying appropriate research goals and questions poses little difficulty. The question of how audiences interpret, decode, and or construct the meaning of texts has fascinated cultural theorists, even if it has remained a difficult topic of study (Fiske, 1991; Hall, 1980; Livingstone, 1993; Steiner, 1991) According to current media theories, consumers of mass media products do not merely decode the messages producers have structured into the text. Rather, readers actively make meaning of the text. They have a stake in the struggle for meaning based on their social location and race, class, gender and sexual identities. In a sense, the text is incomplete until the audience has finished with it. Based on that assumption, some researchers have asked assembled audiences to interpret specific media texts (Condit, 1991; Duncan & Brummett, 1993; Jhally & Lewis, 1992; Morely, 1980). Other researchers have collected "found materials," such as letters to the editor (Ang, 1985; Steiner, 1991) or postings to Internet newsgroups (Mitrano, 1999; Forman & Plymire, in press; 2000; 2001). The latter method has the advantage of spontaneity, as the researcher makes no attempt to guide the authors of found materials to read or interpret given texts.

Collecting Data

Qualitative research has an emergent quality – in many cases, data are only identified in the process of being collected. Though researchers begin their efforts with a plan for data collection, that plan is flexible. As a study progresses, the researcher may repeatedly exercise the option of expanding the pool of data to reflect new understandings of the project and newly identified data possibilities.

Textual Analyses White and Gillett justified their use of *Flex* magazine advertisements because those ads "stress the intrinsic value of bodybuilding practices and the development of a muscular physique" (1994: 21) within the context of a dominant ideology of what it means to be male in contemporary culture. Furthermore, *Flex* has a wide readership, a large percentage of which read the ads and buy the products advertised (White and Gillett 1994: 22). White and Gillett conducted a descriptive analysis of all 916 advertisements that appeared in twelve issues of the magazine. They then completed a close semiotic reading of five selected advertisements that seemed representative of dominant themes they had derived from the larger sample. These strategies work well with textual data because researchers can review a large body of potential data before beginning their work and decide the limits of their investigations.

Production Studies Not all potential "data sets" in qualitative media studies are quite as static as are published texts. Production studies require significant planning, but the dynamic character of the work environments demands far more flexibility of researchers. Theberge and Cronk (1986) spent about a year with the ten full and part-time reporters on the staff of a newspaper in a southwestern US city of about 250,000 people. Theberge and Cronk's study built on Tuchman's (1978) and Fishman's (1980) work and found that the daily routines of sports journalists determine what stories and events are deemed "newsworthy" and create a climate in which women's sports are typically marginalized. Lowes (1997) spent four months as a non-participant observer and interviewer in the sports department of a large newspaper in Canada. He found that reporters' work routines determine that news of commercial sports dominates the papers while non-commercial sports receive little coverage. MacNeill (1996) took a slightly different approach to her study of the production of Olympic ice hockey. In addition to her fieldwork and interviews, she analyzed historical, archival and contemporary documents to understand the political and social contexts of the production of the Olympics and the "historical production of codes of sport and media traditions" (MacNeill 1996: 105). Her study revealed how the television crew constructed a sporting narrative emphasizing hegemonic definitions of nation and masculinity, within a context of labor practices that reinforced specific modes of media production and media power. Silk completed a review of "historical and contemporary documents that outlined the political, economic, and cultural contexts ... [and] industry and network codes of practice" (1999: 115) before embarking on an ethnographic study of Canadian television coverage of the 1995 Canada Cup of Soccer. His ethnographic method was to "immerse" himself in the production process; that immersion developed a particular shape as he gained access to and developed relationships with crew-members and decision-makers for The Sports Network's (TSN) production team. In this setting, Silk could not adequately plan his data collection in advance, as he could not hope to anticipate all of the people and situations he would encounter. Thus he, and other ethnographic researchers, must be alert to the possibility that every new situation is potentially a new set of data that will significantly impact the overall shape of the results and analysis of the research.

Reception Studies As noted above, few empirical studies of sport-media audiences have been completed. On a pragmatic level, the dearth of qualitative audience studies in the sport/media literature is understandable. Audience research techniques include focus groups (Wilson & Sparks, 1996), interviews (Bruce, 1998), ethnographies (Duncan & Brummett, 1993), and discovery of found materials (Mitrano, 1999; Forman & Plymire, in press; Plymire & Forman, 2000; 2001). The strength of these methods is that they provide an in-depth look at the complexities of media consumption within the context of people's daily lives (Morley, 1992; Whannel, 1998). However, these methods set up considerable roadblocks to study. First, media consumption is often a private affair, and the introduction of researchers into the setting may change consumption habits dramatically. Second, these techniques require the mobilization of substantial time and resources, things not always readily available to sport/media researchers, especially those working in departments of Kinesiology and related disciplines. Third, audiences are widely dispersed and must be assembled for a study. The methods used to assemble an audience – "snowballing," advertising, and researcher involvement in social networks – all contribute to the problems of generalizability – the results of audience studies rarely can be generalized since subjects are usually few and in homogeneous group. Fourth, audience members may be shy about speaking out in a "contrived" research setting, especially if the researchers want them to speak about taboo subjects, such as attitudes about race, class and gender (Jhally & Lewis, 1992). Regardless of their personal views, research subjects may understand what sort of comments are politically correct and may edit out incorrect speech, or remain silent, if they wish to cast themselves in a good light.

Reflecting the difficulties and the promise of ethnographic fan research is Duncan and Brummett's (1993) study of male, female and coed groups of football fans. Duncan and Brummett observed three small groups of fans (n=10) watching eleven hours of National Football League broadcasts. The small sample size and short duration of the study greatly reduce the generalizability of Duncan and Brummett's results, but the ethnographic glimpse into the lives of football viewers adds valuable empirical evidence to a discussion of fans of televised sport. Bruce (1998) also relied on a small sample of sports fans in her examination of televised women's basketball, as did Wilson and Sparks (1996) in their examination of fan interpretations of Nike advertisements. Researchers Kelley and Turley (2004) creatively combined textual analysis with effects research, using USA Today Ad Meter scores to judge the impact of Super Bowl commercials on audience affect. This method circumvented the dilemma of producing an audience, whilst offering some insight into the pleasures of viewing.

However, though the results of no single audience study can be generalized widely, the results of the studies combine to offer some important insights that support the theory that fans actively interpret sport-media products using interpretive frameworks shaped by their social locations and life experiences.

One strategy used by media researchers to circumvent some obstacles to audience research is to collect "found" materials such as letters to the editor and/or the producer of television programs (D'Acci, 1994; Hobson, 1982). Linda Steiner (1991), for example, sampled the contents of the "No Comment" section of *Ms.,* which contains print advertisements deemed so sexist and offensive that the *Ms.* reader could interpret their meaning without editorial comment. Ang's (1985) classic study of the Dutch audience for the American television show *Dallas* used found materials as well.

Mitrano (1999) and Plymire and Forman (2000; 2001; Forman & Plymire, in press) have studied postings to Internet newsgroups catering to sports fans as found materials. Newsgroup and/or bulletin board postings are like letters-to-the-editor. They are public materials, even if they are sometimes highly personal (Paccagnella, 1997: 8), and they address an audience of like-minded individuals, which is what letters-to-the-editor do, even if they are addressed to an editor. However, Internet postings have several advantages over traditional found materials. The first advantage is the sheer volume of postings available. Ang's (1985) landmark study of *Dallas* was based on just forty-two letters written by fans. In contrast, Mitrano (1999) collected messages from 112 people during fourteen weeks as a virtual observer on an Internet newsgroup catering to fans of the Hartford Whalers. Plymire and Forman have amassed collections of postings ranging from a low of 72 (2001) to a high of almost 1000 (in press).

Analyzing Data

Every type of qualitative sport-media research utilizes an inductive method of data analysis and interpretation. That is, all derive theoretical statements from an examination of data. However, each type utilizes strategies and methods specific to its particular goals.

Production Studies Ethnographers confront substantial epistemological problems when they begin to analyze and interpret their data. Common sense says researchers "discover" new knowledge through their fieldwork. In stark contrast to that assumption, contemporary ethnographers assume that they actively construct knowledge as they interpret and analyze their field notes and write up their ethnographic text. Meaning is conveyed through the writer's editorial choices and editorial decisions influence the extent to which the author represents the indigenous meanings of the group being studied. Ethnographers must beware of allowing their own interpretive frameworks to obscure indigenous meanings. The writing process must involve a measure of reflexivity as researchers contemplate the extent to which their presence has changed the research setting, their personal perspectives have shaped descriptions of the scene and interpretations of the data, and/or their theoretical and intellectual frameworks have transformed indigenous meanings. Though ethnographic writing always implies a textual construction of reality, ethnographers apply particular strategies to insure a measure of indigenous meaning in the final product. One strategy, outlined by Emerson, Fretz, and Shaw (1995), is to begin with an "open coding" of field notes in which the researchers complete a line-by-line reading of their notes, ask general questions of their notes, and develop a multitude of possible categories of analysis. From this process, ethnographers produce running commentaries on their notes from which they derive themes. Ideally, the themes come not from preset categories but from an open consideration of how events and items in the field notes link together. After identifying themes, ethnographers sort the data again to focus in on core themes, again using a line-by-line analysis, and connect their core themes to more data, if possible, and then theorize patterns and relationships between themes. Having completed this two-step process of close reading and coding, researchers reflect on the data and the process and compose mid-range theories of behavior and meaning grounded in their fieldwork.

A second strategy of contemporary ethnographers is to foreground their presence in the research setting. Sparkes (2002) explains traditional objectivist and positivist science writing encourages researchers to hide their authorial presence using the third person and the passive voice. In this type of writing "data reveal," "themes emerge," and "studies show," as if these inanimate concepts – data, themes and studies – supplant human agency in the production of knowledge. Sparkes identifies several alternative forms of writing that reveal the authority of the researcher in the production of knowledge, one of which is particularly relevant to this discussion: the realist tale. In a realist tale, the author identifies him or herself in the introduction to his or her work in order to reveal his or her perspective and how it motivates and grounds the research and writing process. However, after revealing themselves, realists then retreat behind the façade of the passive voice and the third-person account in order to justify what Sparkes calls "interpretive omnipotence" (2002: 46). The advantage to the realist approach, as opposed to the traditional scientific one, is that realists make significant attempts to privilege the voices of their research subjects; as a result, in a realist tale it is the subjects who reveal the meaning of the situation, not the reified abstraction of the data.

Reception Studies Audience studies pose some of the same challenges to data analysis and interpretation as production ethnographies but with some added twists. The research setting for production ethnography is, typically, naturalistic. Though the presence of the researcher changes the research setting to a greater or lesser degree, people producing a sports program or a newspaper sports page have vested interests in continuing to do their jobs as if the researcher was not present. Too much attention to the researcher would detract from workers' ability to do their jobs, given the pressures of production. Audience studies typically take place in contrived settings; as mentioned above, those settings and the presence of researchers may influence audience reactions to sensitive subjects. Moreover, ethnographic audience studies intrude on leisure time in ways that almost compel participants to change their viewing or reading habits. Far from forgetting the researcher and getting on with business, as participants in production studies may, subjects in audience studies are much less likely to forget the researcher and act as they usually do. Therefore, researchers must necessarily be very skeptical of the data they have collected. Again, the method outlined by Emerson et al. (1995) provides a concrete framework researchers can use to examine their data, but using that framework does not lessen the need for researchers to be reflexive about their impact on their subjects' expressed opinions.

Textual Analyses Fiske identifies content analysis as an empirical method "designed to produce an objective, measurable, verifiable account of the manifest content of messages" (1990: 136). An example of a purely quantitative content analysis of media texts is Lumpkin and Williams' (1991) study of references to race and gender in *Sports Illustrated.* The authors counted the number of times males and females and blacks and whites were showcased in all 3,273 feature articles that appeared in *SI* from 1954 to 1987 and listed the descriptive words used to describe women athletes. Qualitative researchers may not rely on such simple methods, but they rarely "read" a sport-media text without first completing some form of preliminary quantitative analysis.

For example in their qualitative study of anti-drug campaigns in athletics, Davis and Delano report, "A disproportionate number of the images found in the anti-drug media featured white men" (1992: 3), implying that they counted the number of times white men appeared in the materials they examined. Nonetheless, the substance of critical textual analysis is derived using qualitative methods. Most authors using qualitative methods imply that qualitative analysis requires a feel for the subject as well as a rigorous method. To cite Davis and Delano again, "We systematically analyzed all of these texts by teasing out and categorizing various themes, giving special attention to the various assumptions and interpretations that the textual content and structures seemed to suggest" (1992: 3)

From that description, we know that Davis and Delano worked in a systematic fashion (though they give us no details of their system), and the phrase "teasing out" themes implies their method was emergent rather than prescriptive. Themes do not emerge without human assistance, of course, and we may infer that the authors submitted their data to a coding process similar to that outlined by Emerson, et al. We do know the authors validated their findings by comparing the independent readings of two researchers before setting forth the themes and patterns they reported.

Writing Up

The top journals in sport sociology all require authors to adhere to the *Publication Manual of the American Psychological Association.* The American Psychological Association (APA) sets out strict guidelines for manuscript preparation, including an outline of the parts of a manuscript: title page, abstract, introduction, method, results, discussion and references. However, the top journals in sport sociology allow authors a bit more leeway in manuscript organization than does the APA, as many qualitative studies employ methods and rhetorical strategies not anticipated by the APA. The two most prevalent of these rhetorical strategies are the analytical essay and the thematic narrative (Emerson et al., 1995).

An analytical essay begins with a thesis statement that guides the reader through the author's argument. Authors of analytical essays typically will include reviews of literature as bases for their theses and may sketch short outlines of their data collection and analytical methods. The preponderance of the essay, however, will consist of a logical argument reinforced with evidence. The challenge for essayists is to compose their arguments in such a way as to persuade their readers. To facilitate the process essayists must use evidence effectively. Typically authors organize their essays into a series of sections, each of which contains a claim and supporting or refuting evidence. In a textual analysis, the evidence will often be a quotation from or a description of a text or texts that illustrates a general point. Messner et al. (2000) utilize this rhetorical strategy in their analysis of television programming in which they defend the thesis that televised sports construct a version of hegemonic masculinity that champions violence and aggression. They signal their rhetorical intentions early when they assert, "This article, based on a textual analysis, *presents the argument* that televised sports, and their accompanying commercials, consistently present boys with a narrow portrait of masculinity, which we call the Televised Sports Manhood Formula" (Messner et al., 2002: 380, emphasis added).

A thematic narrative contrasts with the analytical essay as it begins with an examination of evidence and builds toward a conclusion in which the authors will express the central ideas they have elaborated throughout the narrative. Whereas an analytical essay will begin with a clearly identifiable thesis statement, a thematic essay will usually begin with a statement of general purpose, such as this,

> The article *considers* the ways in which the Australian print media dealt with issues of gender, femininity, and sexuality to illuminate some of the processes framing women and global sport. Working from the premise that an understanding of the gender dimension of global sport will contribute to more general academic knowledge of global processes, the article thus *seeks to contribute* to debates over global sport, media, and gender. (Stevenson, 2002: 209, emphasis added)

The specific theory proposed by this thematic essay does not emerge (or is not identified), until the end of the essay.

Whether one is writing an analytical essay or a thematic narrative, the central task of the author is to present his or her evidence in a way that convinces the reader of the authority of the text. Effective use of evidence requires organizing the text into a logical format and rigorous citation of sources. Clear and concise strategies for using evidence effectively are outlined by Emerson et al. (1995) and on the website of the Indiana University writing center http://www.indiana.edu/~wts/wts/evidence.html.

Verifying Results

All researchers ultimately must address issues of validity and credibility. Quantitative researchers assume there exists a single paramount reality that can be objectively measured by a scrupulous scientist applying a rigorous method. To ensure, to their own satisfaction, that the results of their research are legitimate, quantitative researchers apply a series of criteria to test the appropriateness of their research design and measuring instruments. First, researchers must ask whether or not their work is valid. Three kinds of validity must be addressed: construct validity, whether or not the study measured what it claimed; internal validity, whether uncontrolled extraneous variables suggest alternative explanations of findings; and external validity, whether a properly chosen random sample allows findings to be generalized to larger population. Second, quantitative researchers must ask whether or not the results of their studies are reliable. That is, whether the instruments used produce accurate and consistent measurements.

In qualitative research, the measuring instrument is the researcher or researchers. It is they who collect and evaluate data. Furthermore, qualitative researchers typically do not assume that a single, objective, paramount reality exists to be measured; instead they assume that reality is constructed through human social interactions. Thus the accuracy and consistency of qualitative data is called into question by the standards of quantitative research. Qualitative researchers have, however, developed their own standards to address validity and reliability. Messner, Dunbar and Hunt (2000) analyzed 23 broadcast hours of the sports most often watched by boys. At least two of the research team watched each hour of programming then compared their independent readings of the programs in order to validate their findings, before the group teased out "common themes and patterns" (Messner et al., 2000: 381) from the data. Like Messner et al., Davis and Delano attempted to anticipate a variety of possible interpretations of each text to help prevent their biases and/or a priori assumptions guiding their analysis. Moreover, they employed a system of categorization that compelled them to consider and reconsider their articulation of themes. Each of these strategies requires researchers to attend to the data rather than to select those pieces of data that fit with their research goals.

Ethnographers and interviewers likewise are scrupulous about listening to their data/subjects and testing their conclusions before finalizing. Though scholars who conduct, write up and publish their research retain a measure of authority not matched by their research subjects, contemporary scholars are more reflexive about the role of the observer/author as a creator as well as an evaluator of ethnographic data. Reflexivity is the process of foregrounding one's participation in the research setting and evaluating how one's social location, perspectives and biases, as well as one's editorial choices, affect one's representations of "reality." Though the field researcher cannot and does not attempt to represent objective reality, the reflexive process is a substantial guard against more egregious misrepresentations of the indigenous perspective of the research subjects.

Exemplary Studies

Production Studies

Silk (1999) studied how a Television Sports Network (TSN) broadcast crew interpreted the Canadian Cup of Soccer for a combined Canadian and international audience. He asked whether the production team would create an image of "nation" for the domestic audience or would appeal to a fragmented international audience using a more "global logic" (Silk 1999: 115). He identified three factors that might explain the logic of production: (1) narrative constructions produced by the crew, (2) the assumed target audience for the telecasts, and (3) the crew's intended or preferred interpretations of events.

He began his research with a content analysis of documents pertaining to the social, historical, economic and cultural contexts of the broadcasts and induced from that examination that the production crew assumed a global audience for their broadcasts. He surmised that the telecasts reflected the crew's intention to address that audience rather than a strictly national Canadian audience. Once versed in the strategic context of the telecasts, he focused on immersing himself in the day-to-day processes of production and in the working lives of the team members. Immersion meant spending substantial time with the crew in every aspect of production for the duration of the event. During the telecasts, he recorded his observations from within the production truck. On other occasions he interviewed the crew formally and informally and sometimes acted as a participant observer when the team asked him to evaluate camera positions and lens-eye views of the action. Silk followed his analysis of field production with a semiotic textual reading of taped telecasts to tease out narrative themes and structures and with observations and interviews at the network's corporate offices.

Silk's multilayered approach breaks new ground in production studies and lends weight to his statement, "These approaches directed attention to preferred readings and positions and, when coupled with an historical analysis, of the material means of the productions and professional discursive practices, offered a robust form of reference for examining cultural production" (1999: 116).

Reception Studies

Bruce (1998) challenged the implication that female consumers of sports texts internalize "trivializing, stereotyping, devaluing, or ambivalent media messages" manifested in televised women's basketball games. She conducted in-depth interviews of six female fans of televised women's basketball. She chose her subjects based on their knowledge of and passion for basketball and on their potential ability to think critically and reflectively about their enjoyment of televised sport, as she wanted subjects "who would be well placed to challenge preferred messages."

She conducted her interviews with individuals or with pairs of women, depending on how the women typically viewed televised women's basketball. She first asked the women open questions about their basketball viewing, then asked the women to comment on her textual and content analyses of programming. She used these comments to amend and adjust her analyses of programming, "to confirm, clarify, and refine major themes, and raise issues that were important to other viewers." This inductive and reflexive process led her to identify themes that connected women's viewing and interpretive practices to their biographies and to cultural histories and values. She concluded that her subjects demonstrated the ability to think critically and read intertextually in order to resist the sexism of preferred or encoded meanings of televised sports texts. She recommended that further studies of audience interpretations of media texts must be "an integral part of research" to correct the overemphasis on identifying the preferred meanings of texts. Bruce's study is a small but significant example of what Morley calls a "parallel analysis," as it tests the researcher's reading of sporting texts against the interpretations of fans.

Textual Analyses

Explanations of textual analysis are typically more complicated than the methods themselves, for example, Plymire (1999) selected her sources based on the assumption that news stories do not transparently represent facts but tend of reproduce the ideological positions of reporters' sources (Tuchman, 1978). She borrowed a method of qualitative discourse analysis from Van Dijk (1991) that pulls apart the rhetorical structure of a text by examining how the "subsequent propositions of a text are bound together" to produce coherent meaning and how readers of a text are able to understand the text using a shared set of meanings. (Plymire, 1999: 163) Van Dijk assumes that details of a story, such as the race, gender and alleged personality characteristics of the people being described, invite the reader to make leaps of logic and create positive or negative associations. These implicit links, as much as any explicit arguments in the text, contribute to the meaning of the text. Plymire collected every available story written about the Chinese women runners in the US press, then selected and analyzed each story that actively "made sense" or "editorialized" about the cause and meaning of the Chinese performances. She read those stories to identify and outline the arguments offered to condemn the Chinese athletes. She then contextualized those news stories and arguments using theoretical and historical writings on ideologies of drugs, race, gender and nation. Moreover she demonstrated that the stories were composed in ways that delegitimated the Chinese achievements in order to protect the imagined superiority and expertise of American track and field, despite the failure of the US to produce equally outstanding performers.

Plymire's process of contextualization was grounded in the set of assumptions explicated by McDonald and Birrell (1999). Plymire assumed the stories of the Chinese women were about social and political power organized along lines of sex, gender, race and nation. The stories attained special importance in the geopolitical climate of the early 1990s when the People's Republic of China was resisting US attempts at global hegemony over military, political and economic policy.

Review

All three types of sport-media study can and have been used to good effect. However, recent studies that cross the boundaries between these categories of analysis highlight the potential of studies that utilize the "robust frame" identified by Silk (1999: 116). Furthermore, the relative lack of audience studies remains a serious lacuna in the sport-media literature. To fill that lacuna and to move in the direction indicated by Silk, researchers need to re-imagine (but not necessarily dispense with) the Gramscian/hegemony framework that has undergirded so much sport-media analysis. Gramscian hegemony theory represented to sports studies scholars an advance beyond theories that conceptualized "mass media" as agents of "cultural imperialism" (Roach, 1997). The fundamental premise of the cultural imperialism paradigm was that powerful media institutions imposed "ideological domination" on passive audiences (Rivera-Perez, 1996: 37). The 1980s saw the development of active audience theories (Ang, 1985; Fiske, 1991; Hall, 1980) that suggested audience members had the power to decode ideological messages in ways that resisted the power of the dominant classes. Fiske, for example, objected to the theoretical contention that television producers encoded dominant ideology into texts where that ideology then "interpellated" or hailed viewers as "Althusserian subject[s]-in-ideology" (1991:

346). Fiske believed Althusser was too pessimistic because he assumed, a priori, that capitalism would homogenize social groups into an "unthinking mass" (1991: 347). Fiske insisted instead that subcultural resistance was alive and well in western societies. According to Fiske, Hall's (1980) essay on encoding and decoding of media texts was an improvement on Althusser, as Hall suggested audience members might read from one of three subject positions, but Fiske contended that empirical testing (e.g., Morley, 1980) showed that audiences had more power to produce meanings that suited them than Hall's theory allowed.

Fiske's theory was well intentioned, but critics immediately attacked him for being overly optimistic about the power of the audience to undermine the power of textual producers. Condit (1991) suggested audience members do not need open or ambiguous texts in order to produce resistant meanings, as Fiske had implied, but that the pleasure and satisfaction of oppositional decoding is limited by the amount of work required to produce a resistant reading. Furthermore, she asserted the amount of interpretive decoding audience members can do is dependent on the strength of their interpretive frameworks – one must have a strong counter-hegemonic framework to successfully resist a text that denotes meanings opposed to one's own interests. Despite continued interest in the active audience (D'Acci, 1994; Jhally & Lewis, 1992; Radway, 1991; Steiner, 1991), questions about audience activity continued. Gibson accused Fiske of "cultural populism" (2000: 253). Morley called Fiske's insistence on textual polysemy and audience resistance "facile" (1993: 14). And Radway demonstrated in her study of romance readers that resistance might a momentary and "mild protest" that might simultaneously "disarm that impulse [for reform]" even as it provided temporary emotional satisfaction (1991: 213).

Recently Rivera-Perez (1996) suggested audience research would benefit from a reintroduction of ideology into the analytical equation. According to Rivera-Perez, Fiske's theory of polysemy encouraged many scholars to focus on audience resistance to the exclusion of consideration of how social institutions and ideologies constrain people's lives and choices. Echoing those sentiments Gibson insists reading practices are "embedded in a network of overdetermined social relations and structures" that are "reproduced within the microprocesses that constitute our daily lives" (2000: 254). The reintroduction of ideology, however, calls for scholarship that is multilayered and contextual, in the fashion of Silk's work, rather than a return to the more deterministic versions of hegemony theory that motivated much sport-media research in the late 1980s and 1990s. Ien Ang (1996) offers perhaps the most useful recent theoretical permutation. Ang suggests that one may assume both that the mass media audience is active and that the media have an unequal power to set the cultural agenda in ways that favor the economic, political and social status quo. Ang argues media producers and their corporate sponsors are cognizant that audiences are both active and fragmented into "niches made up of flexible tastes and preferences" (1996: 11). To cater to this audience, producers, such as those who produced the Canada Cup of Soccer for TSN, create "specialized programming" (Ang, 1996: 12) that caters to both individualized and globalized tastes. Individualized, as no audience member need read from a given or inherent subject position; globalized, as audience members are invited to see themselves as part of identity groups that transcend national boundaries as well as the limits of traditional identity politics. Says Ang, "the active audience has nothing to do with 'resistance', but everything to do with incorporation: the imperative of [consumer] choice *interpellates* the audience as active" (1996: 12, emphasis in original).

Ang's re-conceptualization of the active audience meshes well with recent studies of sport-media production (e.g., Silk, 1999; Silk, 2001; Silk & Amis, 2000). The challenge for sport-media scholars is to create studies that apply Silk's multilayered approach to textual and audience analysis, too.

References

Andrews, D.L. (2003). Sport and the Transnationalizing Media Corporation [Electronic version]. *Journal of Media Economics*, 16, 235–252.

Ang, I. (1985). *Watching Dallas: Soap Opera and Melodramatic Imagination.* New York: Metheun.

—— (1996). *Living Room Wars: Rethinking Media Audiences for a Postmodern World.* London: Routledge.

Bennett, T. (1981). *Popular Culture: Themes and Issues.* Buckingham, UK: Open University Press.

Birrell, S. (1984). Studying Gender in Sport: A Feminist Perspective. In N. Theberge & P. Donnelley (eds). *Sport and the Sociological Imagination.* Fort Worth: Texas Christian University Press.

—— & McDonald, M.G. (2000). *Reading Sport: Critical Essays on Power and Representation.* Boston: Northeastern University Press.

Brohm, J.M. (1978). *Sport: A Prison of Measured Time.* London: Ink Links.

Bruce, T. (1998). Audience Frustration and Pleasure [Electronic version]. *Journal of Sport and Social Issues*, 22.

Condit, C.M. (1991). The Rhetorical Limits of Polysemy. In R.K. Avery & D. Eason (eds). *Critical Perspectives on Media and Society.* New York: Guilford Press.

D'Acci, J. (1994). *Defining Women: Television and the Case of Cagney and Lacey.* Chapel Hill, NC: University of North Carolina Press.

Daddario, G. (1997). Gendered Sports Programming: 1992 Summer Olympic Coverage and the Feminine Narrative Form. *Sociology of Sport Journal*, 14, 103–20.

Davis, L.R. & Delano, L.C. (1992). Fixing the Boundaries of Physical Gender: Side Effects of Anti-Drug Campaigns in Athletics. *Sociology of Sport Journal*, 9, 1–19.

Domingo, B.A. (2003). Stop Slammin' Sammy: A Theoretical Approach to the First 24 Hours of a Communications Crisis in Sport [Electronic version]. *Public Relations Quarterly*, 48, 20–23.

Duncan, M.C. (1990). Sports Photographs and Sexual Difference: Images of Women and Men in the 1984 and 1988 Olympic Games. *Sociology of Sport Journal*, 7, 22–43.

Duncan, M.C. & Brummett, B. (1993). Liberal and Radical Sources of Female Empowerment in Sport Media. *Sociology of Sport Journal*, 10, 57–72.
Duncan, M.C. & Sayaovong, A. (1990). Photographic Images and Gender in Sports Illustrated for Kids. *Play and Culture*, 3, 91–116.
Duquin, M.E. (1989). Fashion and Fitness: Images in Women's Magazine Advertisements. *Arena*, 13, 97–109.
Edwards, H. (1969). *The Revolt of the Black Athlete*. New York: The Free Press.
Emerson, R.M., Fretz, R.I. & Shaw, L.L. (1995). *Writing Ethnographic Fieldnotes*. Chicago: University of Chicago Press.
Fishman, M. (1980). *Manufacturing the News*. Austin, TX: University of Texas Press.
Fiske, J. (1990). *Introduction to Communication Studies*. London: Routledge.
—— (1991). Television: Polysemy and Popularity. In R.K. Avery & D. Eason (eds). *Critical Perspectives on Media and Society*. New York: Guilford Press.
Forman, P.J. & Plymire, D.C. (in press). Amélie Mauresmo's Muscles: The Lesbian Heroic in Women's Tennis. *Women's Studies Quarterly*.
Gantz, W. & Wenner, L.A. (1995). Fanship and the Television Viewing Experience. *Sociology of Sport Journal*, 12, 56–74.
Gantz, W., Wenner, L.A., Carrico, C. & Knorr, M. (1995a). Assessing the Football Widow Hypothesis: A Coorientation Study of the Role of Televised Sports in Long-Standing Relationships. *Journal of Sport and Social Issues*, 19, 352–76.
—— (1995b). Televised Sports and Marital Relationships. *Sociology of Sport Journal*, 12, 306–23.
Gibson, T.A. (2000). Beyond Cultural Populism: Notes Toward the Critical Ethnography of Media Audiences [Electronic version]. *Journal of Communication Inquiry*, 24, 253–73.
Gitlin, T. (1980). *The Whole World is Watching*. Berkeley: University of California Press.
—— (1985). *Inside Prime Time*. New York: Pantheon.
Glasgow Media Group. (1976). *Bad News*. London: Routledge & Kegan Paul.
—— (1980). *More Bad News*. London: Routledge & Kegan Paul.
—— (1982). *Really Bad News*. London: Writers & Readers.
Gramsci, A. (1971). *Selections from the Prison Notebooks of Antonio Gramsci*, Q. Hoare & G. N. Smith (eds and trans.). New York: International Publishers.
Hall, S. (1977). Culture, Media, and the "Ideological Effect." In J. Curran, M. Gurevitch & J. Woollacott (eds). *Mass Communication and Society*. London: Sage.
—— (1980). Encoding/Decoding. In S. Hall, D. Hobson, A. Lowe & P. Willis (eds). *Culture, Media, Language: Working Papers in Cultural Studies, 1972–1979*. London: Hutchinson.
—— (1985). Signification, Representation, Ideology: Althusser and the Post-Structuralist Debates. *Critical Studies in Mass Communication*, 2, 91–114.
Hall, S., Critcher, C., Jefferson, T., Clarke, J. & Roberts, B. (1978). *Policing the Crisis: Mugging, the State, and Law and Order*. London: Macmillan.
Hilliard, D.C. (1984). Media Images of Male and Female Professional Athletes: An Interpretive Analysis of Magazine Articles. *Sociology of Sport Journal*, 1, 251–62.
Hobson, D. (1982). *Crossroads: The Drama of a Soap Opera*. London: Metheun.
Ingham, A. (1976). Sport and the "New Left": Some Reflections upon Opposition without Praxis. In D.M. Landers (ed.). *Social Problems in Athletics*. Champaign, IL: University of Illinois Press.

Jhally, S. & Lewis, J. (1992). *Enlightened Racism: The Cosby Show, Audiences, and the Myth of the American Dream*. Boulder, CO: Westview Press.

Kane, M.J. & Parks, J.B. (1992). The Social Construction of Gender Difference and Hierarchy in Sport Journalism: Few New Twists on a Very Old Theme. *Women in Sport and Physical Activity Journal*, 1, 49–83.

Kelley, S.W. & Turley, L.W. (2004). The Effect of Content on Perceived Affect of Super Bowl Commercials [Electronic version]. *Journal of Sport Management*, 18, 398–421.

Livingstone, S.M. (1993). The Rise and Fall of Audience Research: An Old Story with a New Ending. In M.R. Levy & M. Gurevitch (eds). *Defining Media Studies*. Oxford: Oxford University Press.

Lowes, M.D. (1997). Sports Page: A Case Study in the Manufacture of Sports News for the Daily Press. *Sociology of Sport Journal*, 14, 143–59.

Lumpkin, A. & Williams, L.D. (1991). An Analysis of *Sports Illustrated* Feature Articles. *Sociology of Sport Journal*, 8, 16–32.

MacNeill, M. (1996). Networks: Producing Olympic Ice Hockey for a National Audience. *Sociology of Sport Journal*, 13, 103–24.

Marx, K. & Engels, F. (1981). *The German Ideology: Part One* 8th printing C.J. Arthur (ed.). New York: International Publishers.

McDonald, M.G. & Birrell, S. (1999). Reading Sport Critically: A Methodology for Interrogating Power. *Sociology of Sport Journal*, 16, 283–300.

McKay, J. & Rowe, D. (1987). Ideology, the Media, and Australian Sport. *Sociology of Sport Journal*, 4, 258–73.

Messner, M., Dunbar, M. & Hunt, D. (2000). The Televised Sport Manhood Formula. *Journal of Sport and Social Issues*, 24, 380–94.

Mitrano, J.R. (1999). The "Sudden Death" of Hockey in Hartford: Sports Fans and Franchise Relocation. *Sociology of Sport Journal*, 16, 134–54.

Morley, D. (1980). *The Nationwide Audience: Structure and Decoding*. London: BFI/OU.

—— (1992). *Television Audiences and Cultural Studies*. London: Routledge.

—— (1993). Active Audience Theory: Pendulums and Pitfalls [Electronic version]. *Journal of Communication*, 43, 13–19.

Nelson, C., Treichler, P.A. & Grossberg, L. 1992. Cultural Studies: An Introduction. In L. Grossberg, C. Nelson & P. Treichler (eds). *Cultural Studies*. London: Routledge.

Paccagnella, L. (1997). Getting the Seat of Your Pants Dirty: Strategies for Ethnographic Research in Virtual Communities [Electronic version]. *Journal of Computer-Mediated Communication*, 3, 1. Retrieved April, 27, 2005. http://www.ascusc.org/jcmc/vol3/issue1/paccagnella.html.

Pedersen, P.M., Whisenant, W.A. & Schneider, R.G. (2003). Using a Content Analysis to Examine the Gendering of Sports Newspaper Personnel and their Coverage [Electronic version]. *Journal of Sport Management*, 18, 376–94.

Peters, J.D. (1994). Genealogical Notes on "the Field." In M.R. Levy & M. Gurevitch (eds). *Defining Media Studies: Reflections on the Future of the Field*. Oxford: Oxford University Press.

Plymire, D.C. (1999). Too Much, too Fast, too Soon: Chinese Women Runners, Accusations of Steroid Use, and the Politics of American Track and Field. *Sociology of Sport Journal*, 16, 155–73.

Plymire, D.C. & Forman, P.J. (2000). Breaking the Silence: Lesbian Fans, the Internet, and the Sexual Politics of Women's Sport. *International Journal of Sexuality and Gender Studies*, 5, 141–53.

—— (2001). Speaking of Cheryl Miller: Interrogating the Lesbian Taboo on a Women's Basketball Newsgroup. *National Women's Studies Association Journal*, 13, 1–21.

Radway, J. (1991). *Reading the Romance: Women, Patriarchy, and Popular Literature.* Chapel Hill, NC: University of North Carolina Press.

Rivera-Perez, L. (1996). Rethinking Ideology: Polysemy, Pleasure, and Hegemony in Television Culture. *Journal of Communication Inquiry*, 20, 37–56.

Roach, C. (1997). Cultural Imperialism and Resistance in Media Theory. *Media, Culture, and Society*, 19, 47–66.

Scott, J. (1971). *The Athletic Revolution.* New York: The Free Press.

Silk, M.L. (1999). Local/Global Flows and Altered Production Practices: Narrative Constructions at the 1995 Canada Cup of Soccer. *International Review for the Sociology of Sport*, 34, 113–24.

—— (2001). Together We're One? The "Place" of the Nation in Media Representations of the 1998 Kuala Lumpur Commonwealth Games. *Sociology of Sport Journal*, 18, 277–302.

Silk, M.L. & Amis, J. (2000). Institutional Pressures and the Production of Televised Sport. *Journal of Sport Management*, 14, 267–92.

Silk, M.L. & Andrews, D. (2001). Beyond a Boundary? *Journal of Sport and Social Issues*, 25, 180–202.

Sparkes, A.C. (2002). *Telling Tales in Sport and Physical Activity.* Champaign, IL: Human Kinetics.

Steiner, L. (1991). Oppositional Decoding as an Act of Resistance. In R.K. Avery & D. Eason (eds). *Critical Perspectives on Media and Society.* New York: Guilford.

Stevenson, D. (2002). Women, Sport, and Globalization: Competing Discourses of Sexuality and Nation. *Journal of Sport and Social Issues*, 26, 209–25.

Theberge, N. (1981). A Critique of Critiques: Radical and Feminist Writings on Sport. *Social Forces*, 60, 341–53.

Theberge, N. & Cronk, A. (1986). Work Routines in Newspaper Sports Departments and the Coverage of Women's Sports. *Sociology of Sport Journal*, 3, 195–203.

Tuchman, G. (1978). *Making News: A Study in the Construction of Reality.* New York: The Free Press.

Turner, G. (1990). *British Cultural Studies: An Introduction.* London: Routledge.

Van Dijk, T.A. (1991). The Interdisciplinary Study of News as Discourse. In K.B. Jensen & N. Janowski (eds). *A Handbook of Qualitative Methodologies for Mass Communication Research.* London: Routledge.

Wenner, L. (1989). *Media, Sports, and Society.* London: Sage.

—— (1998). *MediaSport.* London: Routledge.

—— (2004). Recovering from Janet Jackson's Breast: Ethics and the Nexus of Media, Sports, and Management [Electronic version]. *Journal of Sport Management*, 18, 315–35.

Whannel, G. (1998). Reading the Sports Media Audience. In L. Wenner (ed.). *MediaSport.* London: Routledge.

Whisenant, W.A., Pedersen, P.M. & Smucker, M.K. (2004). Referent Selection: How the Women in Sport Journalism Shape their Perceptions of Job Satisfaction [Electronic version]. *Journal of Sport Management*, 18, 368–83.

White, P.G. & Gillett, J. (1994). Reading the Muscular Body: A Critical Decoding of Advertisements in *Flex* Magazine. *Sociology of Sport Journal*, 11, 18–39.

White, P. & Wilson, B. (1998). Distinctions in the Stands: An Investigation of Bordieu's "Habitus," Socioeconomic Status and Sport Spectatorship in Canada [Electronic version]. *International Review for Sociology of Sport*, 34, 245–65.
Williams, R. (1975). *The Long Revolution.* London: Penguin.
Wilson, B. & Sparks, R. (1996). "It's gotta be the shoes": Youth, Race, and Sneaker Commercials. *Sociology of Sport Journal*, 13, 398–427.

7

Sport and the Personal Narrative

Pirkko Markula and Jim Denison

To read the leading journals in sports studies often means reading articles where the researcher deploys a neutral voice written in the third person. In these articles, the researcher acts as an absent, objective observer of social events. In the numerous studies concerning young people and sport, for example, one rarely sees the author reflecting on his or her own childhood experiences in sport. Even apparent qualitative studies around topics such as pain and injury, burnout, winning and losing, and body image tend to be characterized by an absent narrator. Thus, how the author has influenced the text and the conclusions drawn largely remains a secret. Similarly, in all the gender studies done in sport, or the numerous investigations into issues of race and social class in sport, seldom do we come across a position statement from the author where he or she openly discusses the social categories to which he or she belongs.

These concerns over the practices of writing, we believe, are very relevant for qualitative researchers. It is no longer a taken for granted aspect of the research process that for qualitative research to qualify as "real" research it must be written according to the conventions of traditional science. Qualitative researchers are no longer held to such rules as writing objectively in the third person, using the passive voice, or reporting abstracted facts above personal interpretations. This is because qualitative research is fundamentally subjective in nature and takes into account many non-quantifiable elements of experience such as emotions, feelings, desires and dreams. It's important, then, that qualitative researchers celebrate the unique access they have to people's lived experiences and try to evoke those experiences with as much drama and detail as possible. One way of doing this is by crafting stories from people's experiences to show how lives are lived and understood as complete wholes from the inside. These storied accounts then become for qualitative researchers their interpretation and analysis of experience rolled into one.

In addition to considering more carefully how to represent their research subjects' experiences, and considering the possibility of story writing, qualitative researchers today are also concerned with how their own experiences influence the research process. For this reason, many qualitative researchers insert their own selves into their research texts. They do this not only by writing in the first person, but by also discussing how their own biases and values intersect with their research subjects' values. The impact of these changes has spawned a new category of qualitative research known as narrative research. However, the term "narrative" can have different meanings and we believe it is important for any qualitative researcher to clarify the particular way s/he is engaging in narrative research.

For many qualitative researchers the word narrative denotes critical readings of "narratives" – media texts, sporting events or celebrities' lives. The structure of these narratives are analyzed to determine the "preferred reading" as the researcher sees it (McDonald & Birrell, 1999). This understanding of narrative is limited to the analysis of the text and is not concerned with the researcher's subjectivity or how s/he becomes part of his/her research process.

In this chapter, we are not concerned with critical media analyses and we use the term narrative to signify texts that we as qualitative researchers have produced ourselves either through researching and writing up others' experiences or through studying our own lives. Our use of narrative is related to a larger change within the mode of qualitative social science research which we can trace back to the late 1970s, and the connections made by post-structuralist philosophers such as Michel Foucault (1979) and Jacques Derrida (1976) between practices of writing and practices of power.

Relationship between Theory and Method

Derrida (1976) and Foucault (1979) contend that writing is more than a transparent practice of storing information. Modern writing, for them, is invested with dominance; it is a power tool for the capitalist, conquering, male voice that has suffocated the subjective voice of the author and reduced multiple fields of meaning to a singular position. Writing, for them, is not just "writing up" results, but rather indicates a position of power and, therefore, is integral in determining how this power is used. It didn't take long for Foucault's and Derrida's influence to spread beyond philosophy. In fact, their concerns over the transparency of writing created what many have referred to within the social sciences as a "crisis of representation" (e.g., Denzin, 1997).

In anthropology, for example, Edward Bruner (1993) and James Clifford (1986) lifted processes of writing and the act of interpretation to the center of inquiry; language was no longer treated as thin black lines etched on a white surface to describe experience. It was a research issue. We should, therefore, openly discuss the nature of writing in ethnographic research and begin to acknowledge it as a site of power. To acknowledge the partiality, subjectivity and contextuality of social science writing it is, according to Clifford (1986), best to understand research texts as fictions that are ever changing, inventive and invested with literary qualities. From this standpoint, academic and literary writing genres can be seen as the same thing: both are reflexive accounts where the author's personal experiences together with the voices of others are woven into a single polyvocal text. This acknowledgment has led to a profound change in the ways social scientists view their practices. With this change, what Arthur Bochner labels the "narrative turn," qualitative researchers have moved "away from assuming the stance of disinterested spectator toward assuming the posture of a feeling, embodied, and vulnerable observer" (2001: 135).

Clifford (1986), for example, advocates qualitative research writing that, through more literary qualities, recognizes the author's experiences, the experiences of the people studied and the cultural context of interpreting these experiences. Norman Denzin (1994; 1997) and Laurel Richardson (1994; 2000) have also challenged social scientists to think about writing differently. Denzin (1994) argued that there can no longer be a forced scientific separation between the research experience and the resulting interpretation, or between ourselves and our research subjects. Richardson (1994) pointed to the dull and boring nature of sociological writing. Conceiving scholarly interpretation less as a method and more as an art, she argued, would enable researchers to think about creating qualitative research texts that are vital: texts that grip readers and invite them to engage in the subject matter.

Also a number of feminists challenged scientific traditions of reporting experience. These writers lifted women's experiences to the center of inquiry as a deliberate strategy to show how women's everyday, personal experiences reflect the historical, cultural and political contexts of their lives. As a result many feminists began to expand the possibilities of writing feminist research. They promoted ways of writing beyond the monolithic, objective, dominant male voice of traditional social science writing (e.g., Lather, 1992; Probyn, 1993; Richardson, 1997; Stanley, 1992).

These critiques of academic writing practices had a profound impact on the accepted mode of academic writing and theorizing. As Denzin (1994) noted, researchers were now becoming central characters in their research stories, portraying their own experiences in the field through memoirs, fiction or dramatic readings. From these advances came a plethora of new evocative writing practices. Therefore, we further define the term narrative within qualitative research as indicating a distinct writing style: a style that is more storied in nature and that attempts to employ certain literary devices to convey in a rounder, more embodied manner how people's lives are lived into existence and experienced.

We believe the starting point in any research project is when the researcher acknowledges that all research is storied, and that all researchers tell tales, but differ in the extent to which they are explicit about their role in the stories. Moreover, with the narrative turn, research data and the researcher's experiences become weaved into one colorful story. We will return to this point later to explain how a researcher should acknowledge him/herself as a story teller. However, although the researcher's personal experience becomes an integral aspect of the qualitative research process, there are multiple ways of including this experience in the research text. And as narrative ways of writing advance, this task becomes increasingly complicated.

To summarize our position up to this point, we define narrative in this chapter as a shift from a detached, objective researcher who records and reports facts alone, to a researcher who plays an integral part in the research process and whose voice is alive and well in the final written report. Furthermore, narrative, as we will discuss it here, is a style of writing that is interesting, thought provoking, and evocative. It is writing that goes beyond cold-hearted description and includes more than what is directly observable to the human eye to create a more fleshed-out, visceral portrait of the "real." It is a style of writing that moves the reader to think and act critically and reflexively. In this chapter, therefore, we are concerned with how one represents, interprets, or writes one's research results in accordance with the narrative turn. As such, this chapter is not about a specific method of data collection. Rather it is about how data collected in various qualitative ways can be written to represent multiple voices, the researcher's as well as the participants'; and in more of a storied fashion in order that they can be read and understood by multiple audiences.

Data Collection and Analysis for Storied Research

To begin our discussion here, we want to point out that we use the term "story" in a different manner from narrative. If narrative is the general call for attention to writing in social science research, storied writing is the answer to this call. Storied writing captures the nature of the research process and the specific dynamics of the people and the situations we study. If the special subject matter of stories is the changing directions/circumstances and goals of human action, then by utilizing a variety of qualitative date collection techniques – personal recollections, interviews – it is possible to gather material for our stories. However, data alone are not a story. They are the story's raw ingredients. Our primary concern in this chapter is to offer guidance for how to make stories from qualitative data. The first step in this process involves the analysis of one's "raw data," for example, written personal recollections or interview transcripts. This is often an invisible step that goes unrecorded in the final research article. There are no set rules about how one goes on to "translate" this data into a story, and researchers rarely articulate how they move from their data to a story. However, some useful steps exist to guide researchers through this aspect of the research process. We begin by discussing Andrew Sparkes's (1999) advice for how a beginning researcher might analyze his or her data as the first step in writing a story.

Sparkes (1999) believes that one way to analyze data is to detect common themes that emerge through the information that has been collected. This is a frequently used qualitative data analysis technique. It can be deployed to analyze data collected in a range of ways, especially following interviews. Therefore, this technique is not specific to story writing. What is specific for our purposes, however, is that the themes are conveyed in the form of a story. This is more involved than simply quoting one's interview subjects and then providing a brief theoretical discussion. This is not what we would call story making. For our purposes a story, all in one, must capture a sense of the subject's world as well as the researcher's analysis.

A second data analysis technique, according to Sparkes, is to identify the content of the experiences that have been collected to reveal their narrative structure. This analysis includes three steps: (1) collecting information from subjects' concerning past events, (2) making a story out of these events by "the use of plot, set, and characterization that confer structure, meaning, and context on the events selected" (Sparkes, 1999: 21–2), and (3) ordering these events "temporarily": in sequence to create an understanding of how and why these events have unfolded in a particular manner. This will result in a linearly arranged story. However, such a structure doesn't imply cause and effect, but rather shows how people create meaning from a sequence of events.

Sparkes's (1999) final data analysis technique allows for the production of stories organized in a variety of ways. Through this technique, what Sparkes labels narrative analysis, the author aims to detect the setting, characters and plot for his/her story based on the raw data and through these literary devices offer insights into the purpose behind the events, experiences or contexts. We would like to expand upon Sparkes's last data analysis technique to introduce a fourth way of analyzing data to create storied research.

To us, effective story writing involves three analytical steps that need to be taken with one's data: description, interpretation and explanation. To begin, you, as the researcher need to describe the events that took place, who was involved and the setting. This means considering the facts from your data. For example, describe who is speaking and what he or she has said. But remember to consider in the description of your data how people are speaking. Are they whispering or shouting? Do they move their hands around as they speak or sit still? It is important to describe their actions this way to be able to represent them in your story as round not flat characters.

Writing stories, however, means going beyond description. It also involves interpretation. So as well as describing the facts inside your data in as rich a way as possible, consider why those facts are occurring. Try to determine why someone is acting in a specific way. For instance, what does it mean for one of your subject's to say hello angrily or with a smile? What reasons have influenced his or her behavior in a particular situation? Through a mixture of dialogue and exposition it becomes possible to show the goals and motives held by your subjects and create thoughtful, intelligent characters who realize why they behave certain ways.

Finally, after you have interpreted your subjects' goals and intentions you should begin to explain them. Consider the wider implications, tensions or reasons people have for acting in one way or another. Is it to compensate for a personal weakness, or to abide with a societal convention? When you are able to point to these explanations in your story through the use of specific details or images then you are working towards eliciting the larger meaning of your data and creating a text that satisfies the criteria of good narrative research.

After analyzing the data, the researcher can begin to define more specifically how to present his/her story. Storied writing allows for multiple ways of writing up one's results, and in what follows we offer guidance on how to choose among the numerous options available.

Moving into Representation

The result of the narrative turn has been that storied writing now appears more frequently in social science journals. As the ways of writing have multiplied, several categories to describe the forms have emerged. For example, such terms as autobiographical writing, autoethnography, narrative of the self, or ethnographic fiction now exist to describe authors' attempts at storied research. Some scholars make few distinctions between these different terms labeling all storied writing techniques "alternative ways" of representing research. We have, however, opted to organize our discussion of storied writing into two categories which we further divide into two sub-categories. By doing this, we hope to guide researchers and students interested in storied ways of writing to opt for a style of representation that best suits their research goals.

First, we call stories fashioned from data collected about oneself *personal experience narratives*. Second, we call stories fashioned from interviews with others *research stories*. Within these two representational styles we would also like to make two further distinctions, *essayistic* and *literary*. This is because we believe that the ways of writing we are advocating in this chapter are still quite new for many people. Moreover, moving into more literary styles of research can be intimidating and daunting for many. In what follows, therefore, we discuss the variants, procedures and challenges that face both beginning and experienced qualitative researchers interested in personal experience narratives and research stories as a method of interpretation and analysis. To organize our discussion we present a description of each of these forms along with examples of that respective writing style.

Personal Experience Narratives (Essayistic)

Several researchers in sports studies have used personal recollections as the basis of their research narratives (e.g., Denison, 1994; Duncan, 2000; Markula, 2003; Sparkes, 1996; Tsang, 2000). We think this is a good way for a beginning story writer to start. With this data collection method, the researcher usually begins by thinking of moments that have in one way or another been influential in his or her choice of a research topic and the formation of specific research questions. Such as, how did losing the big game affect my views of competition? Or, what effect did my sports injury and my inability to play have on my identity as a man? The moments are written down as personal recollections. These recollections will then begin to explain where, when, why and how events took place. They become the raw data for one's personal experience narrative, not the final results.

To start this process, keep a journal and start with an impression, feeling or observation and see where you go with it. Notice who enters into your recollection and listen to what they say and how they say it. See what issues arise and become important because most likely those are the issues that matter to you. Write close to home, about subjects that really touch the heart of your own life.

When Jim Denison (1994) explored issues concerning his retirement from sport he wrote dozens of recollections related to winning and losing, and his relationships with his coaches and teammates. With these recollections in hand, he worked at synthetizing them into a single story that addressed his central research question concerning how retirement from sport is lived into existence and experienced.

Personal experience narratives can be designed to study any personal experience of the author's life. They can be accounts of suffering from an eating disorder, or more generally mapping one's development as an athlete or physically active person. Laurel Richardson (1994) defines these types of stories as highly personalized and revealing texts in which authors talk openly about their own lived experiences. The idea behind telling revealing personal stories, however, is not to hang your heart out on a sleeve but to enable the reader to share or to learn from how personal experiences are lived. Through such personal stories the social construction of experience becomes more tangible and assumes a sense of the "real."

While essayistic personal experience narratives all begin the same way, with data about yourself, they can be written in a number of ways. For example, some researchers alternate between developed accounts of their personal experiences and theoretical discussions to explain the meaning of their experiences and how their "stories" have been socially constructed. However, what primarily characterizes these essayistic accounts is the author telling about his/her personal experiences in the first person, "truthfully," as they "really happened." Many personal experience narratives are also comprised of several, separate "vignettes": personal experiences or memories that highlight meaningful events or developments that explain the social construction of a person's life experiences. Often, but not necessarily, the vignettes are organized chronologically. There are several examples of these in sports studies and we highlight three to demonstrate the basic qualities.

Tosha Tsang (2000) examines her identity as a high performance athlete through an essayistic personal experience narrative. Her article is comprised of a theoretical discussion followed by four separate vignettes as she reflects upon aspects of her identity as a Canadian-Chinese, female elite rower. All of the personal experiences described what really happened to the author and thus, reflect "truthfully," her own experiences. They also chronologically count the events building up to her participation in the 2000 Olympic games. Here is an example of her writing style:

> One of my teammates, Christine, who is sitting on the grass before me, must have been staring at my legs as I stood before her. She is one of my closer friends on the team and quite the jokester. She squints up at me and half-jokingly says: "So are you going to shave your legs before the Olympics?"
>
> You see, I am a female. More precisely, I am a Canadian female – and I am a Canadian female with hairy legs. I don't shave my legs and haven't for years, and I like it that way. As long as most of my teammates have known me, I have *never* shaved my legs. And really, questions or comments from my rowing friends have rarely come up about my legs . . . until recently. (Tsang, 2000: 48, italics in original)

After each of her personal experiences, Tsang offers a theoretical discussion that explains how her experiences are framed by the social context of being a female athlete.

Margaret Duncan (2000) also reflects on her participation in physical activity through an essayistic personal experience narrative. Unlike Tsang (2000), Duncan does not provide any theoretical grounding for her narratives, but aims to have her recollections speak directly to the reader. Her article includes seven sections organized chronologically: learning to swim as a child, horseback riding, playing games and basketball as a young girl, running, doing martial arts and aerobicizing as an adult. Here is an example of her writing style:

> Alice, my friend in the English Department, encourages me to try her noontime aerobics class at the campus rec center. I temporize. "Uh, maybe next month, when I'm not so busy." Alice persists, and for the sake of our friendship, I finally agree. She attends class three times a week and knows Trish, the doctoral student in Creative Writing who teaches the group. Weird credentials, I think.
>
> Feeling grumpy, I show up for the class in my workout uniform: baggy nylon shorts, oversized T-shirt, running shoes. I'm surprised to note that several people are dressed like I am. I assume our teacher will be willowy and insubstantial, but instead Trish is really ripped. Her quads are beautifully muscled, and she sports what my daughter would call a "six-pack," cut abs. I am unexpectedly envious. (Duncan, 2000: 67)

One relatively early example of an essayistic personal experience narrative that, similar to Duncan's, utilizes separate recollections is Andrew Sparkes's (1996) "Fatal Flaw." In a piece of writing that is both uplifting and disturbing, Sparkes explores his long history with back pain. He draws on medical reports, diary entries, memories, newspaper cuttings, conversations, as well as theories of pain and identity to discuss his relationship with his troubled back. In this highly embodied story, Sparkes explains himself through several separate vignettes, or "moments," that together create a coherent story. Here is an example of his writing style:

> It is May 1994. I have walked down this hospital corridor many times before. The navy blue carpet is familiar as are the polished handrails on either side. Determined not to use these handrails for support, I hobble down an imaginary center line. My body is unable to stand up straight, the hips are pulled to one side, and each time I take a step a searing burst of pain unleashes itself in the lumbar region of my back and travels down my right leg. It's hot in the hospital and I'm sweating. I'm also crying and afraid. In 1988 I had surgery on my lumbar spine here for a prolapsed disc and now I have the feeling that the hospital is soon going to swallow me up again. I want it to; I want this pain to be taken away. (Sparkes, 1996: 465)

Personal Experience Narratives (Literary)

To add to the evocativeness of personal experience narratives, and to expand upon the conventions of an essayistic style, personal experience narratives can also be written in a more literary style. Instead of recounting as "truthfully" as possible what happened, researchers operating within this genre are concerned with time shifts, changing contexts and the use of visual, olfactory, audio and kinaesthetic imagery. Richardson says that while literary personal experience narratives are based on events that really happened to the author, they call "upon such fiction-writing techniques as dramatic recall, strong imagery, fleshed-out characters, unusual phrasings, puns, subtexts, allusion, flashback, flashforward, tone shifts, synecdoche, dialogue, and interior monologue" (2000: 11). Therefore, instead of telling about events in a clear-cut manner, the author aims to show her/his personal experiences. These writers hold "back the interpretation" (Richardson, 2000: 11), inviting the reader to make multiple meanings out of the text. In addition to demonstrating the social construction of identity, self and experience, these stories aim to meet the coherence of good literary writing. For the social science researcher, this genre of writing also allows a simultaneous representation of the researcher's multiple selves: the personal, the professional, the physically active and the gendered, "raced," classed, aged and sexual selves can, like in a true experience, blend meaningfully into an evocative, storied account.

One example of this type of writing in sport is Nate Kohn's and Synthia Syndor's (1998) "How Do You Warm-Up for a Stretch Class." This piece is organized as "a dialogue" between the two authors who, often full of self irony, reflect upon their multiple selves as academics. A separate theoretical narrative runs in footnotes to complement the authors' personal writing. What gives this piece its literary flavor is its extreme fluency as the authors' attempt to show their experiences. Their article, therefore, opens itself up to multiple interpretations rather than positing one clear viewpoint. Here is an example of Kohn's and Sydnor's writing style:

> An innocent adrift in a productive world of conflicting and conflicted signals, I open my mouth and say things that didn't seem to be of me. As I listen to myself speak, I hear the words of a primitive, as if of a child. "How do you," I say to my wife, "warm up for a stretch class?" It is like a Steven Wright joke, a verbal version of a cubist taunt, and at the same time a serious inquiry, something I think I need to know in order not to injure myself in a new enterprise urged upon me by my doctor, family, Richard Simmons and the Nike shoe company. "I can't," I say in reply to the suggestion that I buy a treadmill, "work out at home, I know; I tried some pushups and jumping jacks. I need the gaze of Others, the fear of being laughed at, in order to generate sweat." I look around me and wonder: what is this world I am now living in? How did I get here? The question is not what dream have I awakened from, but what dream have I awakened into. "You wanna feel alive," beat the tom-toms of our times, "you gotta move."
>
> In my work, I now try to journey from consecrating theories that illuminate the "what and how" of studying sport (e.g., Harris, 1989), of documenting the postmodern moment of sport (e.g., Andrews, 1993), to playing with theory and confronting the seduction of a thick sport culture whose temptations and whose tensions I feel in the fundamentally different

> worlds that I transverse daily – the worlds of mother–wife, scholar, and resident of a small community. I yearn for a discourse that moves betwixt and between these worlds, and that answers my neighbors' interrogations: "You must get tickets to all of the games?" "Can you help me with my golf swing?" and challenges colleagues' assertions that national Endowment for the Humanities Grants do not matter in kinesiology. Travelling between these theories and communities I hope, is a grammatology of sport. (Kohn & Sydnor, 1998: 22–3)

Another example of a literary personal experience narrative is Pirkko Markula's (2003) exploration of the contradictions in the life of an eating disordered feminist academic. This story is framed by the author attending a conference. However, the events in the conference evoke her life experience of struggling with food and body dissatisfaction – an experience simultaneously contradicting and underlining her research into women's body image issues. This piece moves between different times of the author's life revealing the interplay of her multiple selves. The text includes a realist theoretical discussion concerning the author's struggle with evocative forms of writing and her experiences as an academic and a contemporary dancer. Here is an example of her writing style:

> After class a student approached me.
>
> "You are so right about the image, it's designed to keep us occupied with trivial body problems when we could be doing many more important things. It makes sense ... I know that, but I still struggle. I go to the gym and do hundreds of awkward outer thigh exercises just to have smaller legs ... I still do it, I still struggle."
>
> "Yes," I nodded, "it is very difficult."
>
> I hesitate a moment, should I tell her how, despite my feminist awareness, I could not disrupt my own disciplining gaze? Or that one of my feminist friends suffered from anorexia when she was a college athlete and felt that she never completely recovered despite her scholarly understanding of eating disorders? She believed instead that she had been permanently left with an "anorexic mind." Perhaps I also possessed an anorexic mind? In fact, I used to be so angry with myself for not having the discipline to become an anorexic. Through feminist research, though, I had become aware of the oppressive nature of the ideal body, yet I still constantly watched what I ate. Even now, as a lecturer, I feel guilty if I am unable to fit my weekly runs into my schedule... So what was I to say to this student in front of me? That she should just be prepared for an ongoing body struggle? And that it just gets worse with age? Or should I tell her that an awareness of the oppressive and constructed nature of the body image was the first step in fighting it? In the end I said, "It is all right to struggle. But you should try to disengage from exercise practices that support the oppressive image." Then I asked her, "Have you tried tai chi?" (Markula, 2003: 38–9)

Personal narratives such as these, written with a certain literary aesthetic, cannot be presented in a static or flat way but must be more sensual in nature. There must be smell and sound and mood present to intensify the feelings. This will give the writing energy and vitality. Writing this way Arto Tiihonen transmits a telling image of what it is to play sport with asthma: "My legs give way. Vision clouds… Over the toilet bowl and hacking. Not just a hack … Tearing lungs … I'm faint" (1994: 51). Using short sentences and relying heavily on verbs and nouns, he creates a sense of urgency and speed. His writing has a powerful emotional effect as we worry if he will be all right. His writing is also very sensual – "vision clouds," "hacking" – which gives us a deeper understanding of the situation he is in and how a body reacts in distress. Furthermore, we can place him – "over the toilet bowl" – and so we begin to formulate a vivid image of a human being experiencing life.

Evocative writing can also provide a strategy to examine so-called taboo topics such as sexuality or abuse. Toni Bruce (2003), in her personal experience narrative titled "Pass," examines issues of sexuality often connected to women's team sport but mostly left undiscussed. Bruce, who sets her story in a bar after a women's basketball game, reflects on the sexual politics of a women's sport team through the eyes of Sam, the main character in the story who confronts issues of sexual identity through her sport participation. By using dialogue and recollections as her main craft techniques, Bruce is able to show several layers of meaning in the formation of sexual identity. Flashbacks also serve as a device to evoke the social context of her sporting experiences. Here is an example of her writing style:

> "Hey, did you hear about Sam's dream last night? She was … Oooooooph." The sharp gust of air escaping from C's diaphragm after Sam's elbow to the ribs only slowed her down momentarily. "She dreamed she was kissing another woman!"
>
> "Good on you girl. That's the second time this month isn't it?" Andie's attempt to high five Sam across the table went begging. "Was it the same women?"
>
> "Oh shut up both of you. And no it wasn't the same one. It was no one." Well, not exactly no one. But no one she knew at least. In the dream, Sam had been at a party, leaning against a hallway wall, observing a parade of young, beautiful women flow from room to room as if on an imaginary stream. One had stopped. Sam's lips tingled again as she relived the sensation as their mouths made contact. Her kiss had been soft, tender, warm, and her breath gently fanned Sam's face. As her tongue slipped between Sam's lips, she had woken with a start, long moments passing as her heart rate slowed to normal and she became fully present in the darkness.
>
> "Well, did you like it?" Andie leaned forward, her knees knocking Sam's beneath the table.
>
> "No!" It came out almost as a shout. She dropped her voice as heads turned towards them. "It felt strange. I didn't even know who she was."
>
> "But weren't you tempted to kiss her back?" Andie was insistent.
>
> "Oh stop it. No. I mean … No. Of course I wasn't."
>
> "Are you sure?" Andie picked up on Sam's hesitation.
>
> "Maybe she's coming around to our way of thinking at last," Diana said, smiling.
>
> "Don't get your hopes up." Sam shook her head in mock despair. "It was only a dream. A bit like that three-pointer you took at the buzzer in last week's game, eh Diana?" (Bruce, 2003: 135)

Research Stories (Essayistic)

Writing social science in more interesting and evocative ways does not have to be limited to the personal experiences of the researcher. All experiences can become more meaningful when careful attention is paid to how they are represented. For example, interview data can be used as raw data for producing what we label research stories.

Toni Bruce (1998) presented the voices of twenty-two women sport writers she interviewed through a single monologue. In this story, Bruce aimed to "illustrate some of the key features of locker room life for women who interview male professional or college athletes" (1998: 6). Here is an example of her writing style:

> The first time I entered a men's locker room, I was 22, and terrified. My mother, a high school English teacher, had attended Catholic high school and Catholic college. My father, raised in the Netherlands, had no notion of what a sportswriter was. The idea that I would willingly walk into a room full of naked men appalled them beyond belief. I remember having a near anxiety attack the first time I had to enter their sacred enclosure. I tried to memorize all the questions I needed to ask, lest I be in the position of glancing around while trying to collect my thoughts. I kept the notebook posed a myopic four inches from my face. And I stared straight into every player's eyes: never below them. (Bruce, 1998: 3–4)

In another experimental piece within the same article, Bruce presents the voices of these women sports writers as a dialogue to further break up her earlier linear monologue and present a conversation where "various interpretations engage with each other on the way to potentially new understandings" (1998: 14):

> *Voice 3*: I always thought NBA players treated women the best and I always thought baseball players, generally speaking, treated women the worst, and football players were somewhere in between. And I decided it was college education – sort of the socialization process – because most baseball players go from high school straight to the minor leagues, never go to college.
>
> *Voice 4*: Except hockey's the same way and I don't hear horror stories about hockey the way I do about baseball and football. And hockey players, very few of them have much of an education. Maybe it's because they're Canadian. Now we'll make a generalization that all Canadians are great (*laughs*).
>
> *Voice 3*: There were probably women covering hockey before women covered anything else, certainly before baseball. I mean, baseball was also sort of the last thing for women to start covering at the major league level.
>
> *Voice 4*: And the NBA as a league is ahead of every other league: on drugs, AIDS awareness, women in the locker room, all kinds of issues.
>
> *Voice 5*: The other thing too though. It's 80 per cent black and I really think the guys are sensitized more to issues like discrimination. (Bruce, 1998: 14)

Jim Denison (1996), similar to Bruce, represented several elite athletes' experiences through the voice of a few composite athletes. Through in-depth interview techniques he studied the retirement experiences of twelve elite athletes, but collapsed all he recorded into three short stories. His stories adhere to the essayistic form by depicting his subjects' experiences in a precise and honest way, and mirroring the language of the everyday with the simple goal of describing and revealing the world as experienced by his subjects in both said and unsaid ways. Here is an example of his writing style:

> Sarah left her watch at home. It was a watch especially designed to take split times to the hundredth of a second and to store them in its memory. But it didn't matter now how long she took to ride around the lake.
>
> Just as she had done thousands of other mornings, Sarah turned left onto Bank street once she was out of town and headed down the Bank street hill towards the bike path that traced the perimeter of Manoa Lake. As she free wheeled past the cars parked along Bank street Sarah checked her form in their windows. She flattened her back, tucked her elbows in closer to her body; all for efficiency's sake. When it dawned on her how meticulous she was being, she laughed. Old habits die hard, she realised. Then she wondered, What do other people think about during their rides? (Denison, 1996: 353)

Karen Barbour (2002), who interviewed women engaged in solo dance making as part of her Ph.D. research, also worked from an essayistic research style by representing her subjects' experiences through "a conversation." Unlike Denison (1996) and Bruce (1998), Barbour includes her own voice as an equal part of the conversation as she, a solo dance maker herself, takes part not only as a researcher but as an artist. While she interviewed each dancer separately, in her story she weaves all the voices together into a coherent story. The conversation takes place in an "imaginary," yet a highly probable setting for such a conversation: the researcher's own home. The direct quotes from the interviews are indicated by italics to give resonance to each dancer's voice. Here is an example of Barbour's writing style:

> It seems to me that Raewyn was using embodied ways of knowing as she valued her own experiential ways of knowing as a dancer and attempted to reconcile these with other knowledge and experiences as she lived her life. She continues
>
> *Related to what you said Susanne, I find that conventions of our culture limit us to a very restricted set of norms. If you do anything outside of that you are classed as a weirdo. But for me, when I have moved away from the norm I feel an incredible expanding of the way I can respond to people and the environment and a sense of freedom and personal well-being.*
>
> "Yes, yes," I hear Susanne agree. She explains how the improvised section in her dance was a freeing experience for her too.
>
> *I had a lot of fun playing as a solo performer, and in my improvisation I could do whatever the hell I liked. With my improvisation I gave myself permission to do whatever I wanted, which was quite liberating and quite powerful. And sometimes I would just walk up to the audience and stare, or go off into a corner and play shadow puppets with my hands and it didn't matter!*

There is lots of laughter at Susanne's story from the three women. Ali and Jan come in to inquire about the joking. We join together to have lunch, and as I am eating, Raewyn remarks to me that there seem to be so few opportunities for her, and perhaps for all of us, to have in-depth discussions about our work. Such discussion creates ripples outwards that help to strengthen the dance community on many levels, she continues. I remember how I felt bereft on the detailed discussion I was used to having in an academic community, when I joined the dance community. Now we are bringing the two communities together and this encourages me. (Barbour, 2002: 208–9)

Research Stories (Literary)

Research stories with a literary bent, resemble, more than any of the other writing styles we have discussed up to this point, the qualities of fiction. For example, they tend to avoid closure, enabling the reader to see that interpretation is never finished, and that life continues on. They also attempt to provide a greater evocative depiction of others' lives through the heightened dramatization of real events using such literary devices as alternative points of view, strong characterization, unusual phrasings and subtexts.

For example, in his literary research story on skateboarders, Robert Rinehart (1998) uses alternative points of view and strong characterization. Rinehart shifts the point of view from which his story is being told numerous times. He begins with an omniscient narrator describing a group of kids working on a skateboarding trick, but then moves the story into a classroom where an angry teacher becomes the new narrator. A few passages later, it's the mother of one of the skateboarder's who assumes the lead role in the story. Despite these shifts in voice, time and place, Rinehart maintains a sense of coherence through his story that enables the reader to stay on track and not lose the plot. He achieves this through strong characterization. This means that he describes in a very rich way the specific features of each one of his central characters. As a result we are able to make an intimate connection between his writing style and his subjects. For example, here is how Rinehart introduces, Bennie, one of the skateboarders at the center of his drama.

He dropped in smooth-like off the slanting concrete, took a quick last puff, then tossed his Marlboro aside and went for the grind. They were skating on the concrete abutment to the library building at the state university. It was 2 a.m., a Wednesday morning, and the pinkish orange halogen lights reflected dully off their faces. A light drizzle fell. The air was thick and wet. He could see the fading lights of the two bicycling campus rent-a-cops as they left for the other side of the school. They had about a half an hour between the cops' rounds.

Three others – Sandy, Josh, and that blonde girl Corky – watched him. The tossing of his smoke was deliberate, and the timing was essential: too early, and he looked like a feeb; too late, he'd miss the trick. Same with the Ollie: to get good air, to ascend magically up to the slight rise of the coping, he timed the heel and toe pops just right, carrying the board, no hands, up with his jumping body. (Rinehart, 1998: 55)

These sentences have a languid, drawn-out feel and capture beautifully the body moving through time and space. Rinehart is able to draw his characters in such a way that we are continually reminded of sport's physical nature and that our bodies aren't short and angular, but long, curved, soft and round. We experience and witness limbs extending and torsos stretching, and in the process Rinehart establishes a memorable character with clear qualities.

Similarly, in his story on football fandom, David Rowe (2000) creates a highly memorable character. Rowe's character assumes the lead narrating role throughout. Therefore, Rowe's piece has an intimate feel as we hear directly the central protagonist's thoughts and feelings. Rowe resorts to absurd phrasings and puns and the very specific language of the insider's understanding of football. The author relies on the everyday speech of the football fan to explain the qualities and characteristics of the life he is attempting to analyze and portray. In addition, several subtexts run beneath Rowe's story. These are the themes running beneath the direct action of the story and include strong commentaries on football, masculinity and Englishness. Rowe deploys an ironic tone to subtly critique the obsessive qualities that many men bring to their appreciation of football. The result is a highly charged stylization of an egotistical, chauvinistic English football supporter whose actions show the roots of football fanaticism that of necessity locate women on the fringes. Rowe's rhythmic, rich prose verges on verse as he hypnotizes us with one delectable sentence after another. Here is an example of his writing:

> When I first saw her I was gobsmacked. I hadn't had the old trembling knee thing since the last minute at Mausoleum Park in '94, when that wanker Broadbent side-footed wide from three yards and the whole End went ape 'cos we knew were "going up, going up, going up, up, up!" Not only was Charmain a real looker, she was also wearing – I reckon it was fate, or maybe just good taste – a dress that was the exact same shade of red as our away strip. It was like we were made for each other, and this time I might really meet my mascot for life.
>
> I snuck up on her blindside, sold the bloke who was chatting her up a dummy and gave her the patter. I couldn't help noticing that she looked a bit like Mandelson's sister, who I met a couple of times before he got transferred to that French club, Abattoir-du-Pres or something. When she said that she'd go to the flicks with me on Saturday, I can tell you I was over the moon. Every cloud, silver lining and that – I didn't have my usual commitments that day. Getting knocked out of the Cup in the first round can have its compensations – I was available for selection, you might say – and for once I could give the reserves a miss. They were playing mid-week anyhow. (Rowe, 2000: 115)

These stories that Rinehart (1998) and Rowe (2000) tell about sport are clearly "moving" pieces. They move quite literally because they evoke a sense of the body in movement, but at the same time they are moving emotionally, rendering for the reader a sense of embodied experience. As with all the authors we have cited above in our examples of personal experience narratives and research stories, Rinehart and Rowe exemplify quite clearly the move we are asking readers to make between the worlds of social science and literature. However, at the expense of being caught in between these worlds, and at the risk of being judged solely by the criteria of one or the other, it is crucial that with new ways of writing – such as we are advocating in this chapter – there also emerge new ways of evaluation and judgement. In the following section we attempt to lay out a judgement criteria to evaluate this highly evocative yet also social scientific writing style.

Judgement Criteria for Storied Writing

Storied research writing has increased the options that social science researchers have to represent their findings. However, relaxing the definition of research writing does not mean relaxing the standards of research. Therefore, while storied writing offers multiple ways of writing up one's analysis, as has already become obvious through the number of examples we have presented, not just any personal experience or story is an acceptable piece of social science research.

Now that there are multiple ways of representing data, there must also be multiple ways of judging "good" research writing from "bad" research writing. Sparkes (2002) presents a comprehensive list of a variety of judgement criteria for storied writing by drawing on the work of a wide range of social scientists (e.g. Ellis, 2000; Lieblich et al., 1998; Lincoln & Guba, 2000; Pelias, 1999; Richardson, 2000). Each one of these criteria calls for an ability to represent, through literary aesthetics, the context of individuals' experiences. These criteria, however, assume a very advanced level of research and writing skills and we have, thus, based on our experiences of assessing students' work, developed our own judgement criteria to encourage students' to experiment with new ways of writing. We present these criteria below in order from the most basic requirements of good storied writing to a more advanced level of storied writing.

When we assess the quality of a storied social science representation, we want to have evidence that it:

1. Clearly captures the lived experiences, sights and sounds of the subject's life through the use of real speech, inside information, contextual details and thick description.
2. Provides a story that is emotionally captivating and doesn't always tell the reader how the characters involved are feeling, but through effective scene setting shows the reader how they are feeling.
3. Depicts through clear exposition the meaning the activities described hold for the subject of the story, and why they behave and act the way they do.
4. Includes an identifiable subject, theme, storyline or plot. It must be more than a descriptive history and consider a specific issue, aspect, conflict, concern or trouble in connection with the experiences described and interpreted in order to connect the subject's story to larger social and cultural issues.

We believe that it also becomes important when judging the merits of a story to ask: does it contain "truthlike statements that produce for readers the feeling that they have experienced, or could experience, the events being described?" (Denzin, 1989: 83). This appearance of truth is often labelled as the verisimilitude that the story carries. If the story resonates with readers then it should be working to bring a previously hidden or submerged reality to light. So conceived, the text then establishes a sense of its own truth.

We also believe that it is appropriate to judge positively a research project incorporating storied techniques if it is somehow able to touch others and serve their needs in ways that other interpretive styles cannot. As Richardson (1990) points out, what is most significant about using stories as a method of social science inquiry is the transformative possibilities of the collective story. She goes on to say:

> At the individual level, people make sense of their lives through the stories that are available to them, and they attempt to fit their lives into the available stories. People live by stories. If the available narrative is limiting, destructive, or at odds with the actual life, peoples' lives end up being limited and textually disenfranchised. Collective stories that deviate from standard cultural plots provide new narratives; hearing them legitimates replotting one's own life. New narratives offer the patterns for new lives. The story of the transformed life, then, becomes a part of the cultural heritage affecting future stories, future lives. (Richardson 1990: 26)

When either personal experience narratives or research stories are working at their best they should, "emotionally bind together people who have the same experiences … thus creating a shared consciousness and providing a sociological community where people can interpret their problems and overcome the isolation and alienation of contemporary life" (Richardson, 1990: 26). As a result of this, for those who actually live within the boundaries of the stories we tell and write, they are true.

Concluding Review

In this chapter, we have discussed the so-called narrative turn in the social sciences, and how it has drawn our attention to the subjective nature of writing research. In light of these changes, educational researchers Jean Clandinin and Michael Connelly (1994) claim that in qualitative social science research it is no longer simply what the writer has to say that is important but how he or she says it. Unlike researchers using methods of writing which emphasize accurate, summative statements, qualitative researchers turning to more storied ways of writing need to be there in the text (Geertz, 1988). Otherwise they will produce silent, impersonal, empty writing that no one will read. However, to create a storied research text means doing more than inserting an "I" or writing in the first person. It does still mean putting forth a reasoned argument. This argument, however, needs to come across in a more subtle way through showing the social context of the experience, issue or problem under investigation. Our goal in this chapter has been to introduce the tradition of storied writing in qualitative sport research for researchers, if they so choose, to adopt these practices.

We have tried to present helpful suggestions on how to produce storied social science research in sport. We presented our advice by creating two main categories of storied sport research, personal experiences narratives and research stories, and two subcategories within these, essayistic and literary. Any story written under these categories, we tried to explain, should meet the judgement criteria of good narrative writing, but at the same time the author does have the freedom to choose how deeply she/he wants to embed her/his argument around the qualities of literature.

We have emphasized that successful storied research writing needs to present vivid accounts of people's experiences that go beyond superficial description to include rich portrayals of people's lives. To move beyond description, the author needs to engage in a variety of writing techniques that involve an attention to style, word choice, description, emotion and tone. This enables these stories to succeed, not only as literary pieces, but as social science research, too. Therefore, storied social science research is not devoid of theory, but by showing not just telling the social context of individual's experiences it aims to explain in a more evocative manner how societal forces impact on our lives.

Storied traditions of research, of course, are new and still evolving. But as this tradition forms, a greater understanding of what we need to do to produce effective storied research will be continually occurring. It is certainly clear at this point in time that this form of research representation cannot be judged based on the criteria designed for objective research writing. Thus, we have included new criteria developed specifically around the unique qualities of storied research writing that can be used to judge the merit and contribution of this way of representation.

Based on our experiences as storied writers and advisors for storied writers, we feel that engaging in this journey is exciting. Becoming a researcher who writes either personal experience narratives or research stories is not easy, and it involves many moments of frustration and long hours of revision. Yet, the rewards can be great.

References

Barbour, K. (2002). The Process of Becoming: Women's Solo Contemporary Dance in Aotearoa/New Zealand. Unpublished doctoral dissertation, University of Waikato, New Zealand.

Bochner, A.P. (2001). Narrative's virtues. *Qualitative Inquiry*, 7, 131–57.

Bruce, T. (1998). Postmodernism and the Possibilities for Writing "Vital" Sports Texts. In G. Rail (ed.). *Sport and Postmodern Times*. Albany, NY: State University of New York Press.

—— (2003). Pass. In J. Denison & P. Markula (eds). *Moving Writing: Crafting Movement in Sport Research*. New York: Peter Lang.

Bruner, E. (1993). Introduction: The Ethnographic Self and the Personal Self. In P. Benson (ed.). *Anthropology and Literature.* Champaign, IL: University of Illinois Press.
Clandinin, J. & Connelly, M. (1994). Personal Experience Methods. In N.K. Denzin & Y.S. Lincoln (eds). *Handbook of Qualitative Research.* London: Sage.
Clifford, J. (1986). Introduction: Partial Truths. In J. Clifford & G.E. Marcus (eds). *Writing Culture.* Berkeley: University of California Press.
Denison, J. (1994). Sport Retirement. Unpublished doctoral dissertation, University of Illinois at Champaign-Urbana.
—— (1996). Sport Narratives. *Qualitative Inquiry,* 2, 351–62.
Denzin, N.K. (1989). *The Research Act* (3rd edition). Englewood cliffs, NJ: Prentice Hall.
—— (1994). The Art and Politics of Interpretation. In N.K. Denzin & Y S. Lincoln (eds). *Handbook of Qualitative Research.* London: Sage.
—— (1997). *Interpretive Ethnography.* London: Sage.
Derrida, J. (1976). *Of Grammatology.* Baltimore, MD: Johns Hopkins University Press.
Duncan, M.C. (2000). Reflex: Body as Memory. *Sociology of Sport Journal,* 17, 60–8.
Ellis, C. (2000). Creating Criteria. *Qualitative Inquiry,* 6, 273–77.
Foucault, M. (1979). What is an Author? In J.V. Harari (ed.). *Textual Strategies.* Ithaca, NY: Cornell University Press.
Geertz, C. (1988). *Works and Lives.* Cambridge: Polity Press.
Kohn, N. & Sydnor, S. (1998). "How do You Warm-Up for a Stretch Class?": Sub/in/di/verting Hegemonic Shoves Toward Sport. In G. Rail (ed.). *Sport and Postmodern Times.* Albany, NY: State University of New York Press.
Lather, P. (1992). Postmodernism and the Human Sciences. In S. Kvale (ed.). *Psychology and Postmodernism.* London: Sage.
Lieblich, A., Tuval-Mashiach, R. & Zilber, R. (1998). *Narrative Research.* London: Sage.
Lincoln, Y. & Guba, E. (2000). Paradigmatic Controversies, Contradictions, and Emerging Confluences. In N.K. Denzin & Y.S. Lincoln (eds). *Handbook of Qualitative Research* (2nd edition). London: Sage.
Markula, P. (2003). Bodily Dialogues: Writing the Self. In J. Denison & P. Markula (eds). *Moving Writing: Crafting Movement in Sport Research.* New York: Peter Lang.
McDonald, M.G. & Birrell, S. (1999). Reading Sport Critically: A Methodology for Interrogating Power. *Sociology of Sport Journal,* 16, 283–300.
Pelias, R. (1999). *Writing Performance.* Carbondale, IL: Southern Illinois University Press.
Probyn, E. (1993). *Sexing the Self: Gendered Positions in Cultural Studies.* London: Routledge.
Richardson, L. (1990). *Writing Strategies: Researching Diverse Audiences.* London: Sage.
—— (1994). Writing: A method of Inquiry. In N.K. Denzin & Y.S. Lincoln (eds). *Handbook of Qualitative Research.* London: Sage.
—— (1997). *Fields of Play: Constructing an Academic Life.* New Brunswick, NJ: Rutgers University Press.
—— (2000). New Writing Practices in Qualitative Research. *Sociology of Sport Journal,* 17, 5–20.
Rinehart, R. (1998). Sk8ting: "Outsider" Sports, At-Risk Youth, and Physical Education. *Waikato Journal of Education,* 6, 55–63.
Rowe, D. (2000). Amour Improper, or "Fever" Sans Reflexivity. *Sociology of Sport* Journal, 17, 95–7.

Sparkes, A.C. (1996). The Fatal Flaw: A Narrative of the Fragile Body-Self. *Qualitative Inquiry*, 2, 463–94.
—— (1999). Exploring Body Narratives. *Sport, Education and Society*, 4, 17–30.
—— (2002). *Telling Tales in Sport and Physical Activity: A Qualitative Journey*. Champaign, IL: Human Kinetics.
Stanley, L. (1992). *The Auto/Biographical I: The Theory and Practice of Feminist Auto/Biography*. Manchester: Manchester University Press.
Tiihonen, A. (1994). Asthma. *International Review for Sociology of Sport*, 29, 51–62.
Tsang, T. (2000). Let Me Tell You a Story: A Narrative Exploration of Identity in High-Performance Sport. *Sociology of Sport Journal*, 17, 44–59.

8

Performed Ethnography

Heather Sykes, Jennifer Chapman and Anne Swedberg[1]

Theoretical Context of Performed Ethnography

Virginia Woolf once said "writing lives is the very devil." She could have been writing about contemporary qualitative research, although she was writing about so much more. Postmodern qualitative research has evolved out of the crisis of representation, which disrupted the notion that researchers could directly capture lived experience, and the crisis of legitimation, which unhinged the traditional criteria of validity and generalizability for assessing the worth of research. During the postmodern, fifth moment of qualitative research (Lincoln & Denzin, 1994), with its experimental texts and multiple voices, life historians had to grapple with the uneasy insight that life stories do not await the researcher "hiding in ethnographic caves or qualitative mountain tops" (Tierney, 1998: 14). Researchers continue to grapple with the crisis of representation, embodiment and post-foundational systems of knowledge. I'm still learning about the devilishness of life history research as my educational qualitative research keeps spinning, through the linguistic turn and now the performance turn (Conquergood, 1992). This chapter follows the performative turn in my life history research about physical education teachers. It describes my collaboration with drama educators to create a performed ethnography based on life history interviews called *Wearing the Secret Out* (Chapman, Swedberg & Sykes, 2005).

Poststructural Interviewing

A life lived.
  Remembering a life lived.
    Interviewing – Retelling li(v)es in speech

I conducted eight life history interviews with physical educators that form the basis of the performance. Life history interviewing, as a method in qualitative and feminist research, has traditionally been rooted in a humanist notion of the individual – a sovereign subject who possesses knowledge which, if skillfully solicited, can be uncovered by the interviewer. In this approach to interview research, the literal translation of talk has been equated with lived experience and its representation (Denzin, 1994). Methodological issues focused on how to accurately represent the lived experience or "reality"; how best to uncover the intended meanings of the researched. My approach to life history refused what Sidone Smith (1993) called the "myth of bourgeois individualism"; that is, a sovereign subject who possesses knowledge which can be skillfully uncovered by the interviewer. Rather, my framework was based on a poststructural notion of subjectivity and identity (Clough, 1993; Scott, 1991; Weedon, 1997). Additionally, queer theories shaped my approach to life history by raising questions about normalcy, heteronormativity and whiteness.

The retelling of lived experience through speech, where speech tries to recreate experience, can only create another moment. As William Tierney emphasized, postmodern life history exists somewhere between history and memory: "Memory is not a spontaneous word association. Speakers and researchers build memory from the shared perspective of the present" (2000: 545). Post-structuralism has radically challenged the humanist logic that separates author, text and reader. In literary theory, Roland Barthes' pronouncement that "the birth of the reader must be at the cost of the death of the author" (cited in Biriotti, 1993: 3) marked a shift away from the intentions of the author towards the response of the reader. Yet, for Elizabeth Grosz, even the birth of the reader simply shifts the position of the sovereign subject from sender to receiver: "the text's materiality exerts a resistance, a viscosity, not only to the intentions of the author but also the readings and uses to which it can be put by readers. In this sense, the text is liable never to arrive at its destination" (1995: 17).

The ripples of this challenge to foundational humanism have spread ever wider across many disciplines in western academia, including sociology, education and performance studies. As performance scholar Elin Diamond observed, "nothing, then, is irreducible or foundational. What appears to be foundational is a discursive effect pretending to be foundational – a pretense that theater understands well" (2000: 32).

Many have been skeptical of the post-structuralist hope that "the death of the author, an attack on the humanist subject, with his implications in racism, sexism and imperialism, can therefore be seen as part of a strategy of political liberation" (Biriotti, 1993: 4). Feminists such as Somir Brodribb (1992) and Teresa Ebert (1996) raised concerns that the post-structuralist death of the author has been championed at a time when the voices of marginalized groups were just beginning to gain authority. The political fall-out, they claim, has not been liberation of subjects experiencing racism, sexism and imperialism but, paradoxically, a well-disguised mechanism to re-silence and de-legitimize their claims to voice and authority. Feminist researchers have been concerned that turning away from the interviewee as sovereign subject and women's testimonies of experience has the potential to disempower women, and jeopardizes the political bite of research.

Within this political context, Biriotti (1993) pointed out that increasingly post-structuralism has directed attention neither at the intentions of the authors or readers, nor interviewees or interviewers but to the workings of texts themselves. Crudely translated into interviewing methodology, this indicated a shift from interpreting what interviewees meant to communicate, as authors of their own life histories, to representing the multiple interpretations available to the researcher and other readers. Writing specifically about artistic representations, Hutcheon acknowledged that feminist and postmodernist politics should not be conflated. Politically, postmodernism is ambivalent, "doubly encoded between complicity and critique, so that it can and has been recuperated by both the left and the right" (1989: 168). In contrast, feminist politics are committed to transforming representations by transforming actual social relations. However, the two are interrelated in that feminism has influenced postmodernism to reconsider it's challenge to the humanist universal "Man" in terms of gender, just as "postmodern parodic representational strategies have offered feminist artists an effective way of working within and yet challenging dominant patriarchal discourses" (1989: 167). More directly related to qualitative research, these productive tensions between feminism and postmodernism compel a reconsideration of the humanist relations between individuals, experience and empowerment in terms of subjectivity, texts and agency. I suggest that performed ethnographies are a vibrant sites for reconsidering how to represent postmodern rather than sovereign subjects. Indeed, in creating *Wearing the Secret Out* we have constantly grappled with these productive tensions between feminism and post-structuralism in our representation of sex, lives and audiotape.

The Performance Turn

The performance turn (Conquergood, 1992) in qualitative research gathered speed throughout the 1990s. In ethnography, the performance turn responded to issues of embodiment (Langellier, 2000) – bodies that looked and were looked at, hands that held the pen to paper and mouths that tried to tell stories of Other's lives. It also emerged within a postmodern ontology that suggests that reality is constituted through performativity (Denzin, 2000), rather than existing or even originating elsewhere. Currently, the performance turn in qualitative research is evolving into a post-interpretive, post-foundational paradigm (Denzin, 2000).

At the 1999 Bergamo Curriculum Theorizing conference I watched two readers theater presentations. I was energized and intrigued by Tara Goldstein's (2001) *Hong Kong, Canada* readers' theater as multicultural curriculum. I left that conference with more than a temporary buzz, determined to explore the simmering potentialities of readers' theater as a way to "translate" my life history interview data into a pedagogical device. Cautiously spurred on by Peter Woods' (1996) *Researching the Art of Teaching*, Norman Denzin's (1997) *Interpretive Ethnography* and especially Laurel Richardson's (1997) *Fields of Play*, I decided to pursue a performance format to represent data from my life history project. There are a number of ethnographic performance texts in anti-racist and health theater (Goldstein, 2001; Mienczakowski, 1997; Pifer, 1999) and growing interest in experimental forms of ethnography within sport sociology, evidenced by the special edition of the *Sociology of Sport Journal* (2000) *Sociological Imaginings, Sociological Narratives* and Andrew Sparkes' (2002) *Telling Tales in Sport and Physical Education*. Brown (1998) developed a performance about the pressures of hegemonic masculinity faced by male students in physical education teacher education called *Boy's Training*.

One of the purposes of ethno-drama is to seek explanation and expression for research in a public form which opens its meanings to its informants as well as to wide audiences (Mienczakowski, 1997: 172) and such performances strive to speak "with informants and audiences rather than speaking for or about them" (Mienczakowski, 1998: 117). Yet, when aligned with post-structuralism, performed ethnography also requires attention "to how stories are told, including how we stage what we represent in the scene of writing" (Lather, 2000b: para 25). Norman Denzin described the unfinished and partial nature of post-structural inquiry: "language and speech do not mirror experience; they create experience, and in the process of creation, constantly transform and defer that which is being described" (1994: 296).

This project took my research beyond the always already fraught moments of interviewing, transcribing and then interpreting data. The collaboration involved translating a transcript into dramatic script, translating that script from page to stage and, with our audiences, translating what happened on stage into learning. Re-presenting interview data as a performed ethnography involved so many moments of telling and re-telling, citing and reciting.

A teaching life lived.
Telling.
Transcribing.
Verifying, anonymizing.
Collaborating.
Interpreting.
Performing.
Screening.
Teaching.

Meaning was and is perpetually being deferred and grasped during this series of translations. The numerous twists and turns of translating data into drama were simultaneously generative and reductive, requiring what Littau called "both a gathering of interpretations and a dispersal of readings" (1993: 52). She described translation as: "That process which underlies any meaning production; it will not be reduced to a merely linguistic motion, nor seen in the form of an obvious reduplication, but as a complex inter-relation between two elements" (1993: 53).

While Littau focused only on translating dramatic script into performance, *Wearing the Secret Out* involved multiple translations because of its genesis in research interviewing and finale in classroom pedagogy. Patti Lather suggested thinking about translation as dissemination rather than containment:

> Translation becomes neither mirror not mimetic copy but, rather, another creation that addresses that which is intranslatable in the original. Remembering, interpreting and becoming, translation is not likeness so much as a transformation... Within/against assumption of "letting the voices speak," translators/historians/ethnographers forge a reciprocal relationship with the original, aware of translation as "violent, forced, and foreign" (Derrida, quoted in Niranjana, 1992, p. 160), supplement rather than mimesis, both inadequate and necessary. (2000b: para 25)

Each stage of this collaborative process added to and took away from earlier moments in the research, although the ghosts of the teachers I'd interviewed were never far away.

Creating a Performed Ethnography

The chapter now recounts the process of developing the ethnographic performance. The performance is based on life history interviews with eight physical educators who self-identified as "lesbian," "gay" and "queer." *Wearing the Secret Out* deals with issues such as coming out, homophobic violence and same-sex desire in physical education. Two actors, my collaborators Anne and Jennifer, perform monologues, short stories and phrases from the interviews using props and dramatic movement. There are long narratives about a middle school teacher who came out to her students, a homophobic verbal and physical assault on a lesbian coach and how a teacher educator deals with same-sex crushes. The actors repeat the following chorus lines throughout the twenty-five-minute performance:

> There have been some efforts to make schools safe for lesbian, gay, transgendered children, but this seems a long way from what we do in the gym sometimes.
> How do you cope with all that stuff in the moment of teaching?

These comments encourage audiences and students to begin thinking and talking about anti-homophobic teaching in the specific context of physical education. Pedagogically, *Wearing the Secret Out* is designed to generate incomplete and multiple meanings. The performance doesn't claim that students will "learn" how to teach in less homophobic or heterosexist ways. Instead, the performance addresses what Elizabeth Ellsworth (1997) refers to as the "multiple who's" in the audience. This mode of address takes into account that each audience member may be simultaneously "ignorant and knowledgeable; resistant and implicated; committed and forgetful; committed and ambivalent, tired, enjoying the pleasures and safety of privilege; effective in one arena and ineffective in another" (Ellsworth 1997: 157). This creates multiple possibilities for identification and dis-identification for each member of the audience. Ultimately, this performed ethnography gives students an obligation to make their own meanings about how to approach anti-homophobic teaching.

Transcribing

I kept hearing ghostly voices that accompanied turning interviews into transcripts and into play scripts, a process so eloquently described by Leas Lockford: "What ultimately appears in performance or print as a seamless whole to the eventual audience or readers is a haunting experience in the somatic and mental memory of the ethnographer as those voices which were made to disappear speak from behind the gaps, the splices and the edits" (2000: 402).

Ghosts of the teachers I interviewed appeared as soon as I boarded my flights home after our interview visits. More of them appeared during the process of transcribing the audiotapes of our interviews. Transcription, where speech is represented as text, is not a straightforward task of capturing the transparent "reality" of speech. As Mishler (1991) noted, it is a critical step in the transformation of speech into a representation – transformation that could lead to many different representations. Indeed, as Lapadat and Lindsay emphasize, it is the process rather than the written product of transcribing that is valuable because "analysis takes place and understandings are derived through the process of constructing a transcript by listening and re-listening, viewing and re-viewing" (1999: 73). I had completed the interviews and transcriptions before Anne and Jennifer started working on the script. When I first started transcribing several years before, I had anticipated transcribing to be a mechanical, laborious task. Yet being re-immersed in the interview during the transcription altered my perceptions quite dramatically at times. I recall leaving one of my very first interviews feeling unsettled for two days afterwards. While transcribing this interview, however, my feelings of disappointment evaporated to reveal some wonderful statements of courage that I had been unable to "hear" during the actual interview. I also became painfully aware of questions that could have been asked if I had been able to "hear" in the interview what I later heard during the transcription. Collaborating with Anne and Jennifer for this project created more cycles of selecting, editing and splicing transcripts. As we worked, Anne, Jennifer and I often heard quite different ghostly voices. Thus even our use of transcripts was theory-laden (Lapadat & Lindsay, 1999) with post-structuralist processes of creation and omission.

Jennifer: I am not always certain what our distance from the primary research brings to the project. If nothing else, it gives us a little less sense of loss when we share what these people said without sharing who they are. I think I might have had a harder time deciding what to delete from Donna's story if I had conducted the interview with her. Her story is so moving; just reading it made it difficult to decide what to cut. I think that if I had had a personal interaction with her, I may not be able to separate my feelings for her from the choices I had to make to best serve the project. So for reasons that are tied to the emotionality of the interview process and the responsibility you come to bear as the interviewer, I suppose it was much easier to make performance choices without having interacted with participants.

Creating the Script

In the early stages, we communicated about the script via e-mail.

Message

From: Heather

Subject: Performed Ethnography Script

To: Anne, Jen

My aim is generate a pedagogy-as-script/play derived from life history interviews, focusing on issues of heterosexism & homo/sexualities, that may be used by teacher educators working with undergraduate student teachers. I envision a montage of the different ways the narrators/characters described how heterosexism and their sexual identities influenced their ways of teaching. I would like you to explore, character by character, how each transcript section could edited for performance to capture/portray the incident or pedagogy being described. The balance here will be between accuracy/verisimilitude and avoiding repetition/excess.

Jennifer: Heather gave us specific sections of each interview that she thought were most important to include. From there, we pulled words, phrases, statement and monologues that we thought were particularly interesting, dramatic or revealing. We wrote up all of these pieces on 3 × 5 notecards so that we could distance ourselves from the individual transcripts. It was difficult to choose just one or two moments – the arc of each person's life experience seemed so integral to the pinnacle moments that we were selecting.

Anne: Throughout the summer, Jennifer and I continued to discuss the transcripts, type up the sections and paste the bits of text onto index cards which we could reshuffle into various configurations. Slowly, something akin to a script began to emerge. Influenced by our reading of Laurel Richardson's (1997) *Fields of Play*, we envisioned five sections of text separated by a series of "choruses." The choruses quickly vanished, although the phrase "how do you cope with all that stuff in the moment of teaching?" functions like a chorus in the current version of the piece. We found ourselves with only three complete monologues or stories. Coach Schneider's story about coming out in class, Donna's story about the student with a crush, Cathy's story about socializing with a group of assistant coaches, one of whom demanded to know her sexuality. We incorporated some of Heather's research questions into the piece, as well as sections where different bits of text were collaged together.

Heather: The early stages of interpretation or scripting are necessarily messy as Donmoyer and Yennie-Donmoyer recounted: "We spent a good amount of time during the early stages of script construction thrashing around like drowning people as we read out data over and over, looking for concepts to grab hold of" (1995: 7). This state of not-knowingness has been, perhaps, one of the most generative aspects of the collaborative relationship. I surprised myself by how easy it was to "let" Anne and Jen work with the interview data. Throughout our collaboration, I have been reticent to change many decisions made by Anne and Jen. For instance, I was uneasy with the early themes developed by Anne and Jennifer – Roll Call, Homophobia, Coming Out, Colleagues, Pedagogy. These themes echoed earlier struggles with "coding" interview data I'd experienced when, writing my dissertation, I'd searched for a way to write more fluid post-structural narratives. Over a period of three years or so, I developed a hybrid methodology saturated with epistemological tensions that moved from trying to accurately re-present any "real" experiences towards cautious discursive analyses of how teachers' stories, my questions, transcripts, quotations and interpretations provide compelling "understandings" and "overstandings" (Sykes, 2001). Being confronted with Anne and Jennifer's "coding" of the data felt, for me, like returning to the beginning of these methodological struggles. As I reflect back on my feeling of calm acquiescence to Anne and Jennifer's interpretative work, I realise that perhaps I was sliding toward Lather's feminist double(d) science where: "the task is to gain new insight into what not knowing means toward the telling of not knowing too much. Here rigor becomes 'something other' than reasserting critical or interpretive mastery" (2000b: para 9). I was thoroughly surprised by how it felt strangely right for me to both relinquish and assert my interpretations throughout the project. It felt easy to defer my concerns about the limitations of "coding" because I didn't know what Anne and Jennifer would make of them. This not-knowingness felt richly productive and exciting.

Verifying and Anonymizing

Anne: I brought up the work of Anna Deavere Smith, a performance artist who interviews her subjects and then "performs" them by taking their speech rhythms, inflections and patterns (including all the pauses, stammers and inconsistencies) into herself. Since Heather had recorded the life history interviews, it might be possible to work from the audio-tapes themselves. Later, when Jennifer and I began to grapple with putting the piece together, we both quickly realized that this approach would not work, in part because we were still envisioning a script as a readers theater piece that would be read by various members of a class, who would never have access to the tapes, and thus never be able to reproduce the interviewee's speech in the way that Smith does in her performance. We also feared that such a degree of mimesis might unintentionally give away the identities of the interviewees, which needed to be protected.

Heather: Earlier in the research process I had returned an anonymized version of the transcripts to each participant for their verification. Participants were encouraged to change, add or remove any sections from the transcripts they felt were inaccurate or potentially dangerous for them. We also used this process to ensure that pseudonyms that we developed jointly would ensure that identities were kept confidential. Protecting participant's identities proved to be an extremely important factor that shaped *Wearing the Secret Out* in the early stages of script development. Also, issues of anonymity were intensified when participants came to see the performance. We changed several performance choices so that colleagues, friends and even partners of participants who were in the audience would not be able to identify anyone's words during the performance. In several cases this was solely my responsibility as the researcher with ethical responsibility to maintain the research terms for informed consent. In cases where the participant had decided to tell people about participating in the research, the need to maintain their anonymity was not so pressing although we still tried to do so.

From Page to Stage

Anne: As the beginning of a new semester approached with terrifying rapidity, Jennifer and I put together the last pieces of the script, and started to, quite literally, "get the script on its feet." We found empty rehearsal space in the basement of a theater building and began to improvise sequences of movement that might accompany the text. We also wanted to make it clear that we were performing stories of people who were not all white, female, and middle class, which we recognized as identities that would be "read" onto our bodies as performers. We originally had concerns about the fact that our bodies don't read as particularly athletic (both Jennifer and I spent a lot of time trying to get out of PE when we were kids), although those concerns vanished over time.

Looking back, I wonder if one of the reasons we didn't end up with a readers' theater piece was our desire to involve the body as text, to find these embodied metaphors for the scripted text, and thus to move rather than remain seated throughout the piece. Originally, we talked about wanting to bring a "rhythm of sport" into the piece, an awareness of the body that is so much a part of physical education, and can make issues of sexuality so volatile and frightening. As we worked, what performance artist Tim Miller calls "metaphors of the body" began to find their way into the piece. For example, the notion of writing on each other's bodies was at least in part prompted by my memories of a workshop I had participated in with Tim. Shayna, one of the other workshop participants, had created a piece in which she wrote a series of "identity" labels on herself (and during the performance invited the audience to write them on her), including "dyke," "lesbian," "bisexual," and "queer." There can be a violence, or an invasion, in writing on the body, as well as a tenderness or an erotic quality, and we played with both.

We also developed a tug-of-war during what we used to call the "coming out" section in which we juxtaposed statements that the interviewees made about how "out" they were willing or able to be in their classrooms or other professional situations. The tug-of-war became a powerful metaphor for the lived experiences of the LGBT teacher in their workplaces.

Heather: Anne and Jennifer created scenes of struggle and dissonance, alongside humor and tenderness. They start the performance wearing several layered T-shirts with racial, sexual and professional identities such as "latina lesbian teacher" written in large black letters on the front and back. These were identities the teachers had used to describe themselves to me at the beginning of the interview process. At various moments Anne and Jennifer take off T-shirts to reveal other identities until they are wearing plain white shirts with no writing. The shirts evoke the title *Wearing the Secret Out* in two ways. Wearing identities of "lesbian," "gay" and "queer" represents being out – wearing the secret *out.* At the same time, removing the T-shirts with labels represents gradually removing the secrecy surrounding these identities – *wearing* the secret out. In a later scene, Anne and Jennifer move around one another to write words on one another's T-shirts and skin as they occur in their lines: "Intervention," "Think," "Teacher," "Love," "Hell." The performance ends with a quiet moment of tender affection between the two female actors.

Jennifer: For the entire piece, we talk a lot about rhythm – how to vary it and how to use it as a way of representing the places these people are coming from. We talk about the rhythm of sport, and how people who engage with sport have a kind of engagement with their bodies that is different from people who don't exercise at all. We hope that we can use rhythm throughout the piece to represent this aspect of identity. This is hard to explain in words – it is a very active concept!

We were keenly aware of the limitations of the ways in which our physical bodies "read" – as white, female, middle class, able and, depending on the crowd, heterosexual. We were also aware that because of our total lack of participation in sport and other forms of organized physical activity, we lacked identification with the one thing all our "characters" had in common. As actors, we were used to representing people who were not us. But what we were creating was not a play with identifiable characters – we were creating a form by which to tell stories that would have to live through our own identities... Do we have a right to let these stories live through our bodies which are not these people? Especially when these stories change based on the body they are read upon. This is a problem. It continues to be a problem.

Issues in Performed Ethnography

The Good Lie of Verbatim Research

Anne: Sometimes, I want to get inside somebody else's head and experience the piece through somebody else's consciousness. The piece is very meaningful to me but when Jennifer and I perform it, what happens then? For example, we announce the fact that the observations, statements, and stories in the piece are culled verbatim from interview transcripts. I've had students we perform for tell me that this was very significant to them, knowing that these were "real" stories, things that truly happened in people's lives. And yet, the stories and their retelling are so far removed from the events and the people who told them that they are also ghosts, shadows, fictions. But that word "verbatim" sets into motion another level or layer of significance that, at least for some viewers, affects the way they receive the stories. I wonder about that.

Heather: One of us usually mentions that the script uses only *verbatim* quotations from interviews. In the video production, this statement rolls up the screen before the performance begins. Using teacher's words verbatim differentiates the script from a fictional play. There is no playwright, only teachers, actors and a researcher. The performance differs from a literary performance by invoking a degree of realism. Mentioning that the script contains teacher's words verbatim offers a useful invitation for students in teacher education classes. It gives momentary legitimacy to the performance as "research" for quantitative and naturalist science-trained students. It permits them to pay attention in a way with which they may be familiar, as highly educated consumers of "research," as teachers seeking to base their teaching on best practices informed by "the research." As one person said, "it really put the issues to the forefront when you can see *real* people talking about *real* issues." As the performance unfolds, this masquerade of realism and naturalism slips away, taking with it the discourses of positivist research and technocratic, prescriptive teaching. Thus using verbatim quotes sets up the "lie of the literal" (Salverson, 1996) only to reveal a certain failure of the mimetic function. The realism promised by a verbatim script that captures the "real" experiences of teachers quickly slips out of sight. Instead, the research presents a montage of stories with inconclusive endings. Consequently, anti-homophobic teaching is not presented as something that can be completely mastered. To this extent, *Wearing the Secret Out* seems to enact a form of post-modern pedagogy, committed to a broad anti-homophobic project while always unsure of itself. Jennifer Simons' expressed this affinity between post-structuralist ethnography and drama pedagogy: "Where science has historically attempted to pin down meaning by definition and analysis, the arts acknowledge and build upon the fact that we can and do hold multiple, even contradictory meanings at the same time, and that sometimes meaning can be physically apprehended although it cannot be verbally expressed" (1997: 5).

Audience Responses as "Angles of Repose"

Heather: Our focus on physical education – a body of knowledge and knowledge of a body – has a curious resonance with performed ethnography. The resonance between performing research and physical education has been noted by Andrew Sparkes, who suggested extending "our understanding of bodies beyond abstract theorizing, by including not just the bodies of our research participants, but also our own bodies as researchers–performers–audience" (2002: 147). Kristin Langellier explained how "the 'performative turn' responds to the twin conditions of bodiless voices, for example, in ethnographic writing; and voiceless bodies who desire to resist the colonizing powers of discourse" (2000: 126). Strangely, *Wearing the Secret Out* evokes resonances between the body and the methodology, between the research focus and its embodied representation. For Langellier, such performance risks both hegemony and resistance, recuperation and transgression, increasing and decreasing domination: "When personal narrative performance materializes performativity – when an orator embodies identity and experience there is always risk and danger. The performance of personal narrative gives shape to the social relations of identity and experience but because such relations are multiple, complexly interconnected and contradictory, it can do so in only unstable ways for participants" (2000: 129).

Perhaps this is what Maxine Greene meant by "making language glow and touch as well as communicate" (cited in Donmoyer & Yennie-Donmoyer, 1995: 6). Yet what meanings are communicated to audiences often feels beyond the reach of our understanding. Jennifer Simons (1997) reported that audiences of her Theater In Education (TIE) research often responded with "I know this is significant but I don't know why." Audiences of *Wearing the Secret Out* often expressed the same sentiment.

Anne: Every audience we've performed for has reacted differently to the piece. I'll never forget the performance at the American Alliance for Health, Physical Education, Recreation and Dance (AAHPERD), for example, where the large audience was composed almost entirely of physical education teachers. There was so much laughter in the room, an almost continuous vocal reaction, acknowledging moments in the piece that slip by with less recognition in other performance contexts. For example, the statement, "Usually I have my rainbow bracelets on, and so it becomes apparent where I'm coming from," drew a huge laugh that rippled throughout the room. So did the moment when Jennifer, retelling Coach Schneider's story about coming out to her sixth grade students, stated, "And about an hour later my principal comes to my room and says, 'How's it going? … Did you happen to talk about your personal life today in class?'" Again, the AAHPERD audience responded with an enormous laugh. By the same token, when we told the story about the coach who was confronted in a bar by her colleague demanding to know, "Do you eat men or do you eat women?" the silence in the room was so intense the air vibrated. Performing at AAHPERD was exciting for us because of this exchange of energy and emotion with the audience. Words and phrases in the piece that hadn't stood out for me suddenly took on new significance. And I was unprepared for the warmth of the reception of the piece, the people who came up afterwards and thanked us for doing it.

Heather: So often, members of the audience rush or meander up to the three us to offer congratulations, handshakes and hugs. Words like "courageous," "wonderful," "brave" bump into one another across most post-performance discussions. Yet audience members are frequently at a loss to quite explain why. Me too, I'm still at a loss to explain why. Julie Salverson suggests full understanding remains out of reach. "Taking responsibility should extend beyond an ongoing inventory of who we are as individuals to an understanding that there are stakes for those with whom we work – stakes that exist, but are never more than partially knowable" (1996: 181).

Acknowledging that all we can look forward to is partial knowledge, or that audiences rarely vocalize their responses, does not dissolve questions about validity. As qualitative research has turned towards anti-foundationalism and performance, construct validity has given way to voluptuous validity, internal validity to triangulation, and positivist validity to rhyzomatic validity. In the context of mixed genre postmodern research, Laurel Richardson (2000) turned from validity as triangulation to the notion of "crystallization" that portends a deepened, complex, thoroughly partial understanding of the topic. She turns our attention away from the triangulation of a fixed "object" through different methods toward crystallization that recognizes there are more than "three sides" from which to approach the world. "The central imaginary is the crystal, which combines symmetry and substance with an infinite variety of shapes, substances, transmutations and angles of approach ... what we see depends upon our angle of repose" (Richardson, 2000: 934). The implications are, she suggests, that we feel how there is no single truth, we know more and doubt what we know. We have observed that students in physical education seem to observe from quite different "angles of repose" (Richardson, 2000: 934) than those in theater or general teacher education. These comments from a group of pre-service elementary teachers (Elsbree, 2001) illustrate their different responses to the same performance:

- "It really put the issues to the forefront when you can see *real* people talking about *real* issues."
- "There weren't a lot of facts, but it hit the audience in an effective way."
- "The movement with words really spoke *loud*!"
- "I did not like the performance art as your medium. I have seen and performed this art form and have always found it more confusing than clarifying."
- "Well thought out and planned. Excellent acting, very dramatic."
- "I was sort of lost because of the style and the randomness of the dialogue, but it was a lot easier to understand after about 5 minutes."
- "Seeing the drama made me feel guilty about my own misconceptions when I was in middle school."
- "Even though I think it worked well for students who feel uncomfortable with the ideas, I wish it were a little less art, a little more guerilla."

From Live Performance to Video Archive

Jennifer: In Spring 2000, we created a video of *Wearing the Secret Out*. This was in response to frequent requests we had received from educators for such a video, and also because Heather and Anne were about to take jobs away from Madison. Anne and I feel the video lacks the "in-your-face" quality of the performance that, although occasionally disliked by students, was a part of what we were going for. It also lacks the intimacy we have with our audiences, since we always perform in non-theater spaces. Furthermore, we fear it lacks the open-ended questioning qualities of the live performance – that meanings are left closed because we the actors are not physically present to engage with the audience afterwards. We believe that essential to the performance are the incomplete meanings that are created when students/audience members experience our bodies moving in space while speaking the interview text. We fear that when the interviewee's words are spoken on screen, perhaps a "truth" or "meaning" is interpreted because video carries a weight of authority that real-live people don't always have.

Heather: We continue to struggle with our different responses to the videotape of the live performance. Now that we are no longer working in the same area, the video allows me to continue sharing the performance with my classes. Yet my very pragmatic reason for using video rather than live performance does not adequately address Jennifer and Anne's concerns about the loss of intimacy and embodiment. Rather, our different opinions indicate the need for ongoing interdisciplinary dialogue about the specific pedagogies in drama education and live performance, which can't be generated from an archived, flat-screen video performance. Meanwhile I continue to explore different pedagogies after screening the videotaped performance to students in my physical education and teacher education classes. In a recent anti-homophobia course, teacher education students also read a complete transcript of the life history interview with one of the teachers featured in the performance. In the following class, students then created and performed their own mini-ethnographies based on the interview transcript as a way of constructing their own meanings. The deferral and regeneration of meanings continues as students juxtapose their own life histories with the play, the interviews and the teachers (Goldstein & Sykes, 2004).

Importance of Collaboration in Performed Ethnography

Heather: This performed ethnography could not have been created without collaboration between the researcher and artists. Our collaboration has a decidedly post-foundational flavor.

Anne: *Wearing the Secret Out* began with a conversation that took place on an old plaid sofa in the teacher education building at the University of Wisconsin-Madison, where I was taking a course in Postmodern Research Methods in the spring of 2000. One of my classmates mentioned she had been transcribing interviews for a professor in Kinesiology who was considering creating a readers' theater piece based on the life history interviews. Since Jennifer and I were doctoral students in Theater and both had a strong interest in education we were indeed interested in the project.

I can't remember at what point I learned that Heather's research focused on the life histories of physical education teachers who do not identify as heterosexual, but this was a huge point of interest for me, for a number of reasons. I first started to teach when I entered the MFA at the University of Louisville. While I had spent many years training as an actor, I had never envisioned myself as a teacher and had no prior preparation for teaching. I had worked in theater or other arts-related organizations for years, environments that attracted many people who did not identify as straight and in which the identities of such people were neither questioned nor censored. Naïve though it may seem, I was unprepared to find myself in teaching situations where students reacted to scripted or improvised same-sex situations by making fun of LBGT relationships or by expressing disgust. Furthermore, at the time I started teaching, I was two years into my first relationship with a woman. When students made homophobic comments in class, I struggled with how best to intervene, and whether or not I should do so from my standpoint as a lesbian. Thus for personal reasons, I very much wanted to read about how other teachers negotiated these tensions in their own lives and in their classrooms, and to explore their stories through drama.

Heather: Inter-disciplinary, inter-departmental, inter-textual, inter-view, inter-pretation. This has been an interdisciplinary collaboration between researcher and actor, between educators and artists, between academics and practitioners. Collaboration between researchers and performance artists is tremendously important (Gray et al., 2002) if not essential "when the risks of producing ethnodrama are considered" (Sparkes, 2002: 147). Furthermore, Michal McCall (2000) suggested that ethnographic performances developed by theater artists and academics in performance studies tend to be more theatrical than those by sociologists. Given this context and agreeing with Snow and Morrill's concern that academics or ethnographers may lack the playwrights "eye and feel for artistry" (1995: 342) and be less able craft a viable performance script, I enthusiastically embarked on a collaboration with Anne and Jennifer across the disciplines of drama education and physical education. While it was more serendipity than method that brought Anne, Jennifer and I together from our different disciplinary homes in Kinesiology and Theater departments, Bagley and Cancienne (2001) raised the issue of whether one needs to be a poet to represent data as poetry or a dramatist to represent data as a play. Now, after several years of collaboration, all of us have come to recognize the need for researchers to work with trained actors. Indeed, this is perhaps our most crucial methodological finding.

Jennifer: One of the most exciting things about creating *Wearing the Secret Out* has been the collaborative process that crosses disciplinary boundaries. As a theater artist, I am well adjusted to collaborating with others in the performing arts; as a drama educator, I am familiar with translating my work for classroom teachers. In both these situations, "collaboration" often translates into each person being in charge of a specific part: the educational component, the choreography, the writing, the directing, the research, and so on. This experience was unique, however, because at some point Anne and I had to make Heather part of the artistic process. At some point we all had to be advocates of the research, the choreography, the representations, and the overall aesthetic. To do that we had to drift through language and experiment with different forms in order to reach our common goal. We had to talk extensively so that we *had* a common goal. It would have been very easy for Heather to "direct" the piece and hold tight to her original idea of a readers' theater piece. But instead she invited us to interact with the material both creatively and intellectually. Through discussion and rehearsal, we also invited her to respond to performance ideas. Although Anne and I introduce ourselves as the "performers" and Heather as the "researcher," the piece is a product of all three of us hammering away at the questions we are collectively interested in.

In/Conclusion

The three of us continue to deliberate about what the performative turns means for our research and teaching. As the researcher, I still hear the teachers' ghosts remarking on how Anne, Jennifer and I have translated face-to-face interviews into transcripts, and those pages onto the stage. Developing a performed ethnography has been a collaborative, uncertain methodological adventure yet I often felt that I, or my research, was somehow getting lost in this performative turn. As a researcher, I experienced intense yet productive losses in authorship and interpretation as I collaborated with Anne and Jennifer. Patti Lather (2000a) suggests getting lost is, perhaps, the best we can do: "Both within and against the 'new ethnography' with its reflexivity, multiple voices and textual experimentation, such practices enact a stammering relationship toward the as yet incompletely thinkable conditions and potential of given arrangements. Here we are all a little lost, caught in the enabling aporias that move us toward practices that are responsible to what is arising out of both becoming and passing away" (2000a: 3).

This feeling of getting lost within postmodern collaborative research has helped me to recognize what can be generated by deliberate openness which, of course, remains a form of inadvertent authority. Translating research interviews about teacher's lives, captured in monotone on audio tape then transcripts, into embodied performance required Anne and Jennifer's skill and artistry as artists. This is perhaps the only thing we are prepared to claim with certainty – the performed ethnography of interview research needed drama specialists. Staging and screening interview data will always involve difficult creations and reluctant losses because of the reductive and generative nature of methodological translation. Our less certain claim is that using performed ethnography, as a postmodern element in teaching, becomes a practice of coping in a fecund and affirmative way without *knowing* what *must* be done (Ellsworth, 1997). Likewise postmodern research has meant presenting stories that *wear the secret out* without always knowing how they do so. We continue to be immersed in the imprecise glow and touch of each performance, wondering what learnings are evoked as this performed research plays out its visceral pedagogy.

Acknowledgment

This research has been generously supported by the Virginia Horne Henry Fund for Issues in Women's Physical Education administered by the University of Wisconsin-Madison, USA.

Note

1. The central part of this chapter was written collaboratively by Heather, Anne and Jennifer. The introductory and concluding sections were written by Heather.

References

Bagley, C. & Cancienne, M. (2001). Educational Research and Intertextual Forms of (Re)Presention: The Case for Dancing the Data. *Qualitative Inquiry*, 7, 2, 221–37.

Biriotti, M. (1993). Introduction: Authorship, Authority, Authorisation. In M. Biriotti & N. Miller (eds.). *What Is An Author?* Manchester: Manchester University Press.

Brodribb, S. (1992). *Nothing Mat(T)Ers: A Feminist Critique of Postmodernism*. Melbourne: Spinitex Press.

Brown, L. (1998). Boy's Training. In C. Hickey, L. Fitzclarence and R. Matthews (eds). *Where the Boys Are*. Geelong: Deakin University Press.

Chapman, J., Swedberg, A. & Sykes. H. (2005). Wearing the Secret Out. In J. Saldana (ed.). *Ethnodrama: An Anthology of Reality Theatre*. Walnut Creek, CA: Altamira Press.

Clough, P. (1993). On the Brink of Deconstructing Sociology: Critical Reading of Dorothy Smith's Standpoint Epistemology. *The Sociological Quarterly*, 34, 169–82.

Conquergood, D. (1992). Ethnography, Rhetoric and Performance. *Quarterly Journal of Speech*, 78, 80–97.

Denzin, N. (1994). The Art and Politics of Interpretation. In N. Denzin and Y. Lincoln (eds). *Handbook of Qualitative Research*. London: Sage.

—— (1997). *Interpretive Ethnography: Ethnographic Practices for the Twenty-First Century*, London: Sage.

Denzin, N. & Lincoln, Y. (2000). The Discipline and Practice of Qualitative Research. In N. Denzin & Y. Lincoln (eds). *Handbook of Qualitative Research:* (2nd Edition). London: Sage.

Diamond, E. (2000). Re: Blau, Beckett, and the Politics of Seeming. *TDR:The Drama Review*, 44, 4, 31–43.

Donmoyer, R. & Yennie-Donmoyer, J. (1995). Data as Drama: Reflections on the Use of Readers Theatre as a Mode of Qualitative Data Display. *Qualitative Inquiry*, 1, 4, 402–29.

Ebert, T. (1996). The Matter of Materialism. In D. Norton (ed.). *The Material Queer: A LesBiGay Cultural Studies Reader*. Boulder, CO: Westview Press.

Ellsworth, E. (1997). *Teaching Positions: Difference, Pedagogy and the Power of Address*, New York: Teachers College Press.

Elsbree, A. (2001). Personal Communication. University of Wiscson-Madison.

Goldstein, T. (2001). Hong Kong, Canada: A One-Act Ethnographic Play For Critical Teacher Education. *Journal of Curriculum Theorizing*, 17, 2, 97–110.

Goldstein, T. & Sykes, H. (2004). From Performed to Performing Ethnography: Translating Life History Research into Anti-Homophobia Curriculum for a Teacher Education Program. *Journal of Teaching Education*, 15, 1, 41–61.

Gray, R., Ivonoffski, V. & Sinding, C. (2002). Making a Mess and Spreading it Around. In A. Bouchner & C. Ellis (eds). *Ethnographically Speaking*. California: Altamira Press.

Grosz, E. (1995). *Space, Time and Perversion*, London: Routledge.

Hutcheon, L. (1989). *The Politics of Postmodernism*, London: Routledge.

Langellier, K. (2000). Personal Narrative, Performance, Performativity: Two or Three Things I Know for Sure. *Theatre and Performance Quarterly*, 19, 2, 125–44.

Lapadat, J. & Lindsay, A. (1999). Transcription in Research and Practice: From Standardization of Technique to Interpretive Positionings. *Qualitative Inquiry*, 5, 1, 64–86.

Lather, P. (2000a). Getting Lost: Feminist Efforts Toward a Double(D) Science. A paper presented at the Journal of Curriculum Theorizing Conference, Bergamo, OH.

—— (2000b). Reading the Image of Rigoberta Menchu: Undecidability and Language Lessons. *International Journal of Qualitative Studies in Education*, 13, 2, 153–62.

Lincoln, Y. & Denzin, N. (1994). The Fifth Moment. In N. Denzin & Y. Lincoln (eds). *Handbook of Qualitative Research*. London: Sage.

Littau, K. (1993). Performing Translation. *Theatre Research International*, 18, 1, 53–60.

Lockford, L. (2000). An Ethnographic Ghost Story: Adapting *What's a Nice Commodity Like You Doing in a Spectacle Like This? Text and Performance Quarterly*, 20, 4, 402–15.

McCall, M. (2000). Performance Ethnography: A Brief History and Some Advice. In N. Denzin & Y. Lincoln (eds). *Handbook of Qualitative Research* (2nd edition). London: Sage.

Mienczakowski, J. (1997). Theatre of Change. *Research in Drama Education*, 2, 2, 159–72.

—— (1998). Interpretive Ethnography: Ethnographic Practices for the Twenty-First Century [Book Review]. *Research in Drama Education*, 3, 1, 116–19.

Mishler, E. (1991). Representing Discourse: The Rhetoric of Transcription, *Journal of Narrative and Life History*, 1, 4, 255–80.

Pifer, D. (1999). Small Town Race: A Performance Text. *Qualitative Inquiry*, 5, 4, 541–62.

Richardson, L. (1997). *Fields of Play: Constructing an Academic Life*, New Brunswick, NJ: Rutgers University Press.

—— (2000). Writing: A Method of Inquiry. In N. Denzin & Y Lincoln (eds). *Handbook of Qualitative Research* (2nd edition). London: Sage.

Salverson, J. (1996). Performing Emergency: Witnessing, Popular Theatre and the Lie of the Literal. *Theatre Topics*, 6, 2, 181–91.

Scott, J. (1991). The Evidence of Experience. *Critical Inquiry*, 17(summer), 773–97.

Simons, J. (1997). Drama Pedagogy and the Art of Double Meaning. *Research in Drama Education*, 2, 2, 193–202.

Smith, S. (1993). Who's Talking/Who's Talking Back? The Subject of Personal Narrative. *Signs: Journal of Women in Culture and Society*, 18, 2, 392–407.

Snow, D. & Morril, C. (1995). New Ethnographies: A Revolutionary Handbook or a Handbook for a Revolution? Journal of Contemporary Ethnography, 24, 3, 341–58.

Sparkes, A. (2002). Telling Tales in Sport and Physical Education: A Qualitative Journey. Champaign, IL: Human Kinetics.

Sykes, H. (2001). Understanding and Overstanding: Feminist-Poststructural Life Histories of Physical Education Teachers. *International Journal of Qualitative Studies in Education*, 14, 1, 13–31.

Tierney, W. (1998). Life History's History: Subjects Foretold. *Qualitative Inquiry*, 4, 1, 49–70.

Tierney, W. (2000). Undaunted Courage: Life History and the Postmodern Challenge. In N. Denzin & Y Lincoln (eds). *Handbook of Qualitative Research:* (2nd edition). London: Sage.

Weedon, C. (1997). *Feminist Practice and Poststructuralist Theory* (2nd edition). Oxford: Blackwell.

Woods, P. (1996). *Researching the Art of Teaching: Ethnography for Educational Use*. London: Routledge.

Index